Injury & Trauma Sourcebook

Learning Disabilities Sourcebook, 2nd Edition

Leukemia Sourcebook

Liver Disorders Sourcebook

Lung Disorders Sourcebook

Medical Tests Sourcebook, 3rd Edition

Men's Health Concerns Sourcebook, 2nd
    Edition

Mental Health Disorders Sourcebook, 3rd
    Edition

Mental Retardation Sourcebook

Movement Disorders Sourcebook

Multiple Sclerosis Sourcebook

Muscular Dystrophy Sourcebook

Obesity Sourcebook

Osteoporosis Sourcebook

Pain Sourcebook, 3rd Edition

Pediatric Cancer Sourcebook

Physical & Mental Issues in Aging
    Sourcebook

Podiatry Sourcebook, 2nd Edition

Pregnancy & Birth Sourcebook, 2nd
    Edition

Prostate Cancer Sourcebook

Prostate & Urological Disorders Sourcebook

Reconstructive & Cosmetic Surgery
    Sourcebook

Rehabilitation Sourcebook

Respiratory Disorders Sourcebook, 2nd
    Edition

Sexually Transmitted Diseases Sourcebook,
    3rd Edition

Sleep Disorders Sourcebook, 2nd Edition

Smoking Concerns Sourcebook

Sports Injuries Sourcebook, 3rd Edition

Stress-Related Disorders Sourcebook, 2nd
    Edition

Stroke Sourcebook, 2nd Edition

Surgery Sourcebook, 2nd Edition

Thyroid Disorders Sourcebook

Transplantation Sourcebook

Traveler's H

Urinary Tra

    Disorders Sourcebook, 2nd Edition

Vegetarian Sourcebook

Women's Health Concerns Sourcebook, 2nd
    Edition

Workplace Health & Safety Sourcebook

Worldwide Health Sourcebook

Teen Health Series

Abuse and Violence Information for
    Teens

Alcohol Information for Teens

Allergy Information for Teens

Asthma Information for Teens

Body Information for Teens

Cancer Information for Teens

Complementary & Alternative
    Medicine Information for Teens

Diabetes Information for Teens

Diet Information for Teens, 2nd Edition

Drug Information for Teens, 2nd Edition

Eating Disorders Information for Teens

Fitness Information for Teens, 2nd
    Edition

Learning Disabilities Information for
    Teens

Mental Health Information for Teens,
    2nd Edition

Pregnancy Information for Teens

Sexual Health Information for Teens,
    2nd Edition

Skin Health Information for Teens

Sleep Information for Teens

Sports Injuries Information for Teens,
    2nd Edition

Stress Information for Teens

Suicide Information for Teens

Tobacco Information for Teens

◆

Eating Disorders Information for Teens

Second Edition

◆

TEEN
HEALTH
SERIES

Second Edition

Eating Disorders Information for Teens

Health Tips about Anorexia, Bulimia, Binge Eating, and Other Eating Disorders

Including Information about Risk Factors, Prevention, Diagnosis, Treatment, Health Consequences, and Other Related Issues

◆

Edited by Sandra Augustyn Lawton

Omnigraphics

P.O. Box 31-1640, Detroit, MI 48231

Bibliographic Note

Because this page cannot legibly accommodate all the copyright notices, the Bibliographic Note portion of the Preface constitutes an extension of the copyright notice.

Edited by Sandra Augustyn Lawton

Teen Health Series

Karen Bellenir, *Managing Editor*
David A. Cooke, M.D., *Medical Consultant*
Elizabeth Collins, *Research and Permissions Coordinator*
Cherry Edwards, *Permissions Assistant*
EdIndex, Services for Publishers, *Indexers*

* * *

Omnigraphics, Inc.

Matthew P. Barbour, *Senior Vice President*
Kevin M. Hayes, *Operations Manager*

* * *

Peter E. Ruffner, *Publisher*

Copyright © 2009 Omnigraphics, Inc.

ISBN 978-0-7808-1044-0

Library of Congress Cataloging-in-Publication Data

Eating disorders information for teens : health tips about anorexia,
bulimia, binge eating, and other eating disorders including information
about risk factors, prevention, diagnosis, treatment, health consequences,
and other related issues / edited by Sandra Augustyn Lawton. -- 2nd ed.
    p. cm. -- (Teen health series)
  Summary: "Provides basic consumer health information for teens about
causes, prevention, and treatment of eating disorders, along with healthy
eating tips. Includes index, resource information and recommendations for
further reading"--Provided by publisher.
  Includes bibliographical references and index.
  ISBN 978-0-7808-1044-0 (hardcover : alk. paper) 1. Eating
disorders--Juvenile literature. 2. Eating disorders in
adolescence--Juvenile literature. I. Lawton, Sandra Augustyn.
  RC552.E18E2836 2010
  616.85'2600835--dc22
                                                    2008049387

This book is printed on acid-free paper meeting the ANSI Z39.48 Standard. The infinity symbol that appears above indicates that the paper in this book meets that standard.

Printed in the United States

Table of Contents

Part Three: Health Consequences Of Eating Disorders And Co-Occurring Concerns

Part Four: Prevention, Diagnosis, And Treatment Of Eating Disorders

Part Five: Healthy Eating And Exercise Plans

Part Six: If You Need More Information

Preface

About This Book

According to the National Association of Anorexia Nervosa and Associated Disorders, approximately eight million people in the U.S. have anorexia nervosa, bulimia, or other eating disorders. Eating disorders often develop during adolescence or young adulthood, but people of all ages can be affected. In addition, eating disorders affect females and males and all races and cultures. Eating disorders frequently co-occur with other mental health disorders, such as depression, substance abuse, and anxiety disorders. If left untreated, eating disorders can result in serious physical health complications.

Eating Disorders Information For Teens, Second Edition provides updated information about anorexia nervosa, bulimia nervosa, binge eating disorder, and other eating disorders. It describes risk factors, health consequences, and co-occurring concerns, and it offers facts about the prevention, diagnosis, and treatment of eating disorders. Body image, self-esteem, and media influences are also discussed, and the book provides information for developing healthy eating and exercise plans. It concludes with suggestions for additional reading and a directory of eating disorders organizations.

How To Use This Book

This book is divided into parts and chapters. Parts focus on broad areas of interest; chapters are devoted to single topics within a part.

Part One: Basic Information About Eating Disorders provides facts about eating disorders, theories about their causes, and the risk factors that may contribute to their development. It also discusses how all ethnic groups are susceptible to eating disorders and that even men, boys, and athletes are at risk.

Part Two: Specific Disorders Related To Eating And Body Image offers details about the three most common eating disorders—anorexia nervosa, bulimia nervosa, and binge eating disorder—and also describes other disorders related to eating and body image.

Part Three: Health Consequences Of Eating Disorders And Co-Occurring Concerns discusses how eating disorders can lead to other health challenges, such as osteoporosis and oral health problems, and how they can complicate existing conditions including diabetes and pregnancy. This section also talks about the link between eating disorders and some mental health disorders.

Part Four: Prevention, Diagnosis, And Treatment Of Eating Disorders provides information about the signs and symptoms of eating disorders and how body image and self-esteem play a significant role in their development. This section also describes how eating disorders are diagnosed and the various forms of treatment that are available.

Part Five: Healthy Eating And Exercise Plans offers facts about eating sensibly and exercising for weight control and physical fitness. It also offers suggestions for choosing safe and successful ways to lose weight.

Part Six: If You Need More Information provides suggestions for additional reading about eating disorders and other related topics. It also provides a directory of organizations able to provide facts about eating disorders, nutrition, fitness, and mental health.

Bibliographic Note

This volume contains documents and excerpts from publications issued by the following government agencies: Center for Disease Control and Prevention (CDC); National Institute of Arthritis and Musculoskeletal and Skin Diseases (NIAMS); National Institute of Diabetes and Digestive and Kidney Diseases (NIDDK); National Institute of Mental Health (NIMH);

National Women's Health Information Center (NWHIC); and the President's Council on Physical Fitness and Sports.

In addition, this volume contains copyrighted documents and articles produced by the following organizations and individuals: A.D.A.M., Inc.; About, Inc.; Academy for Eating Disorders; Anorexia Nervosa and Related Eating Disorders, Inc.; Anxiety Disorders Association of America; Cleveland Clinic; Colorado Department of Public Health and Environment; Eating Disorders Foundation of Victoria, Inc.; Express Scripts; Laura E. Gibson, PhD; Gürze Books; National Eating Disorders Association; National Eating Disorder Information Centre; Nemours Foundation; and the University of Alabama at Birmingham Health System, Office of Medical Publications.

Full citation information is provided on the first page of each chapter. Every effort has been made to secure all necessary rights to reprint the copyrighted material. If any omissions have been made, please contact Omnigraphics to make corrections for future editions.

The photograph on the front cover is from blaneyphoto/iStockphoto.

Acknowledgements

In addition to the organizations listed above, special thanks are due to the *Teen Health Series* research and permissions coordinator, Elizabeth Collins, and to its managing editor, Karen Bellenir.

About the *Teen Health Series*

At the request of librarians serving today's young adults, the *Teen Health Series* was developed as a specially focused set of volumes within Omnigraphics' *Health Reference Series*. Each volume deals comprehensively with a topic selected according to the needs and interests of people in middle school and high school.

Teens seeking preventive guidance, information about disease warning signs, medical statistics, and risk factors for health problems will find answers to their questions in the *Teen Health Series*. The *Series*, however, is not intended to serve as a tool for diagnosing illness, in prescribing treatments, or as a substitute for the physician/patient relationship. All people concerned about medical symptoms or the possibility of disease are encouraged to seek professional care from an appropriate health care provider.

If there is a topic you would like to see addressed in a future volume of the *Teen Health Series*, please write to:

Editor
Teen Health Series
Omnigraphics, Inc.
P.O. Box 31-1640
Detroit, MI 48231

A Note about Spelling and Style

Teen Health Series editors use *Stedman's Medical Dictionary* as an authority for questions related to the spelling of medical terms and the *Chicago Manual of Style* for questions related to grammatical structures, punctuation, and other editorial concerns. Consistent adherence is not always possible, however, because the individual volumes within the *Series* include many documents from a wide variety of different producers and copyright holders, and the editor's primary goal is to present material from each source as accurately as is possible following the terms specified by each document's producer. This sometimes means that information in different chapters or sections may follow other guidelines and alternate spelling authorities. For example, occasionally a copyright holder may require that eponymous terms be shown in possessive forms (Crohn's disease *vs.* Crohn disease) or that British spelling norms be retained (leukaemia *vs.* leukemia).

Locating Information within the *Teen Health Series*

The *Teen Health Series* contains a wealth of information about a wide variety of medical topics. As the *Series* continues to grow in size and scope, locating the precise information needed by a specific student may become more challenging. To address this concern, information about books within the *Teen Health Series* is included in *A Contents Guide to the Health Reference Series*. The *Contents Guide* presents an extensive list of more than 14,000 diseases, treatments, and other topics of general interest compiled from the Tables of Contents and major index headings from the books of the *Teen Health Series* and *Health Reference Series*. To access *A Contents Guide to the Health Reference Series*, visit www.healthreferenceseries.com.

Our Advisory Board

We would like to thank the following advisory board members for providing guidance to the development of this *Series*:

Dr. Lynda Baker, Associate Professor of Library and Information Science, Wayne State University, Detroit, MI

Nancy Bulgarelli, William Beaumont Hospital Library, Royal Oak, MI

Karen Imarisio, Bloomfield Township Public Library, Bloomfield Township, MI

Karen Morgan, Mardigian Library, University of Michigan-Dearborn, Dearborn, MI

Rosemary Orlando, St. Clair Shores Public Library, St. Clair Shores, MI

Medical Consultant

Medical consultation services are provided to the *Teen Health Series* editors by David A. Cooke, M.D. Dr. Cooke is a graduate of Brandeis University, and he received his M.D. degree from the University of Michigan. He completed residency training at the University of Wisconsin Hospital and Clinics. He is board-certified in internal medicine. Dr. Cooke currently works as part of the University of Michigan Health System and practices in Ann Arbor, MI. In his free time, he enjoys writing, science fiction, and spending time with his family.

Part One

Basic Information About Eating Disorders

Chapter 1

Food, Weight, And Eating: Know The Facts

Thoughts, feelings, and behaviors related to managing food and weight can begin to interfere with our everyday activities. When we focus too much attention on our bodies and our eating, these preoccupations can quickly lead to missed opportunities in other parts of our lives. Our personal, school, or professional lives, not to mention our overall well-being, can be drastically affected. Food and weight preoccupation can also lead to severe physical and emotional problems.

Take a few minutes right now to read about the myths of dieting, how these issues affect males and females, cross ethnic, racial and economic lines, and much more.

How Does Someone Develop An Eating Disorder?

There are many societal, familial, and individual factors that can influence the development of an eating disorder. Individuals who are struggling with their identity and self-image can be at risk, as well as those who have experienced a traumatic event. Eating disorders can also be a product of how one has been raised and taught to behave. Usually, an eating disorder signals that the person has deep emotional difficulties that they are unable to face or resolve.

About This Chapter: Information in this chapter is excerpted from "Food and Weight Preoccupation." Reprinted with permission. © 2005 National Eating Disorder Information Centre (www.nedic.ca). All rights reserved.

What's It Like To Have An Eating Disorder?

People with eating disorders often describe a feeling of powerlessness. By manipulating their eating, they then blunt their emotions or get a false sense of control in their lives. In this way, an eating disorder develops out of a method of coping with the world. This coping, however, is merely a mask, as it does not solve the life problems that the person is experiencing.

Clinical Eating Disorders

What exactly are clinical eating disorders? Clinical eating disorders include:

> ♣ **It's A Fact!!**
> **How do I know If I have an eating disorder?**
>
> If the way you eat and think about food interferes with your life and keeps you from enjoying life and moving forward, then that is disordered eating. Take it seriously and talk to someone who can help. You don't need to wait for a diagnosis by a doctor.

- **Anorexia Nervosa:** When you lose a lot of weight because you're hardly eating anything and might over-exercise. You probably can't or don't admit how underweight you are. You may not initially look very thin but may be far too thin to support your health. You can be so thin that every bone in your body shows but still feel "fat." When you feel fat it makes it hard to ask for help or hear advice from others because, to you, "fat" has come to mean "being bad." You could also know that you are much too thin but don't make changes because you're so afraid of food and gaining weight. To you, this would represent losing control over yourself.

- **Bulimia Nervosa:** When you binge and purge. You eat out of control and then try to get rid of the calories. You fast, make yourself vomit, abuse laxatives, or exercise too much. These ways of purging harm your body and don't help you accomplish what you want. Your weight may go up and down a lot.

- **Binge Eating Disorder (BED):** When you eat so much you're uncomfortable, eat to comfort yourself, eat in secret, or keep eating as part of a meal or between meals. You feel a lot of shame or guilt about your eating. Binge eating is also called compulsive eating. It is not the same as bulimia because you do not usually try to get rid of the food you've eaten.

- **Eating Disorder Not Otherwise Specified (EDNOS):** Individuals who experience a mix of anorexia, and/or bulimia, and/or binge eating symptoms, but who don't fall neatly into one of the medical categories, are said to have an Eating Disorder Not Otherwise Specified (EDNOS). These individuals should also receive the help and resources provided to individuals who have a "neat" clinical diagnosis.

Frequently Asked Questions

The following are frequently asked questions relating to eating disorders, dieting, and weight issues. You may find answers to some of your own or similar questions below:

I'm always going on a diet but can't keep the weight off. What's the best way to lose weight?

Diets always work for a little while. If we eat less and stop eating certain foods, we will lose weight. But the weight we lose is mainly water or lean tissue, not just fat. Research consistently shows that only about five percent of us will keep off the lost weight.

Our weight and our body shape and size depend on our genes, our body's metabolism, and the way we live. If we live a generally healthy lifestyle, our body stays within a stable weight range. This is called our "set point," and it is the weight range at which we are healthiest.

☞ **Remember!!**

Any food and weight issues that limit your ability to live a full and pleasurable life are of concern. It doesn't matter if you don't clearly fit one of the clinical categories. You still can, and should, seek help.

Our set point can be changed if we constantly lose and gain weight. If this happens, our bodies could raise their normal set point weights and slow our metabolism to keep it there. This is because our body is trying to protect itself. It doesn't know the difference between a famine and a diet.

Diets set us up to fail. This "failure" makes us feel guilty and adds to bad feelings we may already have, like low self-esteem or dislike of our bodies. We are surrounded by messages that anyone can lose weight as long as we have the right attitude and will power.

This makes it hard to remember just how unhelpful diets really are. Diets are difficult to follow. They restrict what we need or enjoy. So, we start to crave or obsess about the foods we're trying to avoid.

At this point we tend to "break" our diet. And then we feel we have failed rather than recognizing that it is the diet that has failed.

We diet for many different reasons. We may think that being thinner will make us happier. Diets or some other strict routine can also make us feel like we're accomplishing something. By sticking to the rules we are rewarded, at first, by losing weight and by people complimenting us. But, this won't last and nothing else really changes.

So ask, "Why do I want to lose weight?" Are your hopes for a smaller body realistic? How would your life change?

There are realistic ways to get to a healthy weight:

- Learn about healthy eating and establish a pattern of normal eating.

- Try not to label some foods as "good" and some foods "bad." All foods have a place in your life.

- Learn about appropriate portion sizes.

- Be active in ways that you find pleasurable. This will make it more likely that you exercise regularly.

If you do these things, you are likely to find that, after a while, your body will settle at its natural "set weight." Feelings of frustration, tiredness, mood swings and binge eating that you might have experienced while on a diet will lessen and may go away completely.

What's wrong with dieting?

A diet means we eat less to lose weight. It can make both our body and mind hungry. When we go on a diet we often:

- Think about food constantly.

- Over-eat or "binge" on certain foods.

- Over-use condiments, chewing gum, cigarettes, and drinks with caffeine.

- Feel irritable.

- Feel depressed and tired.

- Don't want to be around people.

- Find it hard to concentrate.

The first problem is that when we think about food and weight all the time, we don't deal with the bigger issues we face, like feeling bad about ourselves, or feeling unhappy, or tackling some problem that we have.

A second problem is that a diet can be the first step in developing an eating disorder. By dieting we support the myth that we are only good, attractive, and valuable if we look a certain way. We ignore the research, which shows that healthy, happy, and successful people come in all shapes and sizes.

We might think that we can change our body with a diet. But research shows that:

- 95% to 98% of diets fail.

- Almost all dieters gain back all the weight they lost within five years.

- Many dieters gain back more weight than they lost.

- Children and youth who diet are more likely to be fatter adults.

Diets don't work because our size and shape are largely decided by our genes. Yet, when our diet doesn't work we think it is our fault and that we have failed. This makes us feel even worse about ourselves.

Our body wants to stay at its natural, healthy weight. If we try to go below our natural weight by dieting, our body then starts to burn calories more slowly. We could, therefore, stop losing weight or gain more when we diet. When we stop a diet our body may put on fat to make up for the weight we lost. If we stop and start a diet several times, our body may gain more weight than we lost. This happens because our body doesn't know whether we are dieting or in the middle of a famine, so it tries to protect us.

Can I be addicted to food?

"Bingeing" is a word used to describe eating food uncontrollably. Some people believe they binge because they are addicted to food. Others believe they binge because they are "emotional" eaters. In other words, they eat because the ritual of eating is comforting, or they want the numbness that comes with being too full.

Typically, however, it is starvation or deprivation that causes people to binge. If we are already nutritionally deprived, or eat to comfort ourselves, something as simple as a bad mood or stress can trigger a binge.

In other words, food isn't addictive.

However, disordered eating can become a habit. When we begin to relate to food and eating in particular ways, these habits can be hard to change. So, it is the process (behavior), not the substance (food) that becomes "addictive." Our behaviors meet a need. We may lose control of our eating because we are physically or emotionally deprived, not because we are addicted to food. Once we begin eating in a normal, healthy way again, we won't have the same desire to eat as much high-calorie, high-carbohydrate food, or foods we think are "bad".

I feel fat and unhappy. What can I do?

A lot of people feel this way, especially women. It doesn't matter if we are at a healthy weight or not, we still feel this way. In Western culture, we are taught that fat is bad and that being fat is a sign of poor character. We are expected to feel shame and unhappiness about being fat. As a result, many people who are unhappy about other things, but who don't deal with them, begin to feel bad about themselves more generally, and then they "feel fat."

So, what can you do?

Try to separate what you believe about being fat and other things happening in your life.

Think of it. When do you "feel fat"? Does this feeling come and go or is it always there? Do you feel bad about yourself when certain things happen or when you are around certain people?

Other people, television, and the media more generally tell us what the "perfect" body looks like. They tell us we really need to look that way in order to be happy and successful. Yet the only way in which they are able to portray the ideal body without a blemish is by computer-modifying images or airbrushing out all "imperfections"!

The truth is that there is no one perfect body for everyone. We come in all shapes and sizes. Our weight, shape, and size—like our height—are determined by a mix of genetics, metabolism, and lifestyle. People are naturally thin, average, or fat, and everything in between.

"Feeling fat" is really saying, "I don't like myself." After all, "fat" is not a feeling. If you are able to let go of these ideas about your body, you will be able treat yourself better and value your strengths. Learn to love and treasure your body. Because it is your body.

♣ **It's A Fact!!**
Because we are healthiest at our natural weight, we will also tend to be at our most vibrant, energetic, and attractive.

Can men and boys develop eating disorders?

Yes. Men and boys can have unhealthy eating patterns and eating disorders. An eating disorder is the same illness whether it shows up in a man or woman, although many more women than men have eating disorders. It is estimated that there is one man for every 20 women with anorexia. The estimate is that there is one man for every 10 women with bulimia.

Research has shown that men who endure social pressure in relation to their personal identity or bodies, such as athletes, men in the entertainment and vanity industries, and gay or transgendered men, are more vulnerable to the development of disordered eating. Boys and men who over-exercise or diet are also at increased risk for an eating disorder.

Boys and men have many of the same problems as girls and women:

> ✔ Quick Tip
>
> ### Eating Disorder Self-Check
>
> Read the statements below:
>
> I'm always thinking about food, weight, or the way I look.
>
> I think about food and weight no matter what I'm doing.
>
> I'm ashamed or feel guilty about what I eat.
>
> I eat in secret or lie about what I have eaten.
>
> I plan my day around food or ways to avoid food.
>
> I work, exercise, or see people too much to avoid eating.
>
> I often over-eat or under-eat and don't control it.
>
> I try to make up for eating by purging or eating very little.
>
> I weigh myself every day and my mood depends on the numbers.

- Not feeling "good enough"
- Not feeling in control of their lives
- Feeling depressed, angry, anxious, or alienated
- A history of troubled family or social relationships
- Having difficulties in expressing their feelings
- A history of abuse
- Feeling confused about their sexuality

A lot of people think that only women and girls have eating disorders, so boys and men could be misdiagnosed or might not want to come forward for help. In addition, most support groups and treatment programs are targeted at women and are accessed almost exclusively by women. Males may be uncomfortable being included in such groups. However, treatment providers are increasingly finding ways to ensure that men and boys feel welcome in mixed groups, and also provide programs just for men.

I obsess about parts of my body that are "wrong," no matter my size or how much I weigh.

I count the calories of everything I eat or drink.

I exercise or eat less to punish myself for how much I weigh.

I am very strict about staying a certain weight.

I exercise even if I feel sick.

I exercise to lose weight or because I ate too much.

I call foods "good" and "bad" and feel good or bad depending on which I eat.

Do these sound like you? Be sure to talk to someone who knows about eating disorders. Even if you don't want to change anything at this point in time, it helps to talk to someone. A counselor can support you in choosing actions that won't hurt your body or mind.

The lower number of men with eating disorders is a good reason to examine what helps them avoid developing eating disorders. Understanding what helps males avoid eating disorders can help keep their numbers low as well as help to prevent eating disorders in women.

Ideas For Yourself

Encourage positive body image and healthy attitudes towards food in yourself and those around you. This is part of a healthy lifestyle, which includes working towards physical, emotional, spiritual and mental well-being.

• Criticize the culture that promotes unhealthy body image, not your self.

Look at how encouraging people to dislike their bodies helps to sell products. Even young children can understand this. Encourage children to question, evaluate, and respond to the messages that promote unhealthy body image and low self-esteem.

- Do not encourage or laugh at jokes that make fun of a person's size or body.

  Find a direct and gentle way to say that a person's worth and morality are not related to how they look.

- Avoid labeling food "bad," "sinful," or "junk food."

  Labels like this can make you feel guilty or ashamed for eating "bad food." If we think this way, we can restrict, and then binge, on certain foods. Remember that a healthy diet includes both regularly eating nutritious food and occasionally eating less nutritious, high calorie food. Use different labels for food like "sometimes food" and "everyday food."

- Get rid of your diet!

  Fight against the main cause of eating disorders—dieting. All you need is a trash can. Put one in your office, school, or home. Get rid of all those negative products in your life. Fill it with dieting how-to guides, calorie counters, bathroom scales, diet pills, laxatives, and other diet products. Be real. Free your body and your mind. Spend your money and your passion on something that matters.

- Get rid of your scale!

  Numbers can be deceiving. Listen to your body. Let it tell you how healthy you are. Remember that your weight is not a measurement of your health or self-worth. Make health and vitality your goal, not a specific weight.

Chapter 2

What Are Eating Disorders?

An eating disorder is marked by extremes. It is present when a person experiences severe disturbances in eating behavior, such as extreme reduction of food intake or extreme overeating, or feelings of extreme distress or concern about body weight or shape.

A person with an eating disorder may have started out just eating smaller or larger amounts of food than usual, but at some point, the urge to eat less or more spirals out of control. Eating disorders are very complex, and despite scientific research to understand them, the biological, behavioral, and social underpinnings of these illnesses remain elusive.

Eating disorders frequently appear during adolescence or young adulthood, but some reports indicate that they can develop during childhood or later in adulthood. Women and girls are much more likely than males to develop an eating disorder. Men and boys account for an estimated 5 to 15 percent of patients with anorexia or bulimia and an estimated 35 percent of those with binge eating disorder. Eating disorders are real, treatable medical illnesses with complex underlying psychological and biological causes. They frequently co-exist with other psychiatric disorders such as depression, substance abuse, or anxiety disorders. People with eating disorders also can suffer from numerous

About This Chapter: Information in this chapter is from "Eating Disorders," National Institute of Mental Health, National Institutes of Health, January 2008.

other physical health complications, such as heart conditions or kidney failure, which can lead to death.

Eating Disorders Are Treatable Diseases

Psychological and medicinal treatments are effective for many eating disorders. However, in more chronic cases, specific treatments have not yet been identified.

In these cases, treatment plans often are tailored to the patient's individual needs that may include medical care and monitoring; medications; nutritional counseling; and individual, group, and/or family psychotherapy. Some patients may also need to be hospitalized to treat malnutrition or to gain weight, or for other reasons.

> ♣ It's A Fact!!
>
> The two main types of eating disorders are anorexia nervosa and bulimia nervosa. A third category is "eating disorders not otherwise specified (EDNOS)," which includes several variations of eating disorders. Most of these disorders are similar to anorexia or bulimia but with slightly different characteristics. Binge eating disorder, which has received increasing research and media attention in recent years, is one type of EDNOS.

Anorexia Nervosa

Anorexia nervosa is characterized by emaciation, a relentless pursuit of thinness and unwillingness to maintain a normal or healthy weight, a distortion of body image and intense fear of gaining weight, a lack of menstruation among girls and women, and extremely disturbed eating behavior. Some people with anorexia lose weight by dieting and exercising excessively; others lose weight by self-induced vomiting or misusing laxatives, diuretics, or enemas.

Many people with anorexia see themselves as overweight, even when they are starved or are clearly malnourished. Eating, food, and weight control become obsessions. A person with anorexia typically weighs herself or himself repeatedly, portions food carefully, and eats only very small quantities of only certain foods. Some who have anorexia recover with treatment after only one episode. Others get well but have relapses. Still others have a more chronic form of anorexia, in which their health deteriorates over many years as they battle the illness.

According to some studies, people with anorexia are up to ten times more likely to die as a result of their illness compared to those without the disorder. The most common complications that lead to death are cardiac arrest and electrolyte and fluid imbalances. Suicide also can result.

Many people with anorexia also have coexisting psychiatric and physical illnesses, including depression, anxiety, obsessive behavior, substance abuse, cardiovascular and neurological complications, and impaired physical development.

Other symptoms may develop over time, including the following:

- Thinning of the bones (osteopenia or osteoporosis)
- Brittle hair and nails
- Dry and yellowish skin
- Growth of fine hair over body (for example, lanugo)
- Mild anemia and muscle weakness and loss
- Severe constipation
- Low blood pressure, slowed breathing and pulse
- Drop in internal body temperature, causing a person to feel cold all the time
- Lethargy

Treating anorexia involves the following three components:

1. Restoring the person to a healthy weight

2. Treating the psychological issues related to the eating disorder

3. Reducing or eliminating behaviors or thoughts that lead to disordered eating and preventing relapse

Some research suggests that the use of medications, such as antidepressants, antipsychotics, or mood stabilizers, may be modestly effective in treating patients with anorexia by helping to resolve mood and anxiety symptoms that often co-exist with anorexia. Recent studies, however, have suggested that antidepressants may not be effective in preventing some patients with anorexia from relapsing. In addition, no medication has shown to be effective during the critical first phase of restoring a patient to a healthy weight. Overall, it is unclear if and how medications can help patients conquer anorexia, but research is ongoing.

Different forms of psychotherapy, including individual, group, and family-based, can help address the psychological reasons for the illness. Some studies suggest that family-based therapies, in which parents assume responsibility for feeding their afflicted adolescent, are the most effective in helping a person with anorexia gain weight and improve eating habits and moods.

Shown to be effective in case studies and clinical trials, this particular approach is discussed in some guidelines and studies for treating eating disorders in younger, nonchronic patients.

Others have noted that a combined approach of medical attention and supportive psychotherapy designed specifically for anorexia patients are more effective than just psychotherapy, but the effectiveness of a treatment depends on the person involved and his or her situation. Unfortunately, no specific psychotherapy appears to be consistently effective for treating adults with anorexia. However, research into novel treatment and prevention approaches is showing some promise. One study suggests that an online intervention program may prevent some at-risk women from developing an eating disorder.

Bulimia Nervosa

Bulimia nervosa is characterized by recurrent and frequent episodes of eating unusually large amounts of food (for example, binge eating) and feeling a lack of control over the eating. This binge eating is followed by a type of behavior that compensates for the binge, such as purging (for example, vomiting, excessive use of laxatives or diuretics), fasting, and/or excessive exercise.

Unlike anorexia, people with bulimia can fall within the normal range for their age and weight; but like people with anorexia, they often fear gaining weight, want desperately to lose weight, and are intensely unhappy with their body size and shape. Usually, bulimic behavior is done secretly, because it is often accompanied by feelings of disgust or shame. The binging and purging cycle usually repeats several times a week. Similar to anorexia, people with bulimia often have coexisting psychological illnesses, such as depression, anxiety, and/or substance abuse problems. Many physical conditions result from the purging aspect of the illness, including electrolyte imbalances, gastrointestinal problems, and oral and tooth-related problems.

Other symptoms include the following:

- Chronically inflamed and sore throat

- Swollen glands in the neck and below the jaw

- Worn tooth enamel and increasingly sensitive and decaying teeth as a result of exposure to stomach acids

- Gastroesophageal reflux disorder

- Intestinal distress and irritation from laxative abuse

- Kidney problems from diuretic abuse

- Severe dehydration from purging of fluids

As with anorexia, treatment for bulimia often involves a combination of options and depends on the needs of the individual.

To reduce or eliminate binge and purge behavior, a patient may undergo nutritional counseling and psychotherapy, especially cognitive behavioral therapy (CBT), or be prescribed medication. Some antidepressants, such as fluoxetine (Prozac), which is the only medication approved by the U.S. Food and Drug Administration for treating bulimia, may help patients who also have depression and/or anxiety. It also appears to help reduce binge eating and purging behavior, reduces the chance of relapse, and improves eating attitudes.

CBT that has been tailored to treat bulimia also has shown to be effective in changing binging and purging behavior and eating attitudes. Therapy may be individually oriented or group-based.

Binge Eating Disorder

Binge eating disorder is characterized by recurrent binge eating episodes during which a person feels a loss of control over his or her eating. Unlike bulimia, binge eating episodes are not followed by purging, excessive exercise, or fasting. As a result, people with binge eating disorder often are overweight or obese. They also experience guilt, shame, and/or distress about the binge eating, which can lead to more binge eating.

Obese people with binge eating disorder often have coexisting psychological illnesses including anxiety, depression, and personality disorders. In addition, links between obesity and cardiovascular disease and hypertension are well documented.

Treatment options for binge eating disorder are similar to those used to treat bulimia. Fluoxetine and other antidepressants may reduce binge eating episodes and help alleviate depression in some patients.

Patients with binge eating disorder also may be prescribed appetite suppressants. Psychotherapy, especially CBT, is also used to treat the underlying psychological issues associated with binge eating in an individual or group environment.

How Are Men And Boys Affected?

Although eating disorders primarily affect women and girls, boys and men are also vulnerable. One in four preadolescent cases of anorexia occur in boys, and binge eating disorder affects females and males about equally.

Like females who have eating disorders, males with the illness have a warped sense of body image and often have muscle dysmorphia, a type of disorder that is characterized by an extreme concern with becoming more muscular. Some boys with the disorder want to lose weight, while others want to gain weight or "bulk up." Boys who think they are too small are at a greater risk for using steroids or other dangerous drugs to increase muscle mass.

♣ It's A Fact!!
Boys with eating disorders exhibit the same types of emotional, physical, and behavioral signs and symptoms as girls, but for a variety of reasons, boys are less likely to be diagnosed with what is often considered a stereotypically "female" disorder.

How Are We Working To Better Understand And Treat Eating Disorders?

Researchers are unsure of the underlying causes and nature of eating disorders. Unlike a neurological disorder, which generally can be pinpointed to a specific lesion on the brain, an eating disorder likely involves abnormal activity distributed across brain systems. With increased recognition that mental disorders are brain disorders, more researchers are using tools from both modern neuroscience and modern psychology to better understand eating disorders.

♣ **It's A Fact!!**
Researchers are working to define the basic processes of eating disorders, which should help identify better treatments. For example, is anorexia the result of skewed body image, self-esteem problems, obsessive thoughts, compulsive behavior, or a combination of these? Can it be predicted or identified as a risk factor before drastic weight loss occurs, and therefore avoided?

One approach involves the study of the human genes. With the publication of the human genome sequence in 2003, mental health researchers are studying the various combinations of genes to determine if any deoxyribonucleic acid (DNA) variations are associated with the risk of developing a mental disorder. Neuroimaging, such as the use of magnetic resonance imaging (MRI), may also lead to a better understanding of eating disorders.

Neuroimaging already is used to identify abnormal brain activity in patients with schizophrenia, obsessive-compulsive disorder, and depression. It may also help researchers better understand how people with eating disorders process information, regardless of whether they have recovered or are still in the throes of their illness.

Conducting behavioral or psychological research on eating disorders is even more complex and challenging. As a result, few studies of treatments for eating disorders have been conducted in the past. New studies currently underway, however, are aiming to remedy the lack of information available about treatment.

Questions may be answered in the future as scientists and doctors think of eating disorders as medical illnesses with certain biological causes. Researchers are studying behavioral questions, along with genetic and brain systems information, to understand risk factors, identify biological markers, and develop medications that can target specific pathways that control eating behavior. Finally, neuroimaging and genetic studies may also provide clues for how each person may respond to specific treatments.

Chapter 3
Statistics On Eating Disorders

Anorexia Nervosa

Research suggests that about one percent (1%) of female adolescents have anorexia. That means that about one out of every one hundred young women between ten and twenty are starving themselves, sometimes to death. There do not seem to be reliable figures for younger children and older adults, but such cases, while they do occur, are not common.

Overall, lifetime prevalence estimates are 0.6% for anorexia nervosa, 1.0% for bulimia nervosa, and 2.8% for binge eating disorder. Risk is up to 3 times higher in women versus men. (*American Family Physician*. 2008;77:187-195, 196-197)

Bulimia Nervosa

Research suggests that about four percent (4%), or four out of one hundred, college-aged women have bulimia. About 50% of people who have been anorexic develop bulimia or bulimic patterns. Because people with bulimia are secretive, it is difficult to know how many older people are affected. Bulimia is rare in children.

About This Chapter: "Statistics: How Many People Have Eating Disorders?" Used with permission of ANRED: Anorexia Nervosa and Related Eating Disorders, Inc., http://www.anred.com. © 2008.

Males With Eating Disorders

Many surveys indicate that only about 10% of people with anorexia and bulimia are male. This gender difference may reflect our society's different expectations for men and women. Men are supposed to be strong and powerful. They feel ashamed of skinny bodies and want to be big and powerful. Women, on the other hand, are supposed to be tiny, waif-like, and thin. They diet to lose weight, making themselves vulnerable to binge eating. Some develop rigid and compulsive overcontrol. Dieting and the resulting hunger are two of the most powerful eating disorders triggers known.

Now, that having been said, researchers at Harvard University Medical School have new data that suggests that up to 25 percent of adults with eating disorders are male. Whether that figure indicates that more men are becoming eating disordered, or that men previously escaped attention and diagnosis, or that diagnostic tools have improved and are now catching people who would have escaped detection before has yet to be determined. Preliminary information suggests that men are now more concerned about appearance and body image than they were in the past. The new study was based on information obtained from the National Comorbidity Survey Replication, a mental health survey of nearly 9,000 adults across the U.S.

What Age Groups Are Affected?

Anorexia and bulimia affect primarily people in their teens and twenties, but studies report both disorders in children as young as six and individuals as old as seventy-six. As the Baby Boomers in the U.S. grow older, there seems to be an increase in the incidence of middle-aged women with anorexia and bulimia, possibly because this group has consistently considered image to be of major importance.

Overweight And Obesity

Studies suggest that about sixty percent of adult Americans, both male and female, are overweight. About one third (34%) are obese, meaning that they are 20% or more above normal, healthy weight. Many of these people have binge eating disorder.

In addition, about 31 percent of American teenage girls and 28 percent of boys are somewhat overweight. An additional 15 percent of American teen girls and nearly 14 percent of teen boys are obese (*Archives of Pediatrics and Adolescent Medicine*, January 2004). Causes include fast food, snacks with high sugar and fat content, little physical activity including use of automobiles, increased time spent in front of TV sets and computers, and a generally more sedentary lifestyles than slimmer peers.

Binge Eating Disorder

A study reported in *Drugs and Therapy Perspectives* (15(5):7-10, March 13, 2000) indicates that about one percent of women in the United States have binge eating disorder, as do thirty percent of women who seek treatment to lose weight. In other studies, up to two percent, or one to two million adults in the U.S., have problems with binge eating.

Eating Disorders And Substance Abuse

About 72% of alcoholic women younger than 30 also have eating disorders. (*Health* magazine, Jan/Feb 2002). In addition, people with eating disorders often abuse prescription and recreational drugs, sometimes to numb themselves emotionally, to escape misery and depression, and sometimes in the service of weight loss.

What About Compulsive Exercising?

Because anorexia athletica is not a formal diagnosis, it has not been studied as rigorously as the official eating disorders. We do not know how many people exercise compulsively.

Body Dysmorphic Disorder (Includes Muscle Dysmorphic Disorder)

Body dysmorphic disorder (BDD) affects about two percent of people in the U.S. and strikes males and females equally, usually before age eighteen (70% of the time). Sufferers are excessively concerned about appearance, body shape, body size, weight, perceived lack of muscles, facial blemishes, and so forth. In some cases BDD can lead to steroid abuse, unnecessary plastic surgery,

and even suicide. BDD is treatable
and begins with an evaluation by a
mental health care provider.

Eating Disorders In Western And Non-Western Countries

In a study reported in
Medscape's *General Medicine*
6(3) 2004, prevalence rates in
Western countries for anorexia
nervosa ranged from 0.1% to 5.7%
in female subjects. Prevalence rates
for bulimia nervosa ranged from 0% to 2.1% in males and from 0.3% to 7.3%
in female subjects.

> ♣ **It's A Fact!!**
> **Subclinical Eating Disorders**
>
> We can only guess at the vast numbers of people who have subclinical or threshold eating disorders. They are too much preoccupied with food and weight. Their eating and weight control behaviors are not normal, but they are not disturbed enough to qualify for a formal diagnosis.

Prevalence rates in non-Western countries for bulimia nervosa ranged from 0.46% to 3.2% in female subjects. Studies of eating attitudes indicate abnormal eating attitudes in non-Western countries have been gradually increasing, presumably because of the influence, at least in part, of Western media: movies, TV shows, and magazines. Researchers conclude that the prevalence of eating disorders in non-Western countries is lower than that of Western countries, but it appears to be increasing.

Mortality And Recovery Rates

Without treatment, up to twenty percent (20%) of people with serious eating disorders die. With treatment, that number falls to two to three percent (2–3%). In 2005, Dr. Wright of the Eating Disorders Program at Presbyterian Hospital in Dallas, Texas indicated that the mortality rate for untreated anorexia nervosa may be even higher, up to 25 percent.

With treatment, about sixty percent (60%) of people with eating disorders recover. They maintain healthy weight. They eat a varied diet of normal foods and do not choose exclusively low-cal and non-fat items. They participate in friendships and romantic relationships. They create families and careers.

Many say they feel they are stronger and more competent in life than they would have been if they had not developed confidence in themselves by conquering the disorder.

In spite of treatment, about twenty percent (20%) of people with eating disorders make only partial recoveries. They remain too much focused on food and weight. They participate only superficially in friendships and romantic relationships. They may hold jobs but seldom have meaningful careers. Much of each paycheck goes to diet books, laxatives, Jazzercise classes, and binge food.

The remaining twenty percent (20%) do not improve, even with treatment. They are seen repeatedly in emergency rooms, eating disorders programs, and mental health clinics. Their routinely desperate lives revolve around food and weight concerns, spiraling down into depression, anxiety, loneliness, and feelings of helplessness and hopelessness.

Please Note: The study of eating disorders is a relatively new field. We have no good information on the long-term recovery process. We do know that recovery usually takes a long time, often on average five to seven years of slow progress that includes starts, stops, relapses, and ultimately movement in the direction of mental and physical health.

If you believe you are in the forty percent of people who do not recover from eating disorders, give yourself a break. Get into treatment and stay there. Give it all you have. You may surprise yourself and find you are in the sixty percent after all.

Miscellaneous Statistics

From England: A 1998 survey done by Exeter University included 37,500 young women between twelve and fifteen. Over half (57.5%) listed appearance as the biggest concern in their lives. The same study indicated that 59% of the twelve and thirteen-year-old girls who suffered from low self-esteem were also dieting.

Unrealistic Expectations: Magazine pictures are electronically edited and airbrushed. Many entertainment celebrities are underweight, some anorexically so. How do we know what we should look like? It's hard. Table

✤ It's A Fact!!

Dieting Teens: More than half of teenaged girls are, or think they should be, on diets. They want to lose all or some of the forty pounds that females naturally gain between 8 and 14. About three percent of these teens go too far, becoming anorexic or bulimic.

3.1 compares average women in the U. S. with Barbie doll and department store mannequins. It's not encouraging. (*Health* magazine, September 1997; and NEDIC [National Eating Disorders Information Centre], a Canadian eating disorders advocacy group)

Determining Accurate Statistics Is Difficult

Because physicians are not required to report eating disorders to a health agency, and because people with these problems tend to be secretive, denying that they even have a disorder, we have no way of knowing exactly how many people in this country are affected.

We can study small groups of people, determine how many of them are eating disordered, and then extrapolate to the general population. The numbers are usually given as percentages, and they are as close as we can get to an accurate estimate of the total number of people affected by eating disorders.

Now, that having been said, the journal *Clinician Reviews* [13(9)] 2003] estimates that each year about five million Americans are affected by an eating disorder. But there is disagreement.

The National Association of Anorexia Nervosa and Associated Disorders (ANAD) states that approximately eight million people in the U.S. have anorexia nervosa, bulimia, and related eating disorders. Eight million people represent about three percent (3%) of the total population. Put another way, according to ANAD, about three out of every one hundred people in this country eats in a way disordered enough to warrant treatment.

Table 3.1. Average Women in the U.S. Compared with Barbie Doll and Store Mannequins

	Average Woman	Barbie	Store Mannequin
Height	5' 4"	6' 0"	6' 0"
Weight	145 lbs.	101 lbs.	Not available
Dress size	11 - 14	4	6
Bust	36 - 37"	39"	34"
Waist	29 - 31"	19"	23"
Hips	40 - 42"	33"	34"

Chapter 4

What Causes Eating Disorders?

There are many theories, many interwoven factors, and no one simple answer that covers every person who has an eating disorder. For any particular individual, some or all of the following factors will combine to produce starving, stuffing, and purging.

Biological Factors

According to recent research, genetic factors account for more than half (56 percent) of the risk of developing anorexia nervosa. Work on the genetics of bulimia and binge eating continues. (*Archives of General Psychiatry 2006*; 63:305-312)

Temperament seems to be, at least in part, genetically determined. Some personality types (obsessive-compulsive and sensitive-avoidant, for example) are more vulnerable to eating disorders than others. New research suggests that genetic factors predispose some people to anxiety, perfectionism, and obsessive-compulsive thoughts and behaviors. These people seem to have more than their share of eating disorders. In fact, people with a mother or sister who has had anorexia nervosa are 12 times more likely than others with no family history of that disorder to develop it themselves. They are four times more likely to develop bulimia. (*Eating Disorders Review*. Nov/Dec 2002)

About This Chapter: "What Causes Eating Disorders?" used with permission of ANRED: Anorexia Nervosa and Related Eating Disorders, Inc., http://www.anred.com, © 2008.

Studies reported in the *New England Journal of Medicine* (3/03) indicate that for some, but not all, people heredity is an important factor in the development of obesity and binge eating. Now there are suggestions that women who develop anorexia nervosa have excess activity in the brain's dopamine receptors, which regulate pleasure. This may lead to an explanation of why they feel driven to lose weight but receive no pleasure from shedding pounds. (*Journal of Biological Psychiatry*, July 2005. Guido Frank, et al.)

Also, once a person begins to starve, stuff, or purge, those behaviors in and of themselves can alter brain chemistry and prolong the disorder. For example, both under eating and overeating can activate brain chemicals that produce feelings of peace and euphoria, temporarily dispelling anxiety and depression. In fact some researchers believe that eating disordered folks may be using food to self-medicate painful feelings and distressing moods.

♣ It's A Fact!!

A Note About Stress And Overeating

New research suggests that there is a biological link between stress and the drive to eat. Comfort foods—high in sugar, fat, and calories—seem to calm the body's response to chronic stress. In addition, hormones produced when one is under stress encourage the formation of fat cells. In Westernized countries, life tends to be competitive, fast paced, demanding, and stressful. There may be a link between so-called modern life and increasing rates of overeating, overweight, and obesity. (*Proceedings of the National Academy of Sciences*. Author is Mary Dallman, professor of physiology, University of California at San Francisco [2003].)

Age and brain maturation/impairment play a role also. When an eating disorder begins in childhood or adolescence, it may be especially hard to deal with. Magnetic resonance imaging provides evidence the brain continues to develop and become increasingly complex until people are in their early 20s. The parts of the brain that effectively plan ahead, predict consequences, and manage emotional impulses are just not fully operational in children and teens. Teens may insist they are mature, but the research shows there's a lot more brain wiring that needs to be done before he or she is truly an adult.

Even the U.S. Supreme Court has weighed in on this issue. "Youths are more likely to show a lack of maturity and an underdeveloped sense of responsibility. These qualities often result in impetuous and ill-considered actions and decisions...Juveniles are more vulnerable or susceptible to negative influences and outside pressures, including peer pressure, causing them to have less control...." (Justice Anthony Kennedy writing the majority decision in *Roper vs. Simmons*, March 1, 2005)

Think about it: if teens were truly mature, they would always drive carefully, always wear seatbelts, never consume alcohol or other drugs, and always think about the real-life consequences of their choices and behaviors. Clearly this is not the case. In the same way, teens think their lives are charmed, that they can escape the negative consequences of disordered eating, that they won't get caught in the obsessions and compulsions generated by dieting and the metabolic chaos of binge eating and purging. It is a sad, but predictable, reality that they are mistaken. (David Walsh, *Why Do They Act That Way?* Free Press, Simon & Schuster, 2004.)

And if that were not enough, even when the person is well past 20, starvation, chronic dieting, binge eating, and purging can damage brain wiring and disturb neurochemical processes, impairing the very centers needed to make healthy choices.

Psychological Factors

People with eating disorders tend to be perfectionistic. They have unrealistic expectations of themselves and others. In spite of their many achievements, they feel inadequate and defective. In addition, they see the world as black and white, no shades of gray. Everything is either good or bad, a success or a failure, fat or thin. If fat is bad and thin is good, then thinner is better, and thinnest is best—even if thinnest is sixty-eight pounds in a hospital bed on life support.

Some people with eating disorders use the behaviors to avoid sexuality. Others use them to try to take control of themselves and their lives. They want to be in control and in charge. They are strong, usually winning the power struggles they find themselves in, but inside they feel weak, powerless, victimized, defeated, and resentful.

People with eating disorders often lack a sense of identity. They try to define themselves by manufacturing a socially approved and admired exterior. They have answered the existential question, "Who am I?" by symbolically saying "I am, or I am trying to be, thin. Therefore, I matter."

People with eating disorders often are legitimately angry, but because they seek approval and fear criticism, they do not dare express that anger directly. They do not know how to express it in healthy ways. They turn it against themselves by starving or stuffing.

And then there is pride of achievement. Few things are more satisfying than to succeed in a difficult and dangerous quest, to overcome a challenge that has frustrated others. One does not have to look very far beyond magazine diet articles to see how hard it is to lose weight and maintain a slender figure in today's world of fast food and disappearing time and opportunities to be physically active. Although they usually will not admit it, achieving and maintaining stick thinness is a badge of honor worn with pride by those who can do it. Even if they have earned excellent grades or career honors, being thin may be the only achievement they define as significant. They are not happy and, in fact, may be miserable, but they cling to this achievement as if it validates their existence.

It is often said that the key to understanding an eating disorder is an appreciation of the person's need to control everything: life, schedules, friends, family, food, and especially one's own body. That is true, but there is another factor at least equally important: aspiration to perfection. When people embark on a weight loss program with all the fervor of a pilgrim seeking holiness, it becomes evident that they are hoping for and working to achieve a magical conversion process. By losing weight, they hope to transform their dull caterpillar selves into beautiful butterflies that lead lives of contentment, happiness, confidence, and completion. How sad. If losing weight truly did lead to happiness, we would be a planet of beanpoles.

Happiness, of course, is attainable, but through meaningful work, nourishing relationships, and a connection to something greater than oneself. Magical thinking and simplistic self-improvement programs just aren't up to the challenge.

Family Factors

Some people with eating disorders say they feel smothered in overprotective families. Others feel abandoned, misunderstood, and alone. Parents who overvalue physical appearance can unwittingly contribute to an eating disorder. So can those who make critical comments, even in jest, about their children's bodies.

Families that include a person with an eating disorder tend to be overprotective, rigid, and ineffective at resolving conflict. Sometimes mothers are emotionally cool while fathers are physically or emotionally absent. At the same time, there are high expectations of achievement and success. Children learn not to disclose doubts, fears, anxieties, and imperfections. Instead they try to solve their problems by manipulating weight and food and trying to achieve the appearance of success even if they do not feel successful.

Research at Oregon Health and Science University in Portland has produced strong evidence that exposure to stress (abuse, neglect, loss of a parent) in childhood increases the risk of behavioral and emotional problems (anxiety, depression, suicidality, drug abuse—phenomena frequently associated with eating disorders) in teenagers and young adults.

In addition, other research suggests that daughters of mothers with histories of eating disorders may be at higher risk of eating disorders themselves than are children of mothers with few food and weight issues. Children learn attitudes about dieting and their bodies through observation. When mom is dissatisfied with her body and frequently diets, daughters will learn to base their self-worth on their appearance, says Christine Gerbstadt, spokeswoman for the American Dietetic Association.

Alison Field, lead author of a Harvard study of peer, parent, and media influences on children's dieting behavior and body image attitudes (*Pediatrics*, Vol. 107 No. 1 January 2001, pp. 54-60) adds that "even small cues—such as making self-deprecating remarks about bulging thighs or squealing in delight over a few lost pounds—can send the message that thinness is to be prized above all else."

According to a report published in the April 1999 issue of the *International Journal of Eating Disorders*, mothers who have anorexia, bulimia, or binge eating disorder handle food issues and weight concerns differently than mothers who have never had eating disorders.

Patterns are observable even in infancy. They include odd feeding schedules, using food for rewards, punishments, comfort, or other non-nutritive purposes, and concerns about their daughters' weight.

Still to be determined is whether or not daughters of mothers with eating disorders will themselves become eating disordered when they reach adolescence.

It's important to note that if parents preach and nag about junk food and try to limit their children's access to treats, the children will desire and over-eat these very items. A recent study (*American Journal of Clinical Nutrition.* 2003;78:215) indicates that when parents restrict eating, children are more likely to eat when they are not hungry. The more severe the restriction, the stronger the desire to eat prohibited foods—a classic power struggle and also an illustration of the power of the forbidden. These behaviors may set the stage for a full-blown eating disorder in the future.

Social Factors

People vulnerable to eating disorders, in most cases, are experiencing relationship problems, loneliness in particular. Some may be withdrawn with only superficial or conflicted connections to other people. Others may seem to be living exciting lives filled with friends and social activities, but later they will confess that they did not feel they really fit in, that no one seemed to really understand them, and that they had no true friends or confidants with whom they could share thoughts, feelings, doubts, insecurities, fears, hopes, ambitions, and so forth—the basis of true

♣ **It's A Fact!!**
Sometimes appearance-obsessed friends or romantic partners create pressure that encourages eating disorders. Ditto for sorority houses, theatre troupes, dance companies, school cliques, and online chat rooms that insist extreme dieting is just a lifestyle choice. All these are situations where peers influence one another in unhealthy ways.

intimacy. Often they desperately want healthy connections to others but fear criticism and rejection if their perceived flaws and shortcomings become known.

Cultural Pressures

In Westernized countries characterized by competitive striving for success, and in pockets of affluence in developing countries, women often experience unrealistic cultural demands for thinness. They respond by linking self-esteem to weight.

Cultural expectations can be cruel and unrelenting. "In order for a woman to consider herself happy, she has to be in a good relationship, be happy with her kids, her friends have to like her, her job has to be going well, her house has to look really good—and she has to be thin." (Professor Alice Domar, Harvard Medical School. *Parade* magazine, October 11, 2003)

Media Factors

People in Western countries are flooded by media words and images. An average U.S. child, for example, sees more than 30,000 TV commercial each year (TV-Turnoff Network, 2005). That child sees more than 21 hours of TV each week plus dozens of magazines and many movies every year. In those media, happy and successful people are almost always portrayed by actors and models who are young, toned, and thin. The vast majority is stylishly dressed and has spent much time on hairstyles and makeup.

♣ It's A Fact!!

"Advertising has done more to cause the social unrest of the 20th century than any other single factor."

—Clare Boothe Luce, American author and diplomat (1903-1987)

> **Factoid:** According to *Health* magazine, April 2002, 32% of female TV network characters are underweight, while only 5% of females in the U.S. audience are underweight.

In contrast, evil, stupid, or buffoonish people are portrayed by actors who are older, frumpier, unkempt, or perhaps physically challenged. Many are fat.

Factoid: Again according to *Health* magazine, only 3% of female TV network characters are obese, while 25% of U.S. women fall into that category.

Most people want to be happy and successful, states that require thought, personal development, and usually hard work and reflection. The media, especially ads and commercials for appearance-related items, suggest that we can avoid hard character-building work by making our bodies into copies of the icons of success.

Reading between the lines of many ads reveals a not-so-subtle message—"You are not acceptable the way you are. The only way you can become acceptable is to buy our product and try to look like our model (who is six feet tall and wears size four jeans—and is probably anorexic). If you can't quite manage it, better keep buying our product. It's your only hope."

The differences between media images of happy, successful men and women are interesting. The women, with few exceptions, are young and thin. Thin is desirable, or so they are portrayed. The men are young or older, but the heroes and good guys are strong and powerful in all the areas that matter—physically, in the business world, and socially. For men in the media, thin is not desirable; power, strength and competency are desirable. Thin men are seen as skinny, and skinny men are often depicted as sick, weak, frail, drug addicted, criminal, or deviant.

These differences are reflected in male and female approaches to self-help. When a man wants to improve himself, he often begins by lifting weights to become bigger, stronger, and more powerful. When a woman wants to improve herself, she usually begins with a diet, which will leave her smaller, weaker, and less powerful. Yet females have just as strong needs for power and control as do males.

Many people believe this media stereotyping helps explain why about ninety percent of people with eating disorders are women and only ten percent are men.

In recent years it has become politically correct for the media to make some effort to combat eating disorders. We have seen magazine articles and

TV shows featuring the perils and heartbreak of anorexia and bulimia, but these efforts seem weak and ineffective when they are presented in the usual context. For example, how can one believe that a fashion magazine is truly motivated to combat anorexia when their articles about that subject are surrounded by advertisements featuring anorexic-looking models? How can one believe that the talk show hostess is truly in favor of strong, healthy female bodies when she frequently prods her stick-like thighs and talks about how much she wants to lose weight from her already scrawny body?

In May 1999, research was published that demonstrated the media's unhealthy affect on women's self-esteem and body awareness. In 1995, before television came to their island, the people of Fiji thought the ideal body was round, plump, and soft. Then, after 38 months of Melrose Place, Beverly Hills 90210, and similar western shows, Fijian teenage girls showed serious signs of eating disorders.

In another study, females who regularly watch TV three or more nights per week are fifty percent more likely than non-watchers to feel "too big" or "too fat." About two-thirds of the TV-watching female teens dieted in the month preceding the survey. Fifteen percent admitted vomiting to control their weight. TV shows like the two mentioned above are fantasies, but all over the world young women, and some not so young, accept them as instructions on how to look and act. That's really a shame.

☞ Remember!!

An important question for people who watch TV, read magazines, and go to movies—do these media present images that open a window on the real world, or do they hold up a fun-house mirror in which the reflections of real people are distorted into impossibly tall, thin sticks (or impossibly muscular, steroid-dependent male action figures)? Media consumers need to be wise consumers of visual images.

Even so-called health-oriented magazines can contribute to the problem. Five years after reading magazine articles about dieting, teenage girls were more likely to control weight by fasting, vomiting, smoking cigarettes, or abusing laxatives than girls who never read such articles. The message underlying these articles in many cases is "You should be concerned about your weight, and you should be doing something about it." It's unclear if the toxic message is conveyed in the article itself or the pictures of thin models that accompany the words.

Incidentally, only about 14 percent of teen boys report reading diet articles frequently, compared with 44 percent of girls. And unlike their female peers, those boys do not show long-lasting negative effects on weight control behavior that persist through time. (The study from which these figures come appeared in the January 2007 issue of the journal *Pediatrics*.)

Triggers

If people are vulnerable to eating disorders, sometimes all it takes to put the ball in motion is a trigger event that they do not know how to handle. A trigger could be something as seemingly innocuous as teasing or as devastating as rape or incest.

Triggers often happen at times of transition, shock, or loss where increased demands are made on people who already are unsure of their ability to meet expectations. Such triggers might include puberty, starting a new school, beginning a new job, death, divorce, marriage, family problems, breakup of an important relationship, critical comments from someone important, graduation into a chaotic, competitive world, and so forth.

There is some evidence to suggest that girls who achieve sexual maturity ahead of peers, with the associated development of breasts, hips, and other physical signs of womanhood, are at increased risk of becoming eating disordered. They may wrongly interpret their new curves as "being fat" and feel uncomfortable because they no longer look like peers who still have childish bodies.

Wanting to take control and fix things, but not really knowing how, and under the influence of a culture that equates success and happiness with thinness, the person tackles her/his body instead of the problem at hand. Dieting, bingeing, purging, exercising, and other strange behaviors are not random craziness. They are heroic, but misguided and ineffective, attempts to take charge in a world that seems overwhelming.

♣ **It's A Fact!!**

Multidimensional Risk Factors

A panel at the 2004 International Conference on Eating Disorders in Orlando, Florida, suggested the following spectrum of risk factors. The more any one person has, the greater the probability of developing an eating disorder.

- High weight concerns before age 14
- High level of perceived stress
- Behavior problems before age 14
- History of dieting
- Mother diets and is concerned about appearance
- Siblings diet and are concerned about appearance
- Peers diet and are concerned about appearance
- Negative self-evaluation
- Perfectionism
- No male friends
- Parental control
- Rivalry with one or more siblings
- Competitive with siblings' shape and/or appearance
- Shy and/or anxious
- Distressed by parental arguments
- Distressed by life events occurring in the year before the illness develops
- Critical comments from family members about weight, shape, and eating
- Teasing about weight, shape, and appearance

Sometimes people with medical problems such as diabetes, people who must pay meticulous attention to what they eat, become vulnerable to eating disorders. A certain amount of obsessiveness is necessary for health, but when the fine line is crossed, healthy obsessiveness can quickly become pathological.

Perhaps the most common trigger of disordered eating is dieting. It is a bit simplistic, but nonetheless true, to say that if there were no dieting, there would be no anorexia nervosa. Neither would there be the bulimia that people create when they diet, make themselves chronically hungry, overeat in response to hunger pangs and cravings, and then, panicky about weight gain, vomit or otherwise purge to get rid of the calories.

Feeling guilty and perhaps horrified at what they have done, they swear to "be good." That usually means more dieting, which leads to more hunger, and so the cycle repeats again and again. It is axiomatic in eating disorders treatment programs that the best way to avoid a binge is to never, ever allow oneself to become ravenously hungry. It is far wiser to be aware of internal signals and respond to hunger cues early on by eating appropriate amounts of nourishing, healthy food.

Chapter 5

Genes And Eating Disorders

There is renewed interest and research into genetic influences on the development of eating disorders. This chapter looks at some of the assumptions underpinning this research.

Classical Views On Genes

Most of us are captured by the classical idea of genes as hereditary factors that control the characteristics of living things. With this view, to say that the gene or genes for a characteristic have been found, implies both that certain genes determine or control the characteristic and that they have been identified. Today's molecular biology brings us an understanding of genes that undermines this view. A gene is now understood to be a sequence of deoxyribonucleic acid (DNA) containing the code to make a protein. Very few characteristics or diseases are the direct result of a single, or even several such proteins. In spite of this, the classical view continues to affect the way that genetic influences are seen and discussed.

New Understanding Of Genes

While every analogy has its limits, here is one that might help explain this new understanding. A gene, or set of genes, might be compared to an idea, or set of ideas, for a novel. If the author never writes the novel, the ideas influence nothing. If the author proceeds to write the novel, the ideas have a very strong influence at the beginning of the writing process, but quite early in the process, the characters, setting, and plot may interact and develop according to principles not restricted by the original novel ideas, each influencing the other. J.K. Rowling, for example, recently described the death of a character in *Harry Potter and the Order of the Phoenix* as deeply upsetting to her, perhaps not something that had been part of her original idea, and yet consistent with the logic of the characters and events of the novel. Suppose that our author's novel is published and eventually is to become a Hollywood movie. The screenwriter chosen to adapt the novel for the screen brings his or her own ideas to influence the story. The American studio system brings many other influences to bear as well: economics, ideology, censorship, star promotion, and marketing to name a few. Each new level of operations brings new rules and principles to influence the end result. We may or may not recognize the original author's ideas in the movie version of the novel, however those ideas were involved in the development of the movie. We might say that they made the movie possible, but they definitely did not determine its content.

Similarly with genetic influences, the more complex a level of the organism's functioning we are concerned with, the less direct an influence any proteins coded by genes are likely to have. Eating disorders are complex conditions that involve physiological functioning; thinking processes; behaviors that have individual beneficial effects, like self-comforting; behavioral choices, which have cultural value, like the benefits derived from being thin; and individual meanings, like demonstrating one's strength through self-denial, or communicating distress. There are extremely few diseases, which are the result of a mutation to a single gene, as Huntington disease is. In fact, this is one of the reasons that the classical view of genes was overthrown. While genes will be involved in eating disorders, like the author's initial ideas for a novel are involved in the movie based on it, we will not find a gene or mutation that causes eating disorders.

Susceptibility And Genes

Some researchers have suggested instead that we look for "susceptibility genes" for eating disorders. When an individual has susceptibility genes for a particular disease, he or she is at risk for the disease because it will manifest in a certain environment. Examples given by eating disorders researchers often include the risk of diabetes in people of Asian and Native American ancestry, which becomes manifest in an environment when food is abundant. With some such diseases, we know how to lower or eliminate the risk through environmental changes. For example, phenylketonuria is an hereditary disease caused by the lack of a liver enzyme required to digest phenylalanine, an amino acid most commonly found in protein-containing foods such as meat, cows' milk, and breast milk. This condition can cause brain damage in affected babies, which can be prevented by early detection and manipulation of the feeding environment, that is, eliminating phenylalanine from the child's diet. What these examples have in common is that the illness or disease can be completely defined in physical terms, that bio-chemical processes specific to the illness are candidates for locating genetic contributions, and that the manifesting environment is physical or bio-chemical, rather than interpersonal or sociocultural. Suggesting that these conditions are models for what we might find with eating disorders still plays on the classical idea of genes and fails to take into account their significant and qualitative differences from eating disorders.

Environment And Genes

The effects of genes that may be involved with eating disorders have not been established. Some possibilities researchers are investigating include genes that code for proteins involved in neurotransmitter variations (related to serotonin and dopamine, for instance), which differently affect mood, anxiety, and novelty-seeking; or genes that code for proteins involved in information processing tendencies; or those involved in "traits" like perfectionism or perseverance. No environment or set of environments in which genetic susceptibility would necessarily manifest has yet been specified. There is no reason to believe, that either separately or together, the current candidate genetic influences would be specific to eating disorders, as we know them to be involved in other conditions, and we know that eating disorders often occur along with other conditions. We should be skeptical of the susceptibility model until genetics researchers show us, either directly or in relation to more relevant diseases or disorders, how that model would work with the level of physical, behavioral, interpersonal, and sociocultural complexity at which eating disorders exist.

In some ways, all genes are susceptibility genes for damage, disease, or death given the "right" environmental condition or other. The most extreme example would be the genes that contribute to our needing to breathe oxygen to stay alive. Given an oxygen-deprived environment, the vast majority of us will sustain brain damage or die. The idea of "susceptibility genes" in this case becomes meaningless. It would probably be more accurate just to call the oxygen-deprived environment a poor or poisonous one for human beings.

♣ **It's A Fact!!**
To meaningfully label some set of genes as susceptibility genes for a condition or illness, it should be possible to show that they are specifically connected to the illness or condition and that the environment in which the illness manifests is one that does not harm most people.

Socio-Cultural Environment

Over the past 30 to 35 years, our sociocultural environment has idealized a body shape for women that minimizes body fat to pre-pubertal levels. This is opposite to the most common genetically influenced direction of development for women's bodies, which is increasing body fat at puberty and later. Thus, girls see their bodies developing in ways that they have been socialized to find offensive. It is no wonder that the vast majority of females in our culture react to finding themselves becoming offensive by trying to change themselves to be more acceptable. Although not all develop diagnosable eating disorders, the vast majority are dissatisfied with their bodies and persistently act on this dissatisfaction through a range of body and appetite controlling efforts.

A sociocultural environment does not exist at an abstract external level; rather, it permeates individuals' relationships with one another in institutions like schools and workplaces, in families, in peer groups, and in other interpersonal interactions. When an individual girl is harassed about her body shape, this is not just an individual experience; it is a socioculturally mediated one. Schoolboys can hurt a girl by telling her that she is fat, not because she is actually fat, but because they know it will bother her, giving them the upper hand. Boys doing so are playing on the culture's negative associations with fat, the fact that girls are conditioned to see their personal value as appearance-related, and the power males have in evaluating female bodies. The economic interests satisfied through this culture (and perhaps expanding it currently by creating intense insecurities in boys about their appearances) act as a conservative force against changing it. Sociocultural environments are not neutral; they privilege some people's interests while disadvantaging others, and therefore, have political implications.

Think about this in relation to a different issue. Suppose there are high rates of a criminal behavior like stealing among males living in poverty conditions. We may try to prevent the development of stealing among boys living in poverty by educating them that theft is wrong, teaching them techniques to help them resist impulses to steal, providing them with medications to reduce their impulsive behaviors, and so on. At the same time, let's say we know that a small percentage of them are said to have genetic loading for impulsive behavior and novelty-seeking, and are therefore likely to steal, especially when their culture bombards them with images of consumables that others purchase with ease, and that their culture values men who have big purchasing power. Let's say we also know that in cultures that don't hold these values and in which families are protected from poverty, stealing among males is radically reduced. What would we think about providing millions of dollars for genetics research, while paying lip service to the cultural and poverty issues?

Potential Contributions Of Genetic Research

Researchers in the field of genes and eating disorders suggest a number of potentially helpful contributions from their research. While these are currently appropriately vague, they may become more precise if it becomes possible to specify the involvement of particular genes and particular environments in these disorders. So far, the focus seems to be on refining practices that we already have, or could have, for example developing medications that could more specifically target individuals' neurotransmitter differences; teaching parents how to recognize early signs of perfectionism or obsessiveness, and how to help themselves

♣ **It's A Fact!!**

A culture that sets females at odds with their own development, and which supports industries that exploit the insecurities arising from this (for example, the diet industry), is arguably a poor or poisonous environment for females to live in.

and their children to use these to their own advantage, rather than be dominated by them; and guiding children to choose activities that do not exacerbate the effects of traits like perfectionism. These efforts might increase someone's ability to resist an eating disorder, but they will not provide a genetic prevention or cure in the classical sense.

It is true that if we could specify the genetic influences, we could also learn about protective factors by finding people who have the genes but don't develop eating disorders. While some boys and men do develop eating disorders, being male remains a major protective factor. It is tempting to suggest that the most effective gene therapy for eating disorders would consist of adding a Y chromosome to all "susceptible" females. A modest proposal!

Chapter 6

Who Is At Risk For Developing An Eating Disorder?

These disorders usually appear in bright, attractive young women between the ages of twelve and twenty-five, although there are both older and younger exceptions. At least ten percent (10%) of the people with eating disorders are male, possibly more. Researchers are just now beginning to determine how widespread these problems are in men and boys.

Who Is At Risk For Developing Anorexia Nervosa?

People who become anorexic often are, or were, good children—eager to please, conscientious, hard working, and good students. Typically they are people-pleasers who seek approval and avoid conflict. They may take care of other people and strive for perfection, but underneath they feel defective and inadequate. They want to be special, to stand out from the mediocre masses. They try to achieve that goal by losing weight and being thin.

Some clinicians believe that the symptoms of anorexia are a kind of symbolic language used by people who don't know how to, or are afraid to, express powerful emotions directly, with words. For example, making one's body tiny and thin may substitute for, "I'm not ready to grow up yet," or "I'm

About This Chapter: "Who Is at Risk for Developing an Eating Disorder?" used with permission of ANRED: Anorexia Nervosa and Related Eating Disorders, Inc., http://www.anred.com, © 2008.

starving for attention." Refusing to eat may translate to "I won't let you control me!"

People who develop anorexia often feel stressed and anxious when faced with new situations. Many are perfectionists who have low tolerance for change (including the normal physical changes their bodies experience at puberty), feeling that it represents chaos and loss of control. Some set rigid, unrealistic standards for themselves and feel they have failed totally when they cannot achieve and maintain the degree of excellence they demand of themselves.

In addition to restricting food, classic anorexics also restrict other areas of their lives. They are risk-averse individuals, preferring to live closely circumscribed lives, with few changes in established routines, to which they tightly cling. They need to become more adventurous and learn how to cope with expanded horizons.

Although people who have anorexia nervosa don't want to admit it, many fear growing up, taking on adult responsibilities, and meeting the demands of independence. Many are overly engaged with parents to the exclusion of peer relationships. They use dieting and weight preoccupations to avoid, or ineffectively cope with, the demands of a new life stage such as adolescence, living away from home, or adult sexuality.

Who Is At Risk For Developing Bulimia?

People who become bulimic often have problems with anxiety, depression, and impulse control. For example, they may shoplift, engage in casual sexual activity, indulge in shopping binges, abuse alcohol and other drugs, or cut their flesh and engage in other self-harm behaviors. They do not handle stress gracefully. They may be dependent on their families even though they fiercely profess independence. Many have problems trusting other people. They have few or no truly satisfying friendships or romantic relationships.

They may diet, thinking to improve their lives and feel better about themselves. The deprivation leads to hunger, which leads to powerful cravings, which lead to binge eating. Feeling guilty, and afraid of weight gain, they try to remove calories from their bodies by vomiting, abusing laxatives, fasting, or other methods of purging.

Bulimics binge not only on food but also in other areas of their lives, often taking on more than they can handle: relationships, jobs, responsibilities, family duties, and sometimes possessions and alcohol and other drugs. They need to learn to set limits and boundaries, to slow down and step back a bit so they don't feel so overwhelmed. When they can set appropriate limits, they will have less need to turn to the binge/purge behaviors that serve as a defense against the stress and intensity of being over-involved.

> ♣ It's A Fact!!
> ## Are some people at special risk?
>
> Because of intense demands for thinness, some people are at high risk for eating disorders—wrestlers, jockeys, cheerleaders, sorority members, socialites, dancers, gymnasts, runners, models, actresses, entertainers, and male homosexuals.

Eating Disorders And Abuse

Some clinicians find that a high percentage of their clients with eating disorders also have histories of physical, emotional, or sexual abuse. Research, however, suggests that people who have been abused have about the same incidence of eating disorders as those who have not been mistreated. Nevertheless, the subject arises often enough to warrant discussion here.

People who have survived abuse often do not know what to do with the painful feelings and overwhelming memories that remain, sometimes even many years later. Some try to escape those feelings and memories by numbing themselves with binge food or through starvation. Some try to symbolically cleanse themselves by vomiting or abusing laxatives. Some starve themselves because they believe they are "bad" and do not deserve the comfort of food and the nurture it represents.

As with all eating disorders, the starving and stuffing that follow abuse are coping behaviors. The key to recovery is finding out what the person is trying to achieve, or avoid, with the behaviors. S/he then needs to find, and use, healthier and more effective behaviors to feel better and make life happier. Almost always professional counseling is necessary to complete the process.

Age And Brain Maturation/Impairment Play A Role Too

When an eating disorder begins in childhood or adolescence, it may be especially hard to deal with. Magnetic resonance imaging provides evidence that the brain continues to develop and become increasingly complex until people are in their mid-20s. The parts of the brain that effectively plan ahead, predict consequences, and manage emotional impulses are just not fully operational in children and teens. Teens may insist they are mature, but the research shows there's a lot more brain wiring that needs to be done before he or she is truly an adult. (David Walsh, *Why Do They Act That Way?* Free Press, Simon & Schuster, 2004.)

And if that were not enough, even when the person is well past 20, starvation, chronic dieting, binge eating, and purging can interfere with brain wiring and chemistry, impairing the very centers needed to make healthy choices.

Western Culture—An Incubator For Eating Disorders

People with eating disorders seek external solutions for internal problems. They feel empty, depressed, anxious, fearful, sorrowful, guilty, frustrated, insecure, and depressed. They want to feel better, which is good, but they choose woefully ineffective ways of doing that. In fact, starving and stuffing have the opposite effect; they cause more emotional pain and distress.

Nonetheless, manipulating food and body weight is encouraged by Western culture, which exhorts all of us, and especially women, to improve ourselves by "fixing" the external package, the body. Makeover reality shows on TV are a prime example. The message is, "Change your hair color and style, buy new clothes, paint your face, shove your feet into shoes that hurt, tone your muscles, enlarge your breasts, and lose weight. Then you will be happy, admired, and loved—an instant new identity, a new you.

The problem is, of course, that sprucing up the outside (or starving it to death) does not fix what's wrong on the inside. True happiness and deep contentment are achieved through psychological and spiritual growth and ultimate realization of one's worth and place in the world, not by abusing the body. It takes a lot of wisdom and maturity to realize and accept this hard truth, and the young people most vulnerable to eating disorders are those who most lack those characteristics.

Chapter 7

All Ethnic Groups Are Susceptible To Eating Disorders

At Risk: All Ethnic And Cultural Groups

Boys And Girls Of All Ethnic Groups Are Susceptible To Eating Disorders

Many people believe that eating disorders commonly occur among affluent white females. Although the prevalence of these disorders elsewhere in the population is much lower, an increasing number of males and minorities are also suffering from eating disorders.

Girls and boys from all ethnic and racial groups may suffer from eating disorders and disordered eating. The specific nature of the most common eating problems, as well as risk and protective factors, may vary from group to group, but no population is exempt. Research findings regarding prevalence rates and specific types of problems among particular groups are limited, but it is evident that disturbed eating behaviors and attitudes occur across all cultures.

About This Chapter: Text in this chapter is from the following facts sheets within *BodyWise Handbook*: "At Risk: All Ethnic and Cultural Groups," "African American Girls," "Latina Girls," "Asian and Pacific Islander Girls," and "American Indian and Alaska Native Girls"; produced by the National Women's Health Information Center, a component of the U.S. Department of Health and Human Services, Office on Women's Health, October 2005.

Large percentages of African American, American Indian, and Hispanic females are overweight. Being overweight is a risk factor for engaging in disordered eating behaviors. Risk factors and incidence rates for eating disorders can vary dramatically among subgroups of a specific population.

Cultural Norms Regarding Body Size Can Play A Role In The Development Of Eating Disorders

In Western cultures, the ideal female body is thin. Membership in ethnic groups and cultures that do not value a thin body may protect girls from body dissatisfaction and weight concerns. However, young people who identify with cultures that prefer larger body sizes may be at risk for becoming overweight or obese. Research also suggests that women who think they are smaller than the body size favored by their cultural group may be at risk for binge eating.

Eating Disorders Among Ethnically And Culturally Diverse Girls May Be Underreported And Undetected

Eating disorders among ethnically and culturally diverse girls may be underreported due to the lack of population-based studies that include representatives from these groups. The perception that non-white females are at decreased risk may also contribute to the lack of detection. Stereotyped body images of ethnically diverse women (for example, petite Asian American, heavier African American) can also deter detection. In addition, for some ethnic and cultural groups, seeking professional help for emotional problems is not a common practice.

Girls of different ethnic and cultural groups often receive treatment for the accompanying symptoms of an eating disorder, such as depression or malnutrition, rather than for the eating disorder itself. When these girls are finally diagnosed as having an eating disorder, the disorder (especially anorexia), tends to be more severe. This problem is exacerbated by the difficulty they may have in locating culturally sensitive treatment centers.

African American Girls

African American Girls Are At Risk

After White Americans, African Americans comprise the ethnic and cultural group about which most studies on eating disorders are available.

While there are no incidence or prevalence rates for eating disorders in the African American population, recent studies are providing clinical accounts of eating disorders in African American women.

Numerous studies have documented a high rate of eating disorder behaviors and risk factors, including body dissatisfaction among African American women. More specifically, research demonstrates that binge eating and purging is at least as common among African American women as White women.

Unfortunately, little work has been undertaken regarding differences in presentation of symptoms, cultural-specific risk factors, and effective treatment methods for African Americans.

The belief that African American women do not experience eating disorders contributes to the lack of identification of eating disorder problems among this population. Since the early detection of an eating disorder is very important for its successful treatment, this misperception can result in serious health problems for African American girls.

African American Girls Are Not Immune To The Pressure To Be Thin

The African American culture is more accepting of diverse body sizes and seems to favor a broader beauty ideal. This tolerance may help protect some African American girls from body dissatisfaction and low self-image.

However, as Black girls approach adolescence, they become more concerned with thinness. Studies indicate that when African American girls experience social pressure to be thin, they express the same type of body dissatisfaction and drive for thinness as White girls.

Adolescents from middle class African American families may be particularly vulnerable to the influence of the White beauty ideal. Essence, a magazine that caters to African American women, regularly runs stories on body size anxiety and eating disorders. A survey of its readers indicated that African American women appear to have at least equal levels of abnormal eating attitudes and behaviors as White women. Studies indicate that Blacks who identify with mainstream culture exhibit more eating problems, including dieting and fear of fat.

Media targeting African Americans and other racial and ethnic and cultural groups in this country are increasingly embracing the beauty as thinness ideal. Black female stars in the music, film, and fashion industries are just as thin as their White counterparts. The influence of these role models may contribute to body dissatisfaction and weight control behaviors among African American girls.

African American Women Experience High Rates Of Obesity, A Risk Factor For Eating Disorders

Although the preference for a larger body size may help protect African American girls from body dissatisfaction and dieting, it can encourage obesity, which is also a risk factor for eating disorders. Black women are more than three times as likely as White women to be obese. Black women and girls are also less likely to exercise than their White counterparts. African American families with low incomes are particularly at risk for obesity, due in part to a diet of food that is high in fat.

African American girls are not likely to be heavier than White girls during childhood; but after adolescence their body mass index (BMI) surpasses that of White adolescent girls. This increase may be partially due to metabolic differences, since Black women and girls tend to have lower resting expenditures than their White counterparts. Weight gain during adolescence may contribute to body dissatisfaction, disordered eating, and eating disorders.

Black women who consider themselves heavier than the body ideal preferred by their culture, particularly those who are obese, may experience weight dissatisfaction and a desire to be thinner. Overweight women are more likely than women of normal weight to experience teasing, criticism, or discrimination. These pressures may contribute to binge eating, a disorder that is more common among people who have a history of obesity than others. People with this disorder eat a large amount of food in a short period of time and feel a lack of control over their eating.

Women who consider themselves thinner than the ideal may also be at risk for binge eating. These women may experience body dissatisfaction along with a desire to gain weight in order to approximate their cultural ideal.

African American Women Engage In Binge Eating In High Rates

The first large-scale epidemiological study of recurrent binge eating in Black women indicated that Black women were as likely as White women to report that they had engaged in binge eating and self-induced vomiting. More specifically, a greater number of Black women than White women reported that they had used laxatives, diuretics, or fasting to control their weight. Almost twice as many Black women as White women were identified as probable eating disorder cases. Recurrent binge eaters, regardless of race, are overweight and report a greater number of psychiatric symptoms that those who do not binge eat frequently. In addition, some researchers believe that racial prejudice and discrimination toward African Americans result in a sense of isolation that may contribute to binge eating.

Health professionals must be prepared to respond to this specific health risk behavior and to address possible eating disorders in African American adolescents.

Latina Girls

Latina Girls Are At Risk

Research on eating disorders among Latina girls is limited. However, recent studies indicate that Latina girls are expressing the same concerns about body weight as White girls and that many are engaging in disordered eating behaviors, including dieting and purging, to lose weight.

The myth that Latinas do not experience eating disorders contributes to the lack of identification of the disease among this population. Since the early detection of an eating disorder is very important for its successful treatment, this misperception can result in serious health problems for Latina girls.

Although this chapter addresses eating disorders among Latinas in general, these disorders will affect each subgroup of Latinas in a different way. There is no single Latino standard regarding body size and eating patterns. In addition, within each cultural group, socioeconomic status may also affect the risks for developing eating disorders. For example, Latinas from families with low incomes may face a greater risk for obesity, while those from higher income families may be at a higher risk for dieting to try to fit in with their middle or upper middle class peers.

♣ It's A Fact!!

The terms "Hispanic" or "Latino" encompass diverse groups who immigrated to the U.S. Among the largest Hispanic populations in this country are Mexican Americans, Puerto Ricans, and Cuban Americans. The Hispanic population is growing faster than any other ethnic group in this country; it has more than doubled in the past 20 years. By the year 2020, it is estimated that Hispanics will be the single largest minority group in the U.S. Hispanics are predominantly young, with more than one in three being under the age of 18.

Source: Excerpted from the fact sheet titled "Latina Girls."

Hispanic Girls Express High Levels Of Body Dissatisfaction

Studies show that Latinas express the same or greater concerns about their body shape and weight as White females. In a study of more than 900 middle school girls in northern California, Hispanic girls reported higher levels of body dissatisfaction than any other group. Among the leanest 25% of girls, both Hispanic and Asian girls reported significantly more dissatisfaction than White girls.

Media targeting Latinas, including Hispanic television and magazines, are increasingly reinforcing the ideal of thinness as beauty. For example, although Mexicans have traditionally preferred a larger body size for women, many Mexican American women are idealizing and desiring a thinner figure than the one they currently have. For all racial and ethnic groups, body dissatisfaction is strongly linked with eating disorders.

Low Self-Esteem And Depression Can Contribute To Eating Disorders

Research suggests that Latina girls are at a high risk for mental health problems such as depression. Latina girls also report lower self-esteem and less body satisfaction than girls from other racial and ethnic backgrounds.

Studies indicate that as Latinas move from elementary to middle school and on to high school, they may suffer a greater loss of self-esteem than White or Black girls.

Hispanic girls may lack not only the high sense of self worth demonstrated by many African American girls, but also the academic opportunities available to some White girls. In addition, some Latinas may experience prejudice and discrimination based on ethnicity, language, and social status, which can contribute to low self-esteem and depression.

Obesity Is Also A Risk Factor For Eating Disorders

Hispanics, like African Americans, experience high rates of obesity. Among girls ages 5–17, Black and Hispanic girls have been found to have the highest measures of body mass index (BMI), exceeding those of White and Asian girls. They are also less likely to exercise than their White counterparts.

For Latinas, as well as women from other ethnic and cultural groups, obesity is linked with weight dissatisfaction and with a desire to be thinner. Overweight women are more likely than women of normal weight to experience teasing, criticism, or discrimination.

Obesity is also a risk factor for binge eating. In a recent study of 31 middle schools and high schools in Minnesota, binge eating was more prevalent among Hispanic girls than among those of other cultural backgrounds.

Dieting And Purging Are Widely Prevalent Among Hispanic Girls

Studies indicate that Latinas and White girls have similar rates of disordered eating behaviors. In fact, Latina girls seem to be particularly at risk for two types of disordered eating behaviors: dieting and purging.

♣ It's A Fact!!

Hispanic children consume the most fast food of all ethnic groups. Research has shown that high fat diets greatly contribute to the high rates of obesity among low-income Hispanic families.

Source: Excerpted from the fact sheet titled "Latina Girls."

Hispanic high schoolers have been found to have rates of bulimia comparable to those of Whites. Along with Black girls, Latinas have been found to use laxatives more frequently than girls from other racial groups.

Acculturation May Increase Vulnerability

For Latinas and other groups, acculturation can have an impact on body size preference and body image. Heaviness is seen as a sign of affluence and success in some traditional Hispanic cultures; but as Hispanics acculturate to the standards of beauty in this country, they may seek to achieve thinner bodies. Hispanic women born in the U.S. are more likely to prefer a smaller body size. Those who immigrate after age 17 are less likely to desire a thin body.

High levels of acculturation are associated not only with a drive for thinness but also with less healthy eating behaviors. As a result, second and third generation Hispanic adolescents are more likely to be obese than their first generation peers. Girls who are influenced by more than one race or culture may experience anxiety and confusion about their identity that may also contribute to disturbed eating behaviors.

Asian And Pacific Islander Girls

Asian American Girls Are At Risk

Asian American Girls Express High Levels Of Body Dissatisfaction

Many Asian American girls struggle with self-esteem and identity based largely on issues of attractiveness. Research that included Asian American girls reported that often they are as concerned or more concerned than White girls about their weight and shape.

In a study of more than 900 middle school girls in northern California, Asian American girls reported greater body dissatisfaction than White girls. Among the leanest 25% of girls, Asian girls reported significantly more dissatisfaction than White girls.

Recent research on Asian Americans suggests that body dissatisfaction is increasing due to the promotion of the Western beauty ideal. One study, for example, reported that Japanese Americans desired to be taller, weigh less, and have larger busts and smaller waists and hips. Some researchers believe that racism and sexism may contribute to negative feelings among Asian American women regarding their physical features, such as eye and nose shape, skin color, straight hair, and short stature. Eyelid and nose reconstruction are the most popular types of surgery requested by Asian American women.

♣ It's A Fact!!

The term Asian American/Pacific Islander refers to the more than seven million people from 28 Asian countries and 25 Pacific Island cultures in the U.S. The largest subgroups are Chinese, Filipino, Japanese, Asian Indians, Koreans, and Vietnamese. Hawaiians comprise the largest subgroups of Pacific Islanders (58%), followed by residents of Samoa, Guam, and Tonga. Each subgroup has its own history, language, and culture.

Excerpted from the fact sheet titled "Asian and Pacific Islander Girls."

Perfectionism And Need For Control Can Also Contribute To Eating Disorders

Asian Americans are often perceived as the "model minorities" and are expected to be successful and high achieving. Asian American girls may try to seek power and identity through the pursuit of a physically ideal body. The drive to become the "perfect Asian woman" can lead to perfectionism, which is linked to eating disorders, particularly anorexia. In addition, the cultural value of "saving face," which promotes a façade of control, may also contribute to disordered eating or eating disorders.

Acculturation May Increase Vulnerability

Adapting to a new culture creates a set of stressors that for Asian American and immigrant girls may cause confusion about identity, including gender roles. For example, an adolescent girl raised by her family to be obedient and demure may experience emotional turmoil in a Western culture that prizes independence and individualism.

For Asian American girls, acculturation can lead to feelings of isolation, low self-esteem, and the devaluation of native cultural identity, which can increase their vulnerability to eating disorders.

Highly acculturated Chinese females are more likely to report bulimic behaviors and a drive for thinness than those who stay closer to their family values. One report found that the more acculturated Asian American girls were at greatest risk for adopting the "dysfunctional" behaviors of White American society, including poor eating habits and accepting media messages regarding standards of beauty.

> ♣ **It's A Fact!!**
> Many Asian Americans equate psychological problems with weakness and shame; therefore, women and girls may avoid seeking treatment.
>
> Excerpted from the fact sheet titled "Asian and Pacific Islander Girls."

Obesity Is Also A Risk Factor

Rates of obesity are very high for some Asian/Pacific Islanders, such as Hawaiians and Samoans. Overweight and obesity are risk factors for disordered eating behaviors, such as bingeing and purging. Dieting for weight loss is also associated with the development of eating disorders and other unhealthy behaviors, including skipping meals and diet-binge cycles. One study, in fact, revealed that binge eating was more prevalent in Asian American than White females.

American Indian And Alaska Native Girls

American Indian Girls Are At Risk

Studies indicate that American Indian and Alaska Native adolescents are increasingly exhibiting disturbed eating behaviors and using unhealthy practices to control their weight. Disordered eating has been shown to occur more often among this group than among White, Hispanic, African American, or Asian girls.

In a large study involving 545 Hispanic, American Indian, and White high school students, American Indians consistently scored the highest on each of seven items representing disturbed eating behaviors and attitudes.

This study, which included 129 American Indians, also found very high rates of self-induced vomiting and binge eating among this group. Other small studies of American Indian adolescents also indicate high rates of disordered eating, including dieting and purging.

American Indian Youth Express High Levels Of Body Dissatisfaction

The largest and most comprehensive survey undertaken to date on the health status of Native American youths living on or near reservations involved 13,454 American Indians and Alaska Natives in grades 7 through 12. Approximately 41% of the adolescents reported feeling overweight, 50% were dissatisfied with their weight, and 44% worried about being overweight.

Among American Indian youth, body dissatisfaction is associated with unhealthy weight control behaviors. In the Indian Adolescent Health Study mentioned above, almost half of the girls and one-third of the boys had been on weight loss diets in the past year, with 27% reporting self-induced vomiting and 11% reporting the use of diet pills. Girls who reported feeling overweight were more likely to engage in unhealthy weight control practices.

Acculturation May Increase Vulnerability

Increased contact with the mainstream culture that equates thinness with beauty seems to contribute to higher rates of disordered eating among American Indian girls. In one study, anorexic Navajo girls from Arizona were more likely to come from upwardly mobile families who moved off the reservation. In a second study, child and adolescent members of a tribe were much more likely to prefer thinner body sizes than elder tribe members.

Eating disturbances have also been associated with racism, social isolation, low self-worth, and pressure to look a certain way, which may increase vulnerability to developing eating disorders.

Obesity Is Also A Risk Factor

American Indians have a high prevalence of obesity in all age groups and both sexes. Children who are obese are at risk for developing eating disorders and for becoming obese adults. More specifically, being overweight is a risk factor for eating disturbances in ethnically diverse women. Attention needs to be focused, therefore, on the prevention and treatment of obesity in American Indian adolescents.

Among American Indian Youth, Disordered Eating Is Linked To Other Harmful Behaviors

The Indian Adolescent Health Study indicates that disordered eating behaviors are related to other health compromising behaviors. Frequent dieting and purging among American Indian girls was associated with a wide range of risk factors, such as high emotional stress, binge eating, alcohol and tobacco use, thoughts and attempts of suicide, delinquent behaviors, and physical and sexual abuse.

The early identification of disordered eating behaviors may help uncover risk factors for other unhealthy and possibly more serious behaviors among these adolescents.

Chapter 8

Males With Eating Disorders

The stereotypical anorexic, bulimic, and binge eater is female. The stereotype is misleading.

What Eating Disorders Do Men And Boys Get?

Just like girls and women, boys and men get anorexia nervosa and bulimia nervosa. Many males describe themselves as compulsive eaters, and some may have binge eating disorder. There is no evidence to suggest that eating disorders in males are atypical or somehow different from the eating disorders experienced by females.

How Many Males Have Eating Disorders?

The numbers seem to be increasing. Twenty years ago it was thought that for every 10–15 women with anorexia or bulimia, there was one man. Today researchers find that for every four females with anorexia, there is one male, and for every 8–11 females with bulimia, there is one male. (*American Journal of Psychiatry*, 2001: 158: 570-574)

Binge eating disorder, the most common eating disorder, seems to occur almost equally in males and females, although males are not as likely to feel guilty or anxious after a binge as women are sure to do.

About This Chapter: "Males with Eating Disorders," used with permission of ANRED: Anorexia Nervosa and Related Eating Disorders, Inc., http://www.anred.com, © 2008.

Clinics and counselors see many more females than males, but that may be because males are reluctant to confess having what has become known as a "women's problem." Also, health professionals do not expect to see eating disorders in males and may therefore under-diagnose them.

♣ It's A Fact!!

Researchers at Harvard University Medical School have new data that suggests that up to 25 percent of adults with eating disorders are male. Whether that figure indicates that more men are becoming eating disordered, or that men previously escaped attention and diagnosis, or that diagnostic tools have improved and are now catching people who would have escaped detection before has yet to be determined. Preliminary information suggests that men are more concerned about appearance and body image than they were in the past. The new study was based on information obtained from the National Comorbidity Survey Replication, a mental health survey of nearly 9,000 adults across the U.S.

Are The Risk Factors For Males Any Different Than The Ones For Females?

Some are the same; others are different. Risk factors for males include the following:

- They were fat or overweight as children.

- They have been dieting. Dieting is one of the most powerful eating disorder triggers for both males and females, and one study indicates that up to seventy percent of high school students diet at one time or another to improve their appearance. (Theodore Weltzin, MD; Rogers Memorial Hospital)

- They participate in a sport that demands thinness. Runners and jockeys are at higher risk than football players and weight lifters. Wrestlers who try to shed pounds quickly before a match so they can compete in a lower weight category seem to be at special risk. Body builders are at risk if they deplete body fat and fluid reserves to achieve high definition.

- They have a job or profession that demands thinness. Male models, actors, and entertainers seem to be at higher risk than the general population.

- Some, but not all, males with eating disorders are members of the gay community where men are judged on their physical attractiveness in much the same way that women are judged in the heterosexual community.

- Living in a culture fixated on diets and physical appearance is also a risk factor. Male underwear models and men participating in reality show makeovers lead other males to compare themselves with these so-called ideal body types. So do ads for male skin and hair care products. Weight loss and workout programs, as well as cosmetic surgery procedures, whose goal is chiseled muscularity, can lead to the same sort of body dissatisfaction that afflicts women who read fashion magazines and watch movies and TV shows featuring so-called perfect people.

  In May 2004, researchers at the University of Central Florida released a study saying men who watched TV commercials with muscular actors felt unhappy about their own physiques. This "culture of muscularity" can be linked to eating disorders and steroid abuse, the researchers said.

  Much has been made of the effect the Barbie doll has on the body image of a young girl. Now we have the Wolverine action figure (and others) marketed to boys. If Wolverine were life size, his biceps would be 32 inches around. Advertisers are marketing to males the same way they have pitched goods to females, with apparently many of the same related problems.

Males And Females With Eating Disorders: Similar But Different

Males often begin an eating disorder at older ages than females do, and they more often have a history of obesity or overweight.

Heterosexual males are not exposed to the same intense cultural pressures to be thin that women and girls endure. A casual review of popular magazines and TV shows reveals that women are encouraged to diet and be thin so they can feel good about themselves, be successful at school and at work, and attract friends and romantic partners. Men, on the other hand, are exhorted to be strong and powerful, to build their bodies and make them large and strong so they can compete successfully, amass power and wealth, and defend and protect their frail, skinny female companions.

It's interesting to note that when women are asked what they would do with one magic wish, they almost always want to lose weight. Men asked the same question want money, power, sex, and the accessories of a rich and successful lifestyle. They often think their bodies are fine the way they are. If they do have body concerns, they usually want to bulk up and become larger and more muscular, not tiny like women do. Males usually equate thinness with weakness and frailty, things they desperately want to avoid.

Treatment Of Males With Eating Disorders

Because eating disorders have been described as female problems, males are often exceedingly reluctant to admit that they are in trouble and need help. In addition, most treatment programs and support groups have been designed for females and are populated exclusively by females. Males report feeling uncomfortable and out of place in discussions of lost menstrual periods, women's sociocultural issues, female-oriented advertising, and similar topics.

Nevertheless, like females, males almost always need professional help to recover. The research is clear that males who complete treatment given by competent professionals have good outcomes. Being male has no adverse affect on recovery once the person commits to an effective, well-run program.

The wisest first step is a two-part evaluation: one component done by a physician to identify any physical problems contributing to, or resulting from, the eating disorder; and a second part done by a mental health therapist to identify psychological issues underlying problematic food behaviors.

When the two parts of the evaluation are complete, treatment recommendations can be made that address the individual's specific circumstances.

It is important to remember that eating disorders in males, as well as in females, can be treated, and people of both genders do recover. Almost always, however, professional help is required.

If you are concerned about yourself, find a physician and mental health therapist who will be sympathetic to the male perspective. The sooner treatment is begun, the sooner the person can turn the problem around and begin building a happy, satisfying life. The longer symptoms are ignored or denied, the harder that work will be when it is finally undertaken.

Chapter 9

Athletes With Eating Disorders

In a sense, eating disorders are diets and fitness or sports programs gone horribly wrong. A person wants to lose weight, get fit, excel in his or her sport, but then develops obsessive thoughts about food and training, ultimately losing control and ending up with body and spirit ravaged by starvation, binge eating, purging, and frantic compulsive exercise. What may have begun as a solution to problems of low self-esteem has now become an even bigger problem in its own right.

Several studies suggest that participants in sports that emphasize appearance and a lean body (for example, figure skating and cheer leading) are at higher risk for developing an eating disorder than are non-athletes or folks involved in sports that require muscle mass and bulk (for example, football and weight lifting).

Statistics

One study of 695 male and female athletes found many examples of bulimic attitudes and behavior. A third of the group was preoccupied with food. About a quarter binged at least once a week. Fifteen percent thought they were overweight when they were not. About twelve percent feared losing

About This Chapter: "Athletes with Eating Disorders: An Overview" used with permission of ANRED: Anorexia Nervosa and Related Eating Disorders, Inc., http://www.anred.com, © 2008.

✤ **It's A Fact!!**

Eating disorders are significant problems in the worlds of ballet and other dance, figure skating, gymnastics, running, swimming, rowing, horse racing, ski jumping, and riding. Wrestlers, usually thought of as strong and massive, may binge eat before a match to carbohydrate load and then purge to make weight in a lower class.

control, or actually did lose control, when they ate. More than five percent ate until they were gorged and nauseated.

In this study, five and a half percent vomited to feel better after a binge and to control weight. Almost four percent abused laxatives. Twelve percent fasted for twenty-four hours or more after a binge, and about one and a half percent used enemas to purge.

Another research project done by the National Collegiate Athletic Association (NCAA) looked at the number of student athletes who had experienced an eating disorder in the previous two years. Ninety-three percent of the reported problems were in women's sports. The sports that had the highest number of participants with eating disorders, in descending order, were women's cross country, women's gymnastics, women's swimming, and women's track and field events.

The male sports with the highest number of participants with eating disorders were wrestling and cross country track.

Male And Female Athletes: Different Risk Factors

The female athlete is doubly at risk for the development of an eating disorder. She is subject to the constant social pressure to be thin that affects all females in western countries, and she also finds herself in a sports milieu that may overvalue performance, low body fat, and an idealized, unrealistic body shape, size, and weight. Constant exposure to the demands of the athletic subculture added to those bombarding her daily on TV, in movies, in magazines, and transmitted by peers, may make her especially vulnerable to the lure of weight loss and unhealthy ways of achieving it.

Males also develop eating disorders but at a much reduced incidence (approximately 90% female; 10% male). Males may be protected somewhat by their basic biology and different cultural expectations.

Many sports demand low percentages of body fat. In general, men have more lean muscle tissue and less fatty tissue than women do. Males also tend to have higher metabolic rates than females because muscle burns more calories faster than fat does. So women, who in general carry more body fat than men, with slower metabolisms and smaller frames, require fewer calories than men do.

All of these factors mean that women gain weight more easily than men, and women have a harder time losing weight, and keeping it off, than men do. In addition, women have been taught to value being thin. Men, on the other hand, usually want to be big, powerful, and strong; therefore, men are under less pressure to diet than women are—and dieting is one of the primary risk factors for the development of an eating disorder.

Special Concerns

Female Athletes, Disordered Eating, And Increased Risk Of Injury

According to a study published in the *American Journal of Sports Medicine*, female athletes who restrict calories to keep weight down seem to be vulnerable to leg pain, stress fractures, and other injuries that cause people to miss practices and competitions. (*Am J Sports Med* 2006 34: 1500-1507). The pain is not significantly eased by running less, working out fewer days, and wearing different shoes. Eating a normal, healthy diet and maintaining normal, healthy weight appear to be the most important factors in relieving this kind of pain.

Some coaches tell their female athletes, "You know when you're training hard enough. It's when your periods stop." In fact, if a woman is physically stressing herself that much, and if she has pared her body fat down below a level that is healthy, absent periods mean caloric deficiency and too-low estrogen levels that can leave bones fragile, weak, and prone to fracture. Carried far enough, this pattern can result in female athlete triad, three related problems that include (1) eating disorders and low energy, (2) menstrual disorders or absent periods, and (3) weak bones or even osteoporosis, which until recent years was seen primarily in post menopausal elderly women.

Wrestlers And Quick Weight Loss

Everyone who uses drastic and unhealthy methods of weight loss is at risk of dying or developing serious health problems, but the deaths of three college wrestlers in the latter part of 1997 triggered re-examination of the extreme weight-loss efforts common in that sport. Athletes in other sports have died too; runners and gymnasts seem to be at high risk. The deaths of three young men in different parts of the U.S. in the late 1990s have put the problem once again before the public.

News reports say that the three were going to school in North Carolina, Wisconsin, and Michigan. Authorities believe they were trying to lose too much weight too rapidly so they could compete in lower weight classes. The wrestling coach at Iowa State University has been quoted as saying, "When you have deaths like this, it calls into question what's wrong with the sport. Wrestlers believe that, foremost, it's their responsibility to make weight, and that mind set may come from the fact that they believe themselves invincible." They share that mind set with others who use dangerous methods of weight loss, both athletes and non-athletes.

Two of the young men were wearing rubber sweat suits while they worked out in hot rooms. One died from kidney failure and heart malfunction. The other succumbed to cardiac arrest after he worked out on an exercise bike and refused to drink liquids to replenish those he lost by sweating. One was trying to lose four pounds, the other six.

Wrestlers share a mentality with people who have eating disorders. They push themselves constantly to improve, to be fitter, to weigh less, and to excel. They drive themselves beyond fatigue. One coach reports that "wrestlers consider themselves the best-conditioned athletes that exist, and they like the fact they can go where no one's gone before. The instilled attitude among these kids is that if they push and push, it'll pay off with a victory." No one expects to die as a consequence of weight loss, but it happens.

When a clamor arose for the NCAA to do something, to make rules prohibiting drastic methods of weight loss, a representative said, "We could make every rule in the book, but we can't legislate ethics. That's where the wrestlers and coaches have to put the onus on themselves."

What price victory? It takes maturity and wisdom to realize that in some circumstances the price is too high.

Chapter 10

How To Tell Someone You Have An Eating Disorder

When you begin to notice that disordered eating habits are affecting your life, your happiness, and your ability to concentrate, it is important that you talk to somebody about what you're going through.

What is disordered eating?

Disordered eating is when a person's attitudes about food, weight, and body size lead to very rigid eating and exercise habits that jeopardize one's health, happiness, and safety. Disordered eating may begin as a way to lose a few pounds or get in shape, but these behaviors can quickly get out of control, become obsessions, and may even turn into an eating disorder.

When you begin to notice that disordered eating habits are affecting your life, your happiness, and your ability to concentrate, it is important that you talk to somebody about what you're going through. Although you might not be struggling with an eating disorder, sometimes it is necessary to recognize disordered eating tendencies and address them before they escalate into a life-threatening problem.

About This Chapter: Information in this chapter is from "Sharing with EEEase," © 2005 National Eating Disorders Association. Reprinted with permission. For additional information, visit www.NationalEatingDisorders.org, or call the toll-free Information and Referral Helpline at 800-931-2237.

If you are able to recognize disordered eating attitudes and behaviors in yourself, you have already taken the first step toward a happy, healthy, balanced way of life. The second step—telling a trusted friend, family member, or professional counselor/nutritionist—is equally important.

Because many individuals who are dealing with disordered eating have found it difficult to tell somebody what they are going through and what behaviors they've adopted, this chapter provides a guideline of things to say in order to make the initial conversation a bit easier. Remember that this is not a script and that everyone's situation is different.

> ✔ **Quick Tip**
> You should not attempt to address your disordered eating alone. You will benefit from the support of others and the comfort of discussing the feelings you're experiencing.

What are the Three Es of expression?

Establish A Safe Environment

Once you have decided to tell somebody about the habits you have adopted, identify someone that you trust and feel comfortable talking to. Next, set aside a specific time with that person so you can discuss your situation. To make things most comfortable for you, try to find a private, comfortable place away from other people and distractions. This will help you talk openly about your concerns and feelings. Both before and during this conversation, it is normal for you to experience a range of feelings including fear, shame, anger, embarrassment, or nervousness. To keep up the courage to talk about what you're going through, remember that you are doing the right thing. It is important to talk about this and ask for help.

You should be proud of yourself for taking the first steps toward a healthy, well-balanced lifestyle.

Explain The Situation

Using specific details, explain the thoughts and feelings that you are having and the behaviors you have developed. Starting from the beginning, talk about how you began the disordered eating habits and why you feel pressured to continue them (It is a good idea to prepare yourself ahead of time and write these things down or practice saying them aloud). Although you may not be able to fully explain the reasons for your eating and exercise rituals, attempting to do so may help you recognize some of the connections you make between eating, exercise, and self-esteem.

It is important to keep in mind that the person you have confided in may not completely understand exactly how you are feeling or the reasons for your behavior. They may demonstrate shock, denial, fear, or even anger. Be patient and remain calm. Remember that they may not automatically know the best way to respond and support you, but you can help them learn how. Educate them with the facts and explain what you need from them during your recovery process.

Educate With The Facts

Give the person you confide in some information regarding the prevalence of eating disorders and tips for how to best support somebody who is struggling with food, weight, or body image issues. Share facts with them that include the physical and emotional effects of eating disorders, along with the steps involved in recovery. Be sure to let this person know how they can help and what you need, and keep them informed as your needs change throughout your recovery process. Remind them that recovery is a gradual process, there may even be some setbacks, and you will require patience and understanding along the way.

Who should I tell?

In addition to a trusted friend or family member, it is advisable to seek help from a professional counselor and/or nutritionist. Getting help from a professional who understands and specializes in eating, weight, and body image issues is essential during recovery from an eating disorder. Confiding in a counselor or nutritionist can feel less threatening and more objective because they are familiar with situations like your own. These are people that specialize in the treatment of eating disorders and offer support services, medical advice, and nutritional therapy.

What should I say?

Be as specific as possible when explaining what you are going through. It may be helpful to develop a script based on the following questions. Include whatever answers you are comfortable revealing and remember that the more you include, the better the person you're speaking with will understand and be able to help.

- When did you begin having different thoughts regarding food, weight, or exercise? What were the thoughts?

- When did the different behaviors start? What was the behavior? How were you feeling at the time? Did you hope to accomplish something specific (for example, lose weight, maintain weight, gain control of something, get somebody's attention, see what it was like) in doing this behavior?

- Have you noticed any physical health effects? (It may include fatigue, loss of hair, digestive problems, loss of menstrual cycle, heart palpitations, etc.) Have you noticed any emotional effects?

- How are you currently feeling physically? Emotionally? Do you feel ready to stop the disordered eating behaviors?

- How can the people in your life best support you? Do you want them to monitor your behavior? Do you want them to ask you how you are doing with your recovery or would you rather tell them about it when you're ready?

- What changes are you willing to make in your life to establish a healthy lifestyle?

✤ It's A Fact!!
It is important to realize that you are not alone in your struggle. Studies have shown that 5–10 million girls and women, and 1 million boys and men, are struggling with eating disorders including anorexia, bulimia, binge eating disorder, and related conditions.

As you begin to address your eating concerns, keep in mind that you are a special and unique individual. Regardless of the numbers on the scale, the size, shape, and curve of your body, you have qualities about you that nobody else has. As you begin to let go of the dieting mindset, you will notice how wonderful it can be to enjoy life without being consumed with thoughts of food and weight.

Rest assured that you can return to a mindset where your happiness and self-image are not based on your reflection in the mirror or your weight on the scale.

Chapter 11

How An Eating Disorder Affects Family Members

When Caregivers Feel Like Food

Caregiving for someone with an eating disorder requires being close to the person, and caregivers may feel the effects of the disorder personally. It's important to understand how these disorders can affect relationships.

Restricting Food Often Means Restricting Relationships With Caregivers

If someone in your life has anorexia nervosa and restricts her food intake, it is very likely that she doesn't allow anything (or anyone) else to "get in" either. She loses the capacity for intimacy with others. If her father asks her about something important to her, she may deflect the question and ask another question in return to distract him. In short, anorexia eventually leads a person to treat others as she treats food—by avoiding.

About This Chapter: Information in this chapter is from "Relationships With Eating Disorder Caregivers Suffer." © 2008 by Matthew Tiemeyer (http://eating disorders.about.com/od/informationforparents/a/projectsymptoms.htm). Used with permission of About, Inc., which can be found online at www.about.com. All rights reserved.

✔ **Quick Tip**
Living With Someone With An Eating Disorder

It's not always easy to feel certain about what you can do to help the person you care about. Here are some ideas:

- **Encourage the person to seek professional help.** Overcoming an eating disorder can be very difficult without assistance, so accessing professional help is an important goal.

- **Encourage the person to recognize their other skills and attributes.** Use your knowledge of the person to encourage them to see the positive effects change can bring and to see the benefits of a life without an eating disorder.

- **Try to keep communication positive and open.** Take time to talk, but not always about the eating problem.

- **Try to take the focus off food and weight.** The person with the eating disorder is already likely to be over focused on food and weight issues.

- **Mealtimes should not become a battleground.** Frustrations and emotions need to be expressed but not at meal times; this is already likely to be a difficult time.

- **Accept limitations and responsibilities.** The support and encouragement of family and friends is vital, however, it is the person with the eating disorder's responsibility to take the necessary steps towards recovery.

- **Independence.** The person with the eating disorder has the right to lead an independent life and make decisions for themselves and in their own time. This can be difficult especially if the person is younger or quite sick; however, recovery often involves the person learning to become more self-sufficient.

- **Set boundaries.** If someone is behaving in a way that is difficult for you, it is okay to let them know that their behavior is not acceptable. Only set boundaries you can enforce.

- **Do things as you usually would.** The person with the eating disorder needs to learn to co-exist with food and with other people, rather than others learning to co-exist with the eating disorder. Try not to make any changes to meal times, food shopping, outings, topics of conversation, or other interests.

- **Separate the person from the disorder.** Remind yourself that the person's behavior is often more a symptom of the eating disorder than a reflection of their character.

- **Enjoy things together.** It is important not to let the eating disorder become the focus of the family or relationship. Continue to enjoy things together that you have always done.

- **Build the person's self-esteem.** Try and focus on their positive behaviors rather than the more destructive ones.

- **Spend time with other members of the family or friendship group.** The person with the eating disorder is important, but no more so than other people. Try to avoid a situation where siblings or partners feel neglected.

- **Accept your limitations.** As a family member or friend, you cannot deal with all the problems associated with the disorder. Your role as a family member or friend is unique and something that a therapist can't be, just as the therapist's role is something a family member or friend can't take on.

- **Become informed.** Information about eating disorders, recovery stories, and strategies can be useful. There are several books written for families and friends.

- **Look after yourself.** Get as much support and information as you need. Support groups, relatives, friends, counselors, telephone support lines, and other professionals may be useful.

- **Be patient.** Eating disorders are complicated, and recovery can take some time. Sometimes it's important to remind yourself that the person does not want to be unwell either, but they lack the ability to overcome the disorder straight away.

Source: "Living with Someone with an Eating Disorder," © 2006 Eating Disorders Foundation of Victoria, www.eatingdisorders.org.au. Reprinted with permission.

♣ **It's A Fact!!**

How Are Family And Friends Affected

Parents, siblings, partners, friends, extended family, work colleagues, and others often experience many different feelings as they learn to cope with the effects of the eating disorder on the person, and on their own lives. The strain of living with the eating disorder can create tensions and divisions within the family. Each person involved will be affected in different ways. There may be feelings of:

- **Confusion** about:

    - the eating disorder and recovery process

    - why this has happened

    - the best way to handle the illness in the family, partnership, or friendship circle, etc.

- **Grief And Anger** about:

    - loss of the person's mental and physical health

    - change in the person's behavior/denial of problem, refusal to get help

    - the difficulties or changes the illness is creating in the family, partnership, or friendship circle, etc.

    - not being able to make the person well

    - loss of time alone and/or with other family members/friends

    - loss of trust for the person who may behave deceptively

- **Guilt Or Fear** about:

    - possibly causing the illness in some way

    - not recognizing the illness earlier

    - not dealing with the illness differently

    - that the person may not recover or may die

Source: "How Are Family and Friends Affected," © 2006 Eating Disorders Foundation of Victoria, www.eatingdisorders.org.au. Reprinted with permission.

Chaos With Food Translates To Relationship Chaos With Others

The dynamic with food is different when bulimia nervosa is present.

One moment, food is demanded and devoured. The next moment, it seems disgusting and must be purged.

Often, a person with bulimia will treat loved ones in the same way. In one moment, friends and family feel incredibly close. In the next, they seem untrustworthy and uncaring. Just as there is behavior to eliminate food, there is then clear behavior to create distance with people. Erratic anger and betrayal are two examples. Having people emotionally close becomes uncomfortable.

Shame Of Eating Disorder Becomes Shame In Caregivers And Loved Ones

Even though a person with anorexia often seems to be in control and gives those around her a sense of being indestructible, she usually has a great deal of shame underneath. This is what drives her to want to change herself so dramatically.

Among family and friends, she is able to make herself feel better, in some ways, by making others feel worse. This is not her intent; normally, a person with anorexia wants everyone to do well. But she also believes that she is stronger than other people. When she sees loved ones crumble as they watch her lose weight, it tells her that she is stronger than they are. This makes her feel good on some level, but on another level, she believes that these "weaker" people could never protect and care for her well. This reinforces the sense that she is the only one who can care for herself.

With bulimia, shame is more on the surface. A son with bulimia will not want his parents to know that he is binging and purging; and if he is hiding food, he does not want that to be discovered either. So he carries the shame of his actions constantly. But when family members know of the disorder and see him head to the bathroom after a meal, they can feel their own shame at being part of a family that is not functioning entirely well.

Working On The Real Issue: Avoiding Relationship Distractions

It's important to remember that all of these problems are really reflections of the inner world of the person with the disorder. This can help you to maintain a compassionate perspective and keep your focus on what's important—making sure that the person gets the help she needs.

But it isn't easy, and you may need help. Even though you're not the one with the eating disorder, you may benefit from counseling. A support group is another great resource. Knowing that others are facing the same things you are is often relieving. When you find out that others feel like relationships make no sense, or that they feel shame just as you do, it can give you courage to take the actions you need to take.

Part Two

Specific Disorders Related To Eating And Body Image

Chapter 12

Anorexia Nervosa

What is anorexia nervosa?

A person with anorexia (a-neh-RECK-see-ah) nervosa, often called anorexia, has an intense fear of gaining weight. Someone with anorexia thinks about food a lot and limits the food she or he eats, even though she or he is too thin. Anorexia is more than just a problem with food. It is a way of using food or starving oneself to feel more in control of life and to ease tension, anger, and anxiety. Most people with anorexia are female. An anorexic:

- has a low body weight for her or his height;

- resists keeping a normal body weight;

- has an intense fear of gaining weight;

- thinks she or he is fat even when very thin; and

- misses three menstrual periods in a row for girls who have started having their periods.

About This Chapter: Text from "Anorexia Nervosa," National Women's Health Information Center, 2006, which was adapted from "What Should I Say? Tips for Talking to a Friend Who May Be Struggling with an Eating Disorder" from the National Eating Disorders Association.

Who becomes anorexic?

While anorexia mostly affects girls and women (90–95 percent), it can also affect boys and men. It was once thought that women of color were shielded from eating disorders by their cultures, which tend to be more accepting of different body sizes. Sadly, research shows that as African American, Latina, Asian/Pacific Islander, and American Indian and Alaska Native women are more exposed to images of thin women, they also become more likely to develop eating disorders.

What causes anorexia?

There is no single known cause of anorexia, but some things may play a part, such as the following:

- **Culture:** Women in the U.S. are under constant pressure to fit a certain ideal of beauty. Seeing images of flawless, thin females everywhere makes it hard for women to feel good about their bodies. More and more, men are also feeling pressure to have a perfect body.

- **Families:** If you have a mother or sister with anorexia, you are more likely to develop the disorder. Parents who think looks are important, diet themselves, or criticize their children's bodies are more likely to have a child with anorexia.

- **Life Changes Or Stressful Events:** Traumatic events like rape, as well as stressful things like starting a new job, can lead to the onset of anorexia.

- **Personality Traits:** Someone with anorexia may not like her or himself, hate the way she or he looks, or feel hopeless. She or he often sets hard-to-reach goals for her or himself and tries to be perfect in every way.

- **Biology:** Genes, hormones, and chemicals in the brain may be factors in developing anorexia.

What are signs of anorexia?

Someone with anorexia may look very thin. She or he may use extreme measures to lose weight by:

- making her or himself throw up;

- taking pills to urinate or have a bowel movement;

- taking diet pills;

- not eating or eating very little;

- exercising a lot, even in bad weather or when hurt or tired;

- weighing food and counting calories; and

- moving food around the plate instead of eating it.

Someone with anorexia may also have a distorted body image, shown by thinking she or he is fat, wearing baggy clothes, weighing her or himself many times a day, and fearing weight gain.

Anorexia can also cause someone to not act like her or himself. She or he may talk about weight and food all the time, not eat in front of others, be moody or sad, or not want to go out with friends.

What happens to your body with anorexia?

With anorexia, your body does not get the energy from foods that it needs, so it slows down. Figure 12.1 shows how anorexia affects your health.

Can someone with anorexia get better?

Yes. Someone with anorexia can get better. A health care team of doctors, nutritionists, and therapists will help the patient get better. They will help her or him learn healthy eating patterns, cope with thoughts and feelings, and gain weight. With outpatient care, the patient receives treatment through visits with members of their health care team. Some patients may need "partial hospitalization." This means that the person goes to the hospital during the day for treatment but lives at home. Sometimes, the patient goes to a hospital and stays there for treatment. After leaving the hospital, the patient continues to get help from her or his health care team.

Individual counseling can also help someone with anorexia. If the patient is young, counseling may involve the whole family too. Support groups may

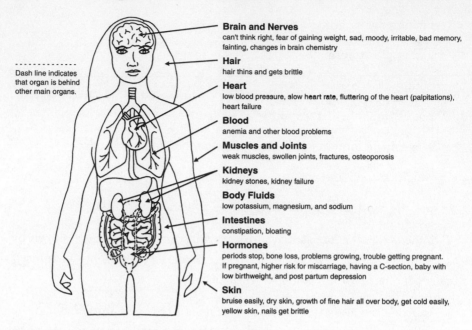

Brain and Nerves
can't think right, fear of gaining weight, sad, moody, irritable, bad memory, fainting, changes in brain chemistry

Hair
hair thins and gets brittle

Heart
low blood pressure, slow heart rate, fluttering of the heart (palpitations), heart failure

Blood
anemia and other blood problems

Muscles and Joints
weak muscles, swollen joints, fractures, osteoporosis

Kidneys
kidney stones, kidney failure

Body Fluids
low potassium, magnesium, and sodium

Intestines
constipation, bloating

Hormones
periods stop, bone loss, problems growing, trouble getting pregnant. If pregnant, higher risk for miscarriage, having a C-section, baby with low birthweight, and post partum depression

Skin
bruise easily, dry skin, growth of fine hair all over body, get cold easily, yellow skin, nails get brittle

- - - - - - - - - - - - -
Dash line indicates that organ is behind other main organs.

Figure 12.1. Anorexia Affects Your Whole Body

also be a part of treatment. In support groups, patients and families meet and share what they have been through.

Note: Adapted from "What Should I Say? Tips for Talking to a Friend Who May Be Struggling with an Eating Disorder" from the National Eating Disorders Association.

♣ It's A Fact!!

Often, eating disorders happen along with mental health problems such as depression and anxiety. These problems are treated along with the anorexia. Treatment may include medicines that fix hormone imbalances that play a role in these disorders.

Chapter 13

Bulimia Nervosa

What is bulimia?

Bulimia (buh-LEE-me-ah) nervosa is a type of eating disorder. It is often called just bulimia. A person with bulimia eats a lot of food in a short amount of time. This is called binging. The person may fear gaining weight after a binge. Binging also can cause feelings of shame and guilt. So, the person tries to "undo" the binge by getting rid of the food. This is called purging. Purging might be done by:

- making yourself throw up;

- taking laxatives (LAX-uh-tiv)—pills or liquids that speed up the movement of food through your body and lead to a bowel movement;

- exercising a lot;

- eating very little or not at all; and

- taking water pills to urinate.

About This Chapter: Text from "Bulimia Nervosa," National Women's Health Information Center, 2006, which was adapted from "What Should I Say? Tips for Talking to a Friend Who May Be Struggling with an Eating Disorder" from the National Eating Disorders Association.

Who becomes bulimic?

Many people think that only young, upper class, white females get eating disorders. It is true that many more women than men have bulimia. In fact, 9 out of 10 people with bulimia are women; but bulimia can affect anyone. Men, older women, and women of color can become bulimic. It was once thought that women of color were protected from eating disorders by their cultures. These cultures tend to be more accepting of all body sizes, but research shows that as women of color are more exposed to images of thin women, they are more likely to get eating disorders. African-American, Latina, Asian/Pacific Islander, and American Indian and Alaska Native women can become bulimic.

What causes bulimia?

Bulimia is more than just a problem with food. Dieting or stress can set off a binge. Painful emotions, like anger or sadness, also can bring on binging. Purging is how people with bulimia try to gain control and to ease stress and anxiety. There is no single known cause of bulimia, but these factors might play a role:

- **Culture:** Women in the U.S. are under constant pressure to be very thin. This "ideal" is not realistic for most women; but seeing images of flawless, thin females everywhere can make it hard for women to feel good about their bodies. More and more, men are also feeling pressure to have a perfect body.

- **Families:** It is likely that bulimia runs in families. Many people with bulimia have sisters or mothers with bulimia. Parents who think looks are important, diet themselves, or judge their children's bodies are more likely to have a child with bulimia.

- **Life Changes Or Stressful Events:** Traumatic events like rape can lead to bulimia. So can stressful events like being teased about body size.

- **Psychology:** Having low self-esteem is common in people with bulimia. People with bulimia have higher rates of depression. They may have problems expressing anger and feelings. They might be moody or feel like they cannot control impulsive behaviors.

- **Biology:** Genes, hormones, and chemicals in the brain may be factors in getting bulimia.

What are signs of bulimia?

A person with bulimia may be thin, overweight, or normal weight. This makes it hard to know if someone has bulimia, but there are warning signs to look out for. Someone with bulimia may do extreme things to lose weight, such as the following:

- using diet pills or taking pills to urinate or have a bowel movement
- going to the bathroom all the time after eating to throw up
- exercising too much, even when hurt or tired

Someone with bulimia may show signs of throwing up, such as the following:

- swollen cheeks or jaw area
- rough skin on knuckles (if using fingers to make one throw up)
- teeth that look clear
- broken blood vessels in the eyes

Someone with bulimia often thinks she or he is fat, even if this is not true. The person might hate his or her body or worry a lot about gaining weight. Bulimia can cause someone to not seem like him or herself. The person might be moody or sad. Someone with bulimia might not want to go out with friends.

What happens to someone who has bulimia?

Bulimia can hurt your body. Figure 13.1 shows how bulimia harms your health.

Can someone with bulimia get better?

Yes. Someone with bulimia can get better with the help of a health care team. A doctor will provide medical care. A nutritionist (noo-TRISH-un-ist) can teach healthy eating patterns. A therapist (thair-uh-pist) can help the patient learn new ways to cope with thoughts and feelings.

Therapy is an important part of any treatment plan. It might be alone, with family members, or in a group. Medicines can help some people with

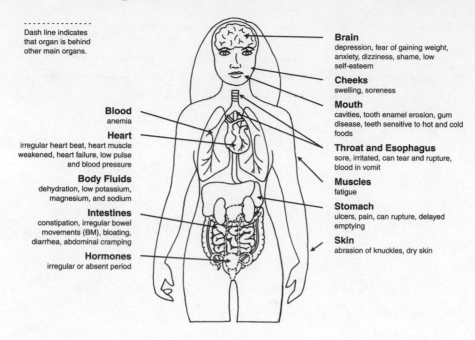

Dash line indicates that organ is behind other main organs.

Brain
depression, fear of gaining weight, anxiety, dizziness, shame, low self-esteem

Cheeks
swelling, soreness

Mouth
cavities, tooth enamel erosion, gum disease, teeth sensitive to hot and cold foods

Blood
anemia

Heart
irregular heart beat, heart muscle weakened, heart failure, low pulse and blood pressure

Throat and Esophagus
sore, irritated, can tear and rupture, blood in vomit

Muscles
fatigue

Body Fluids
dehydration, low potassium, magnesium, and sodium

Stomach
ulcers, pain, can rupture, delayed emptying

Intestines
constipation, irregular bowel movements (BM), bloating, diarrhea, abdominal cramping

Skin
abrasion of knuckles, dry skin

Hormones
irregular or absent period

Figure 13.1 How Bulimia Affects Your Body

bulimia. These include medicines used to treat depression. Medicines work best when used with therapy.

Note: Adapted from "What Should I Say? Tips for Talking to a Friend Who May Be Struggling with an Eating Disorder" from the National Eating Disorders Association.

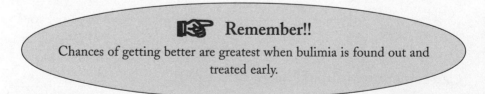

☞ Remember!!

Chances of getting better are greatest when bulimia is found out and treated early.

Chapter 14

Binge Eating Disorder

Walker's room is his oasis. It's where he listens to music, does his homework, and talks online with his friends. For the most part, it looks like a typical teen bedroom—except for what's under the bed. That's where Walker keeps his secret stash of snacks and tosses the empty candy wrappers, chip bags, and cookie boxes.

Walker has just polished off a whole package of cookies and a large bag of chips—and he hasn't even finished his homework yet. He's searching for more chips to eat while he does his math. He hates that he's overweight, but he can't seem to stop bingeing. In the back of his mind, he knows that in an hour or so he's going to feel guilty and disgusted with himself, but right now it feels like he just can't stop eating.

Understanding Binge Eating

If you gorged yourself on chocolate during Halloween or ate so much of your grandma's pumpkin pie at Thanksgiving that you had to wear elastic-waist pants afterwards, you know what it feels like to overeat. It's perfectly normal to overeat from time to time—most people do.

About This Chapter: "Binge Eating Disorder," July 2006, reprinted with permission from www.kidshealth.org. Copyright © 2006 The Nemours Foundation. This information was provided by KidsHealth, one of the largest resources online for medically reviewed health information written for parents, kids, and teens. For more articles like this one, visit www.KidsHealth.org, or www.TeensHealth.org.

Teens are notorious for being hungry a lot. That's because the body demands extra nutrients to support the major growth of muscle and bone that's happening. So if you go through phases where you feel like eating more sometimes, that's usually why, and it's absolutely natural.

But binge eating is different from normal appetite increases or overeating from time to time. People with a binge eating problem consume unusually large amounts of food on a regular basis. They often eat quickly, and they don't stop eating when they become full.

Binge eating involves more than just eating a lot. With binge eating, a person feels out of control and powerless to stop eating while he or she is doing it. That's why binge eating is also called compulsive overeating.

People with a binge eating problem may overeat when they feel stressed, upset, hurt, or angry. Many find it comforting and soothing to eat, but after a binge they are likely to feel guilty and sad about the out-of-control eating. Binge eating is often a mixed-up way of dealing with or avoiding difficult emotions.

How Is Binge Eating Different From Other Eating Disorders?

Anorexia nervosa, bulimia nervosa, and binge eating are all considered eating disorders because they involve unhealthy patterns of eating.

Both binge eating and bulimia involve eating excessive amounts of food, feeling out of control while eating, and feeling guilty or ashamed afterward. But bulimia nervosa (sometimes called binge-purge syndrome) is different from binge eating disorder because people with bulimia vomit or use laxatives to try to keep themselves from gaining weight after eating. They may also try to burn off the extra calories by exercising compulsively as a way of making up for overeating. People with binge eating disorder do not have these "purge" characteristics.

Unlike bulimia and binge eating, which involve out-of-control overeating, people with anorexia are preoccupied with thinness and starve themselves to feel more in control. People with anorexia have a distorted body image and believe they're fat—even though they actually may be dangerously thin. Like people with bulimia, some people with anorexia may also exercise compulsively to lose weight.

All three of these eating disorders involve unhealthy eating patterns that begin gradually and build to the point where a person feels unable to control them. All eating disorders can lead to serious health consequences, and all involve emotional distress.

✦ It's A Fact!!

A Vicious Cycle

Binge eating can lead to other problems, such as weight gain, unhealthy dieting, and emotional problems. Most people who binge eat are overweight or obese. Concerns about weight gain may lead them to go on extreme diets that they can't stick to, so they return to their old behavior. Binge eating can leave a person feeling helpless, hopeless, and depressed. These painful feelings may make the binge eating worse if the person turns to food as a way of dealing with such feelings.

Source: The Nemours Foundation.

Why Do Some People Binge Eat?

Most experts believe that it takes a combination of things to develop an eating disorder—including a person's genes, emotions, and behaviors (such as eating patterns) learned during childhood.

Some people may be more prone to overeating because of biological reasons. For example, the hypothalamus (the part of the brain that controls appetite) may fail to send proper messages about hunger and fullness. And serotonin, a normal brain chemical that affects mood and some compulsive behaviors, may also play a role in binge eating.

In most cases, the unhealthy overeating habits that develop into binge eating start during childhood, sometimes as a result of eating habits learned in the family. It's normal to associate food with nurturing and love. But some families may overuse food as a way to soothe or comfort. When this is the case, kids may grow up with a habit of overeating to soothe themselves when they're feeling pressured because they may not have learned healthier ways to deal with stress. Some kids may grow up believing that unhappy or upsetting feelings should be suppressed and may use food to quiet these emotions.

Both guys and girls can have eating disorders. Anorexia and bulimia appear to be more common among girls. But binge eating seems to be just as likely to affect guys as girls.

It's hard to know just how many teens may have a binge eating problem. Because people often feel guilty or embarrassed about the out-of-control eating, many don't talk about it or seek help.

What Are The Signs A Person Has A Binge Eating Problem?

Someone with a binge eating problem might:

• eat much more rapidly than normal

• eat until uncomfortably full

• eat large amounts of food even when not hungry

• eat alone because of embarrassment

• feel disgusted, depressed, or guilty after a binge eating episode

• gain weight excessively

A person who binge eats usually does so more than twice a week over a period of six months or more, and often feels upset, embarrassed, ashamed, or angry about the out-of-control eating.

Getting Help

For many people with binge eating problems, it can seem hard to reach out for help because of the embarrassment they may feel and the stigma that society places on overeating and being overweight. Many people don't get treatment for binge eating until they're adults and trying to lose weight. But getting professional help as a teen can reduce some of the long-term health problems.

People with eating disorders need professional help because problems like binge eating can be caused by brain chemistry and other things that are beyond someone's control. Doctors, counselors, and nutrition experts often work together to help those with eating disorders manage their eating, weight, and feelings.

Nutrition specialists or dietitians can help them learn about healthy eating behaviors, nutritional needs, portion sizes, metabolism, and exercise. They can also help design an eating plan that's specially designed for someone's needs and help the person stick with it and make progress.

Unlike a problem with drugs or alcohol where part of the treatment is avoiding the substance altogether, people still have to eat. This can make it harder for someone with a binge eating problem to overcome it because the temptation to overeat is always there. So part of dealing with a binge eating disorder is learning how to have a healthy relationship with food.

Psychologists and other therapists can help people learn healthy ways of coping with emotions, thoughts, stress, and other things that might contribute to a person's eating problem.

Sometimes certain family members can help by talking with the person and his or her therapist about shared eating patterns, feelings (and beliefs about how feelings should be expressed), and family relationships. Doing this can help someone examine how certain eating patterns may have been influenced by family—and to stop the patterns that aren't healthy.

Depending on what's behind someone's binge eating, doctors may prescribe medications along with therapy and nutrition advice.

People with binge eating disorder may find it helpful to surround themselves with supportive family members and friends. It's best to avoid people who make negative comments about eating or weight because they can add to someone's feelings of self-criticism, making matters worse.

Another thing that can help build self-confidence and take a person's mind off eating is trying a new extracurricular activity or hobby. Finding a way to express feelings, such as through music, art, dance, or writing, can also help someone deal with difficult emotions in a healthy way.

As with any eating disorder, there is no quick fix for binge eating. Treatment can take several months or longer while someone learns a healthier approach to food. But with the right guidance, commitment, and practice, it is possible to overcome old habits and replace them with healthier behaviors.

✔ Quick Tip
Helping A Friend

If you think a friend has a problem with binge eating, it may be difficult to talk about it, but your concern and support may be just what your friend needs to get help. Showing you care, listening, and just being there for support can help a friend get through any difficult situation.

Source: The Nemours Foundation.

Chapter 15

Emotional Eating

Understanding Emotional Eating

Emotional eating is a common phenomenon in which the urge to eat is not due to physiological hunger. In a culture in which food is incredibly abundant, emotional eating represents a convenient way for individuals to manage emotions that are uncomfortable.

Why Call It Emotional Eating?

To be clear, the term emotional eating is not eating with your emotions openly displayed. It is rare for most people to consciously feel their emotions while eating.

Instead, emotional eating occurs in response to emotions that often go unnoticed. Though they may be under the surface, emotions become too difficult to control in the normal course of the day, and food provides a powerful distraction.

What Feelings Are Avoided With Emotional Eating?

Anxiety, fear, loneliness, anger, and guilt—any uncomfortable emotion may be at the root of emotional eating.

A man might eat more and more as his home business earns less and less money. Another person might return home from a date feeling worthless and turn to ice cream for comfort. The possibilities are endless.

How Does Emotional Eating Soothe Negative Feelings?

Eating does several things to relieve anxiety and other negative emotions:

- Food changes the chemical balance in the body. Some foods increase endorphin levels, which in turn, creates a sense of happiness or contentment.

- We associate being full with comfort. Fullness increases comfort, which counteracts negative emotions. And if a person eats past fullness to discomfort, the physical sensation distracts the mind from other problems.

- Eating takes time that might otherwise be spent thinking negative thoughts. A person uses even more time in preparing food and cleaning up after eating.

- Celebrations usually involve food, and a person may therefore be conditioned to be in a more celebratory mood when eating.

♣ It's A Fact!!

Emotional eating can contribute to other eating disorders (anorexia nervosa, bulimia nervosa, and binge eating disorder, for example).

Source: Excerpted from "Understanding Emotional Eating," © 2008 by Matthew Tiemeyer (http://eatingdisorders.about.com/od/othereatingdisorders/a/emotionaleat.htm). Used with permission of About, Inc., which can be found online at www.about.com. All rights reserved.

Maybe I Eat Emotionally. So What?

Emotional eating can have a profound effect on quality of life.

But there are ways to treat emotional eating and the underlying problems that fuel it. Taking a step toward greater health may mean speaking with a counselor, learning more about solid nutrition, getting medical attention for chemical imbalances, or finding a support group.

Breaking Free From Emotional Eating

Emotional Eating Treatment Options

If you're concerned that you or someone you love may be stuck in emotional eating patterns, you have to make treatment choices.

Why "treatment?" The word may sound extreme given that emotional eating is not a diagnosable eating disorder. But there is no reason to deal with this difficult problem alone.

Emotional Eating Treatment With A Dietitian

A dietitian will help you identify your eating patterns. When you match these patterns with your emotional conditions throughout each day, you may be able to find consistent ways in which emotions lead you to eat when you aren't really hungry. Also, dietitians can help you learn ways to eat that minimize the emotional highs and lows of some diets, which can reduce your need to soothe yourself with food (or with anything else, for that matter).

Emotional Eating Treatment With A Counselor

It's no secret that counselors (therapists) work in the area of emotions all the time.

A good counselor (someone with whom you can connect and make progress) will be fluent in language that will help you identify emotions that may lead to emotional eating. Often, negative emotions are somewhat hidden. Finding ways to express these feelings constructively can help clear unwanted eating patterns.

Emotional Eating Treatment With A Doctor Or Psychiatrist

In general, doctors and psychiatrists will approach eating disorders with a focus on biological issues. These physicians may prescribe medications to bring the brain's chemistry back into balance.

We would all like to be able to function well without medication, but our bodies sometimes need help to get back on track. Medication is not designed to be a "crutch," and those who take medications are not failures. If you don't make or absorb certain neurotransmitters well, you simply won't feel good emotionally. However, if you're concerned about drugs, make sure your prescribing clinician understands and addresses your questions to your satisfaction.

Emotional Eating Treatment With Yourself

While treatment providers are often involved when lasting change occurs, there are things you can do for yourself. You'll need to care for yourself well no matter what treatment course you may choose. Self-care includes a number of strategies:

- **Exercise:** Using your body feeds your brain good chemicals, so you don't have to soothe it with food.

- **Investing In Healthy Relationships:** This is the direct way to deal with loneliness.

- **Actively Pursuing Things You Enjoy:** It might be a manicure, a bubble bath, or a drive to a favorite scenic area. Not all of life will be enjoyable, but where have you hurt yourself through deprivation?

- **Stop Dieting:** Dieting (deprivation) leads to eating rebounds far more often than it works—*far* more often.

- **Get Good Sleep:** Tiredness can look a lot like hunger.

Chapter 16

Night Eating Syndrome

People indulging in midnight snacks may have more than a bad habit. They may actually have a real clinical illness identified as night eating syndrome (NES), a disorder in which affected people have little appetite during the morning but wake up two or more times a night, taking in more than 30% to 50% of their calories before the sun rises. As the day wears on, their mood worsens and they become more and more depressed, only to raid the refrigerator and cupboards for high-carbohydrate snacks again during the night. As anxiety and depression increases throughout the night, so does the eating, leading to a vicious cycle.

Researchers from the University of Pennsylvania Medical Center have found some clues as to what causes this baffling condition. NES is not only an eating disorder, they say, but also a disorder of mood and sleep, occurring as a result of hormonal changes related to sleep, hunger, and stress. It appears sufferers have abnormal blood levels of the hormone leptin, which helps regulate appetite. They also tend to have low blood levels of melatonin, a hormone believed to play a role in maintaining normal sleep patterns. Other hormones may play a role as well, including glucose, insulin, cortisol, and adrenocorticotropic hormone, which stimulates the production of cortisol, a stress hormone.

About This Chapter: Information in this chapter is from "Night-Eating Syndrome a Mood, Eating, and Sleep Disorder," January 10, 2005. © University of Alabama Board of Trustees for the University of Alabama at Birmingham. Reprinted with permission.

♣ It's A Fact!!

Night Eating Syndrome Tied To Obesity

People suffering from night eating syndrome are at higher risk than normal for obesity and substance abuse, according to recent research. The study also found that night eating syndrome is a common condition among psychiatric patients.

Characterized by excessive eating in the evening (hyperphagia) and nocturnal awakening with ingestion of food, night eating syndrome affects approximately 1.5 percent of the U.S. population. The condition was first observed among obese patients, but it also affects people who are not obese.

In a study partly supported by the National Institute of Diabetes and Digestive and Kidney Diseases, 399 psychiatric outpatients were screened for the eating disorder via a night eating questionnaire. Investigators inquired about hunger and craving patterns, percentage of calories consumed after the evening meal, insomnia and awakenings, nocturnal food cravings and ingestions, and mood. Participants who scored above cutoff on the questionnaire were interviewed by phone and received a night eating syndrome diagnosis if they reported having evening hyperphagia or nocturnal awakenings with ingestions of food three or more times a week.

The researchers also found that only 1% to 2% of adults have the problem, but about 6% to 9% of people who seek treatment for obesity have NES, and the disorder may run in families. Additionally, the body's "internal clock" or circadian rhythm of food intake is disturbed, while the circadian sleep rhythm remains normal. Currently, NES appears to respond to treatment with selective serotonin reuptake inhibitors antidepressants, such as Prozac, Zoloft, and Paxil.

In summary, night eating syndrome is characterized by five primary signs:

1. Not feeling hungry in the morning. Those with NES often lack the desire to eat until lunchtime or the afternoon.

2. Overeating in the evening. For NES sufferers, hunger significantly picks up in the evening and causes them to overeat.

3. Difficulty falling asleep. NES sufferers often find it hard to fall off to sleep and may need to eat something before going to bed in order to drift off.

Results placed the prevalence of night eating syndrome at 12.3 percent. Further, investigators noted that obese psychiatric patients were five times more likely to suffer from night eating syndrome than normal-weight patients, with obesity present in 57.1 percent of diagnosed night eaters. Although this study found an association between obesity and night eating syndrome, investigators did not conclude that night eating syndrome might lead to obesity, or vice-versa. Approximately 79 percent of the obese patients enrolled in this study were not night eaters.

Substance abuse was another behavior associated with night eating syndrome, and alcohol was noted as the most commonly abused substance. The investigators observed that mental health professionals will probably encounter patients suffering from night eating syndrome in their practice and should be aware of available treatment options.

Source: Excerpted from "Night Eating Syndrome Tied to Obesity," *WIN Notes*, Summer 2006, Weight-control Information Network, an information service of the National Institute of Diabetes and Digestive and Kidney Diseases (NIDDK).

4. Waking at night and eating. Night eaters wake up at least once a night and are often unable to go back to sleep unless they have something to eat.

5. Feeling depressed. Night eaters have a higher rate of depression than non-night eaters and often report feeling sad and stressed.

If you are seeking help for night eating syndrome, schedule an appointment with your family doctor for a complete physical examination and ask for a referral to a doctor or psychologist trained in the field of eating disorders.

Chapter 17

Orthorexia Nervosa

The term orthorexia nervosa is an invention of Steven Bratman, MD, a specialist in alternative medicine. Orthorexia is essentially an obsession with healthy eating. The emphasis is on the presence of an obsession. A commitment to eating well is not orthorexia. Orthorexia is present when eating healthy food dominates a person to such an extent that the person lets other areas of life suffer.

Orthorexia is not an officially recognized disorder. Whether it deserves this status is open for debate.

Symptoms Of Orthorexia

According to Bratman, orthorexia may look like anorexia nervosa, but it has significant differences. Maintaining an obsession with health food may cause a restriction of calories merely because available food isn't "good enough." Those with orthorexia may lose enough weight to give them a body mass index consistent with someone with anorexia (for example, less than 18.5).

Is Orthorexia A Form Of Obsessive-Compulsive Disorder?

Orthorexia certainly has some of the features of obsessive-compulsive disorder (OCD). As with OCD, those with orthorexia take actions that are aimed at

About This Chapter: Information in this chapter is from "Orthorexia Nervosa." © 2008 by Matthew Tiemeyer (http://eatingdisorders.about.com/od/othereatingdisorders/p/orthorexia.htm). Used with permission of About, Inc., which can be found online at www.about.com. All rights reserved.

> ### ♣ It's A Fact!!
> Eating only the "right foods" (and perhaps only at the "right times") can give those with orthorexia a sense of superiority to others. Relationships suffer as they become less important than holding to dietary patterns.

preventing or reducing distress or preventing some dreaded event or situation. A key part of the definition of OCD is that the person struggling with the disorder recognizes that the repetitive behaviors or recurrent thoughts he has affect him in negative ways. Whether this occurs for those with orthorexia is unclear.

Vegetarians And Vegans Need Not Be "Orthorexic"

It's true that, based on some societal norms, vegetarian and vegan diets are restrictive. But if a person on such a diet does not allow it to become a dominant obsession, orthorexia is by definition not present.

On the other hand, vegetarian and vegan diets have been starting points for some who have developed eating disorders. Someone with orthorexia will naturally have strong dietary restrictions. Such restrictions can adhere to vegetarian or vegan standards, among many other possibilities.

An Example Of Orthorexia

One dietary plan that may be a form of orthorexia is calorie restriction, an organized plan in which participants reduce their calories by 20 to 40%, but make sure they get all required nutrients. The plan rigidly enforces reducing calories and getting the necessary nutrients. Proponents of the plan have a powerful allegiance to it.

Controversy

Some believe that orthorexia is a myth and that Bratman is out to make a buck (he's written a book on the topic that is now out of print). The reality is that very little peer-reviewed research exists on orthorexia. On the other hand, the phenomenon of food purity dominating a person's thoughts and life is not far-fetched. We know that eating disorders exist and that there are various kinds of obsessions. The question is whether this proposed disorder can stand on its own as an independent diagnosis in the future.

Chapter 18

Pica: Eating Things That Aren't Food

Pica is a disorder marked by the eating of substances that provide no nutritional value, such as dirt. Of course, it is common for babies to put all kinds of things in their mouths, but a diagnosis of pica is valid only when eating a substance is not appropriate for the person's age.

Substances Eaten In Pica

Substances that a person with pica might eat include the following:

- Clay or soil
- Paint chips
- Leaves
- String
- Hair
- Sand
- Pebbles
- Animal droppings
- Chalk

- Burned match heads or cigarette butts
- Rust
- Library paste
- Cornstarch, laundry starch, or baking soda
- Light bulbs
- Pencil erasers

Adolescents and adults more commonly ingest clay or soil.

Older children might eat sand, pebbles, or leaves. Younger children and infants normally choose plaster, string, or paint.

Who Gets Pica?

Pica is most often found in children—most commonly children between one and three years of age. Estimates of the percentage of children who have pica at some point in their lives range from 10% to 33%.

Older persons can develop pica as well. Among adults, it is common in pregnant women, particularly those in their first pregnancy in late adolescence. The disorder occurs more frequently in those with psychiatric or developmental problems.

Also, individuals living in difficult socioeconomic conditions are more likely to have pica. This can be due to malnutrition, lack of adequate supervision, or both.

Causes Of Pica

A common assumption is that people eat these substances to make up for deficiencies in their diets, a thought supported by the finding that some pregnant women stopped struggling with pica when they were given iron supplements. However, other factors can be at work as well.

♣ It's A Fact!!

Those who diet may try to fill their stomachs with no-calorie substances to satisfy cravings.

Some cultures believe that ingesting certain substances can help them "incorporate magical spirits into their bodies." In other cases, certain kids of clay are assumed to be helpful for treating morning sickness. And some children may eat non-food substances to imitate a pet.

Dangers Of Pica

Though pica is common and often harmless, it can be very dangerous. Several potential problems are associated with pica:

- Eating something toxic (for example, lead poisoning)
- Infections
- Presence of parasites
- Blockage of the intestines or other gastrointestinal problems

Treatment

Treatment may involve several kinds of professionals, depending on the reasons for the disorder and the symptoms. A doctor will be necessary for physical problems caused by pica. If there are socioeconomic issues involved, a social worker may be able to provide guidance that alleviates underlying problems. Finally, if psychological issues are present, a therapist or psychiatrist is helpful.

Chapter 19

Laxative Abuse

People who abuse laxatives often find themselves in a no-win situation. They use laxatives to "feel thin," which is an immediate, positive result. Eventually, however, the exact opposite occurs. They find themselves "feeling fat" from excessive water retention—a delayed, negative result. Here are some steps to stop abusing laxatives:

1. Stop taking laxatives right now, and do not take any more unless your physician instructs you to do so. Remember that stimulant-type laxatives are especially harmful to the body.

2. Drink at least six to ten cups of water (and decaffeinated beverages—not caffeinated beverages because they act like a diuretic, promoting loss of fluid) a day. Restricting your fluid intake at this time promotes dehydration and only worsens the constipation.

3. Including some physical activity in your regular daily pattern can also help to regulate your bowel function, although you should discuss the intensity and type of activity first with your health care provider or therapist. Too much or too vigorous exercise can worsen constipation, due to the effects on your metabolism and fluid balance.

About This Chapter: Information in this chapter is from "How to Stop Abusing Laxatives," *Eating Disorders Review*, © 2000 Gürze Books. Reprinted with permission. Reviewed August 13, 2008 by David A. Cooke, M.D., Diplomate, American Board of Internal Medicine.

4. Eat regularly. It is important that you spread the amount of food recommended to you on your meal plan across at least three meals a day, and to eat these meals at regular intervals.

5. Eat more foods that promote normal bowel movements. The healthiest dietary approach to promoting normal bowel function is to eat more whole-grain breads, cereals, and crackers, and wheat bran or foods with wheat bran added. This dietary approach should be done in tandem with drinking more fluids. Vegetables and fruits also contribute to normal bowel function. Prunes and prune juice are not recommended because the ingredient in prunes that promotes bowel movements is actually an irritant laxative, and long-term use of prunes and prune juice can result in the same problem as long-term use of laxatives.

6. Write down the frequency of your bowel movements on a sheet of paper. If you are constipated for more than three days, call your physician, dietitian, or psychotherapist.

What To Expect From Laxative Withdrawal

There is no way to predict exactly how stopping laxatives will affect you. For example, the amount or length of time laxatives have been used is not an indicator of how severe the withdrawal symptoms will be. The best way to lessen the unpleasant effects of laxative withdrawal is to prepare yourself for these effects and to develop an action plan for coping in case the unpleasant side effects do occur.

Common side effects of laxative withdrawal are:

- constipation;
- fluid retention;
- feeling bloated;
- temporary weight gain.

Just reading this list, you can see that laxative withdrawal is especially difficult for people with eating disorders. You already are highly reactive to "feeling fat," and the symptoms of laxative withdrawal only worsen this feeling.

To help you get through the process of laxative withdrawal, it is essential to remember that any weight gain associated with laxative withdrawal is only temporary. Symptoms of laxative withdrawal do not lead to permanent weight gain.

How long will laxative withdrawal last? This varies greatly. A few people have these symptoms for two days; a few others have had them for two to three months. Most people have symptoms of laxative abuse for one to three weeks after stopping laxatives.

♣ It's A Fact!!

Myth: If you induce diarrhea with laxatives, you can prevent the absorption of food and avoid body weight gain.

Fact: Inducing diarrhea by laxatives does not significantly change the absorption of food in the body. Consequently, laxatives do not significantly prevent weight gain. What appears to be weight loss is actually dehydration or water deprivation. Laxatives work near the end of the bowel, where they primarily affect absorption of water and electrolytes (like sodium and potassium). They thus work after most of the nutrients from the food have been absorbed into the body.

Laxative Abuse: Myths And Medical Complications

Myth: You need to use a laxative every time you feel constipated.

Fact: "Feeling" constipated does not necessarily mean that you are constipated. This is especially true of people who have problems with eating. Eating too little food or eating sporadically can result in the sensation of constipation. In this case, the problem is not constipation but poor eating habits.

Myth: When you actually are constipated, you need to use a laxative.

Fact: People who use excessive amounts of laxatives will eventually find the exact opposite happening—the laxatives will cause reflex constipation.

Myth: All laxatives are alike.

Fact: There are many different types of laxatives that are taken by mouth or as a suppository. The ones most commonly used are:

- Stimulant-type laxatives, including Ex-Lax®, Correctol®, Senokot®, Ducolax®, Feen-a Mint®, and some of the so-called herbal laxatives. Osmotic-type laxatives, including Milk of Magnesia®.

- Bulk agents, including Metamucil®, Colace®, and unprocessed bran. Bulk agents promote bowel movement. When bulk agents are used as directed (with large amounts of water), they don't have the same physical effects on the bowel as the stimulant and osmotic laxatives. However, when these bulk agents are misused, they have the same psychological consequences as regular laxatives. Misusing these agents must be discontinued.

Myth: Laxatives, particularly over-the-counter products, are safe.

Fact: Laxative abuse can be medically dangerous. Laxative abuse is defined as (1) use of laxatives for weight control, or (2) frequent use of laxatives over an extended period of time.

Medical Complications Of Laxative Abuse

The medical complications of laxative abuse depend on several factors, including the type of laxatives used, the amount used, and how long they have been used. Some of the more common complications of laxative abuse follow.

Constipation: Repeated use of laxatives actually causes constipation. This may lead people to increase the dosage of the amount of laxative, which in turn only worsens the constipation problem.

Dehydration: Laxatives cause fluid loss through the intestines. Dehydration then impairs body functioning.

Electrolyte Abnormalities: Many people who abuse laxatives often demonstrate electrolyte imbalances. Electrolytes such as potassium, sodium, and chloride are important to life functions. With chronic diarrhea, electrolytes are drawn out of the body through the feces. This leads to an electrolyte imbalance in the body.

Edema: As noted before, laxatives cause fluid loss. Dramatic changes or fluctuations in fluid balance confuse the body's self-regulating protective mechanisms by retaining fluid. As a result, prolonged laxative abuse frequently leads to fluid retention or edema.

Bleeding: People who abuse laxatives, especially the stimulant-type laxatives, can develop blood in their stools. Chronic blood loss associated with laxative abuse can lead to anemia.

Impaired Bowel Function: People who abuse stimulant-type laxatives can develop permanent impairment of bowel function.

Chapter 20

Compulsive Exercise

Rachel and her cheerleading team practice three to five times a week. Rachel feels a lot of pressure to keep her weight down—as head cheerleader, she wants to set an example to the team. So she adds extra daily workouts to her regimen. But lately, Rachel has been feeling worn out, and she has a hard time just making it through a regular team practice.

You may think you can't get too much of a good thing, but in the case of exercise, a healthy activity can sometimes turn into an unhealthy compulsion. Rachel is a good example of how an overemphasis on physical fitness or weight control can become unhealthy. Read on to find out more about compulsive exercise and its effects.

Too Much Of A Good Thing?

We all know the benefits of exercise, and it seems that everywhere we turn, we hear that we should exercise more. The right kind of exercise does many great things for your body and soul. It can strengthen your heart and muscles, lower your body fat, and reduce your risk of many diseases.

Many teens who play sports have higher self-esteem than their less active pals, and exercise can even help keep the blues at bay because of the endorphin rush it can cause. Endorphins are chemicals that naturally relieve pain and lift mood. These chemicals are released in your body during and after a workout and they go a long way in helping to control stress.

So how can something with so many benefits have the potential to cause harm?

Lots of people start working out because it's fun or it makes them feel good, but exercise can become a compulsive habit when it is done for the wrong reasons.

Some people start exercising with weight loss as their main goal. Although exercise is part of a safe and healthy way to control weight, many people may have unrealistic expectations. We are bombarded with images from advertisers of the ideal body: young and thin for women; strong and muscular for men. To try to reach these unreasonable ideals, people may turn to diets, and for some, this may develop into eating disorders such as anorexia and bulimia. And some people who grow frustrated with the results from diets alone may over exercise to speed up weight loss.

Some athletes may also think that repeated exercise will help them to win an important game. Like Rachel, they add extra workouts to those regularly scheduled with their teams without consulting their coaches or trainers. The pressure to succeed may also lead these people to exercise more than is healthy. The body needs activity, but it also needs rest. Over exercising can lead to injuries like fractures and muscle strains.

Are You A Healthy Exerciser?

Fitness experts recommend that teens do at least 60 minutes of moderate to vigorous physical activity every day. Most young people exercise much less than this recommended amount (which can be a problem for different reasons), but some—such as athletes—do more.

Experts say that repeatedly exercising beyond the requirements for good health is an indicator of compulsive behavior. Some people need more than the average amount of exercise, of course, such as athletes in training for a big event. But several workouts a day, every day, when a person is not in training is a sign that the person is probably overdoing it.

People who are exercise dependent also go to extremes to fit activity into their lives. If you put workouts ahead of friends, homework, and other responsibilities, you may be developing a dependence on exercise.

If you are concerned about your own exercise habits or a friend's, ask yourself the following questions. Do you:

- force yourself to exercise, even if you don't feel well?
- prefer to exercise rather than being with friends?
- become very upset if you miss a workout?
- base the amount you exercise on how much you eat?
- have trouble sitting still because you think you're not burning calories?
- worry that you'll gain weight if you skip exercising for a day?

If the answer to any of these questions is yes, you or your friend may have a problem. What should you do?

How To Get Help

The first thing you should do if you suspect that you are a compulsive exerciser is get help. Talk to your parents, doctor, a teacher or counselor, a coach, or another trusted adult. Compulsive exercise, especially when it is combined with an eating disorder, can cause serious and permanent health problems, and in extreme cases, death.

Because compulsive exercise is closely related to eating disorders, help can be found at community agencies specifically set up to deal with anorexia, bulimia, and other eating problems. Your school's health or physical education department may also have support programs and nutrition advice available. Ask your teacher, coach, or counselor to recommend local organizations that may be able to help.

You should also schedule a checkup with a doctor. Because our bodies go through so many important developments during the teen years, guys and girls who have compulsive exercise problems need to see a doctor to make sure they are developing normally. This is especially true if the person also has an eating disorder. Female athlete triad, a condition that affects girls who over exercise and restrict their eating because of their sports, can cause a girl to stop having her period. Medical help is necessary to resolve the physical problems associated with over exercising before they cause long-term damage to the body.

Make A Positive Change

Changes in activity of any kind—eating or sleeping, for example—can often be a sign that something else is wrong in your life. Girls and guys who exercise compulsively may have a distorted body image and low self-esteem. They may see themselves as overweight or out of shape even when they are actually a healthy weight.

Compulsive exercisers need to get professional help for the reasons described above. But there are also some things that you can do to help you take charge again:

- **Work on changing your daily self-talk.** When you look in the mirror, make sure you find at least one good thing to say about yourself. Be more aware of your positive attributes.

- **When you exercise, focus on the positive, mood-boosting qualities.**

- **Give yourself a break.** Listen to your body and give yourself a day of rest after a hard workout.

- **Control your weight by exercising and eating moderate portions of healthy foods.** Don't try to change your body into an unrealistically lean shape. Talk with your doctor, dietitian, coach, athletic trainer, or other adult about what a healthy body weight is for you and how to develop healthy eating and exercise habits.

♣ It's A Fact!!
Exercise and sports are supposed to be fun and keep you healthy. Working out in moderation will do both.
Source: The Nemours Foundation.

Chapter 21

Female Athlete Triad

With dreams of college scholarships in her mind, Hannah joined the track team her freshman year and trained hard to become a lean, strong sprinter. When her coach told her losing a few pounds would improve her performance, she immediately started counting calories and increased the duration of her workouts. She was too busy with practices and meets to notice that her period had stopped—she was more worried about the stress fracture in her ankle slowing her down.

Although Hannah thinks her intense training and disciplined diet are helping her performance, they may actually be hurting her—and her health.

What Is Female Athlete Triad?

Sports and exercise are part of a balanced, healthy lifestyle. Girls who play sports are healthier; get better grades; are less likely to experience depression; and use alcohol, cigarettes, and drugs less frequently than girls who aren't athletes. But for some girls, not balancing the needs of their bodies and their sports can have major consequences.

About This Chapter: "Female Athlete Triad," October 2006, reprinted with permission from www.kidshealth.org. Copyright © 2006 The Nemours Foundation. This information was provided by KidsHealth, one of the largest resources online for medically reviewed health information written for parents, kids, and teens. For more articles like this one, visit www.KidsHealth.org, or www.TeensHealth.org.

Some girls who play sports or exercise intensely are at risk for a problem called female athlete triad. Female athlete triad is a combination of three conditions: disordered eating, amenorrhea, and osteoporosis. A female athlete can have one, two, or all three parts of the triad.

Triad Factor #1: Disordered Eating

Most girls with female athlete triad try to lose weight primarily to improve their athletic performance. The disordered eating that accompanies female athlete triad can range from avoiding certain types of food the athlete thinks are "bad" (such as foods containing fat) to serious eating disorders like anorexia nervosa or bulimia nervosa.

Triad Factor #2: Amenorrhea

Because a girl with female athlete triad is simultaneously exercising intensely and not eating enough calories, when her weight falls too low, she may experience decreases in estrogen, the hormone that helps to regulate the menstrual cycle. As a result, a girl's periods may become irregular or stop altogether. Of course, it is normal for teen girls to occasionally miss periods, especially in their first year of having periods. A missed period does not automatically mean a girl has female athlete triad. A missed period could mean something else is going on, like pregnancy or a medical condition. If you have missed a period and you are sexually active, talk to your doctor.

Some girls who participate intensively in sports may never even get their first period because they've been training so hard. Other girls may have had periods, but once they increase their training and change their eating habits, their periods may stop.

Triad Factor #3: Osteoporosis

Low estrogen levels and poor nutrition, especially low calcium intake, can lead to osteoporosis, the third aspect of the triad. Osteoporosis is a weakening of the bones due to the loss of bone density and improper bone formation. This condition can ruin a female athlete's career because it may lead to stress fractures and other injuries.

Usually, the teen years are a time when girls should be building up their bone mass to their highest levels—called peak bone mass. Not getting enough calcium during the teen years can also have a lasting effect on how strong a girl's bones are later in life.

Who Gets Female Athlete Triad?

Most girls have concerns about the size and shape of their bodies, but girls who develop female athlete triad have certain risk factors that set them apart. Being a highly competitive athlete and participating in a sport that requires you to train extra hard is a risk factor.

Girls with female athlete triad often care so much about their sports that they would do almost anything to improve their performance. Martial arts and rowing are examples of sports that classify athletes by weight class, so focusing on weight becomes an important part of the training program and can put a girl at risk for disordered eating.

Participation in sports where a thin appearance is valued can also put a girl at risk for female athlete triad. Sports such as gymnastics, figure skating, diving, and ballet are examples of sports that value a thin, lean body shape. Some girls may even be told by coaches or judges that losing weight would improve their scores.

Even in sports where body size and shape aren't as important, such as distance running and cross-country skiing, girls may be pressured by team-mates, parents, partners, and coaches who mistakenly believe that "losing just a few pounds" could improve their performance.

The truth is, though, that losing those few pounds generally doesn't im-prove performance at all. People who are fit and active enough to compete in sports generally have more muscle than fat, so it's the muscle that gets starved when a girl cuts back on food. Plus, if a girl loses weight when she doesn't need to, it interferes with healthy body processes such as menstruation and bone development.

In addition, for some competitive female athletes, problems such as low self-esteem, a tendency toward perfectionism, and family stress place them at risk for disordered eating.

What Are The Signs And Symptoms?

If a girl has risk factors for female athlete triad, she may already be experiencing some symptoms and signs of the disorder, such as:

- weight loss

- no periods or irregular periods

- fatigue and decreased ability to concentrate

- stress fractures (fractures that occur even if a person hasn't had a significant injury)

- muscle injuries

Girls with female athlete triad often have signs and symptoms of eating disorders, such as:

- continued dieting in spite of weight loss

- preoccupation with food and weight

- frequent trips to the bathroom during and after meals

- using laxatives

- brittle hair or nails

- dental cavities because in girls with bulimia tooth enamel is worn away by frequent vomiting

- sensitivity to cold

- low heart rate and blood pressure

- heart irregularities and chest pain

How Doctors Help

An extensive physical examination is a crucial part of diagnosing female athlete triad. A doctor who thinks a girl has female athlete triad will probably ask questions about her periods, her nutrition and exercise habits, any medications she takes, and her feelings about her body. This is called the medical history.

Poor nutrition can also affect the body in many ways, so a doctor might order blood tests to check for anemia and other problems associated with the triad. The doctor also will check for medical reasons why a girl may be losing weight and missing her periods. Because osteoporosis can put a girl at higher risk for bone fractures, the doctor may also request tests to measure bone density.

Doctors don't work alone to help a girl with female athlete triad. Coaches, parents, physical therapists, pediatricians and adolescent medicine specialists, nutritionists and dietitians, and mental health specialists can all work together to treat the physical and emotional problems that a girl with female athlete triad faces.

It might be tempting for a girl with female athlete triad to shrug off several months of missed periods, but getting help right away is important. In the short term, she may have muscle weakness, stress fractures, and reduced physical performance. Over the long term, she may suffer from bone weakness, long-term effects on her reproductive system, and heart problems.

A girl who is recovering from female athlete triad may work with a dietitian to help get to and maintain a healthy weight and ensure she's eating enough calories and nutrients for health and good athletic performance. Depending on how much the girl is exercising, she may have to reduce the length of her workouts. Talking to a psychologist or therapist can help a girl deal with depression, pressure from coaches or family members, or low self-esteem and can help her find ways to deal with her problems other than restricting her food intake or exercising excessively.

Some girls with female athlete triad may need to take hormones to supply their bodies with estrogen so they can get their periods started again. In such cases, birth control pills are often used to regulate the menstrual cycle. Calcium and vitamin D supplementation is also common for a girl who has suffered bone loss as the result of female athlete triad.

What If I Think Someone I Know Has It?

A girl with female athlete triad may try to hide it, but she can't just ignore the disorder and hope it goes away. She needs to get help from a doctor and other health professionals. If a friend, sister, or teammate has signs and symptoms of female athlete triad, discuss your concerns with her and encourage her to seek treatment. If she refuses to seek treatment, you may need to mention your concern to a parent, coach, teacher, or school nurse.

You may worry about being nosy when you ask questions about a friend's health, but you're not. Your concern is a sign that you're a caring friend. Lending an ear may be just what your friend needs.

✔ Quick Tip
Tips For Female Athletes

Here are a few tips to help teen athletes stay on top of their physical condition:

- **Keep track of your periods.** It's easy to forget when you had your last visit from Aunt Flo, so keep a calendar in your gym bag and mark down when your period starts and stops and if the bleeding is particularly heavy or light. That way, if you start missing periods, you'll know right away, and you'll have accurate information to give to your doctor.

- **Don't skip meals or snacks.** Girls who are constantly on the go between school, practice, and competitions may be tempted to skip meals and snacks to save time. But eating now will improve performance later, so stock your locker or bag with quick and easy favorites such as bagels, string cheese, unsalted nuts and seeds, raw vegetables, granola bars, and fruit.

- **Visit a dietitian or nutritionist who works with teen athletes.** He or she can help you get your dietary game plan into gear and determine if you're getting enough key nutrients such as iron, calcium, and protein. And if you need supplements, a nutritionist can recommend the best choices.

- **Do it for you.** Pressure from teammates, parents, or coaches can turn a fun activity into a nightmare. If you're not enjoying your sport, make a change. Remember: It's your body and your life. You—not your coach or teammates—will have to live with any damage you do to your body now.

Source: The Nemours Foundation.

Chapter 22

Body Dysmorphic Disorder And Bigorexia

Body Dysmorphic Disorder

What is body dysmorphic disorder?

Body dysmorphic disorder (BDD) is a type of somatoform disorder, a mental illness in which a person has symptoms of a medical illness, but the symptoms cannot be fully explained by an actual physical disorder. People with BDD are preoccupied with an imagined physical defect or a minor defect that others often cannot see. People with this disorder see themselves as "ugly" and often avoid social exposure to others or turn to plastic surgery to try to improve their appearance.

BDD shares some features with eating disorders and obsessive-compulsive disorder. BDD is similar to eating disorders in that both involve a concern with body image. However, a person with an eating disorder worries about weight and the shape of the entire body, while a person with BDD is concerned about a specific body part. BDD is a long-term (chronic) disorder that affects men and women equally. It usually begins during the teen years or early adulthood.

About This Chapter: This chapter begins with "Body Dysmorphic Disorder," © 2008 The Cleveland Clinic Foundation, 9500 Euclid Avenue, Cleveland, OH 44195, www.clevelandclinic.org. Additional information is available from the Cleveland Clinic Health Information Center, 216-444-3771, toll-free 800-223-2273 extension 43771 or at http://www.clevelandclinic.org/health. Text by Matthew Tiemeyer, under the heading "Bigorexia," is cited separately within the chapter.

Obsessive-compulsive disorder (OCD) is an anxiety disorder that traps people in endless cycles of thoughts and behaviors. People with OCD have recurring and distressing thoughts, fears, or images (obsessions) that they cannot control. The anxiety (nervousness) produced by these thoughts leads to an urgent need to perform certain rituals or routines (compulsions). Similarly, with BDD, a person's preoccupation with the defect often leads to ritualistic behaviors, such as constantly looking in a mirror or picking at the skin. The person with BDD eventually becomes so obsessed with the defect that his or her social, work, and home functioning suffers.

The most common areas of concern for people with BDD include:

- **Skin Imperfections:** These include wrinkles, scars, acne, and blemishes.

- **Hair:** This might include head or body hair or absence of hair.

- **Facial Features:** Very often this involves the nose, but it also might involve the shape and size of any feature.

Other areas of concern include the size of the penis, muscles, breasts, thighs, buttocks, and the presence of certain body odors.

What are the symptoms of BDD?

People with BDD have distorted views of themselves, which can lead to harmful or socially avoidant behaviors or repeated attempts to correct perceived problems through surgery. Some of the warning signs that a person may have BDD include the following:

- Engaging in repetitive and time-consuming behaviors, such as looking in a mirror, picking at the skin, and trying to hide or cover up the defect

- Constantly asking for reassurance that the defect is not visible or too obvious

- Repeatedly measuring or touching the defect

- Experiencing problems at work or school, or in relationships, due to the inability to stop focusing on the defect

- Feeling self-conscious and not wanting to go out in public, or feeling anxious when around other people

- Repeatedly consulting with medical specialists, such as plastic surgeons or dermatologists, to find ways to improve his or her appearance

What causes BDD?

The exact cause of BDD is not known. One theory suggests the disorder involves a problem with certain neurotransmitters in the brain. Neurotransmitters are chemicals that help nerve cells in the brain send messages to each other. The fact that BDD often occurs in people with other mental health disorders, such as major depression and anxiety, further supports a biological basis for the disorder.

Other factors that might influence the development of, or trigger, BDD include:

♣ **It's A Fact!!**

Pressure from peers and a society that equates physical appearance with beauty and value can have an impact on the development of body dysmorphic disorder (BDD).

Source: © 2008 The Cleveland Clinic Foundation.

- Experience of traumatic events or emotional conflict during childhood

- Low self-esteem

- Parents and others who were critical of the person's appearance

How is BDD diagnosed?

The secrecy and shame that often accompany BDD make its diagnosis difficult. Most experts agree that many cases of BDD go unrecognized. People with the disorder often are embarrassed and reluctant to tell their doctors about their concerns. As a result, the disorder can go unnoticed for years or never be diagnosed. One red flag to physicians or family members is when patients repeatedly seek plastic surgery for the same or multiple perceived physical defects.

In diagnosing BDD, the physician will begin his or her evaluation with a complete history and physical examination. If the doctor suspects BDD, he or she might refer the person to a psychiatrist or psychologist, health care professionals who are specially trained to diagnose and treat mental illnesses. The psychiatrist or psychologist makes a diagnosis based on his or her assessment of the person's attitude, behavior, and symptoms.

How is BDD treated?

Treatment for BDD likely will include a combination of the following therapies:

- **Psychotherapy:** This is a type of individual counseling that focuses on changing the thinking (cognitive therapy) and behavior (behavioral therapy) of a person with body dysmorphic disorder. The goal is to correct the false belief about the defect and to minimize the compulsive behavior.

- **Medication:** Certain antidepressant medications, called selective serotonin reuptake inhibitors (SSRIs), are showing promise in treating body dysmorphic disorder.

- **Group And/Or Family Therapy:** Family support is very important to treatment success. It is important that family members understand body dysmorphic disorder and learn to recognize its signs and symptoms.

What are the complications associated with body dysmorphic disorder?

Social isolation can occur if the person becomes too self-conscious to go out in public. This also can have a negative impact on school or work. People with BDD also are at high risk for developing major depression, and the distress associated with the disorder puts people with BDD at high risk for suicide. Further, people with this disorder might undergo many surgical procedures in an attempt to correct their perceived defect.

What is the outlook for people with BDD?

The outlook is promising for people with BDD who receive and follow treatment. The support of family members and other loved ones can help ensure that the person receives and stays with treatment, and might help to improve outcomes.

Can BDD be prevented?

There is no known way to prevent BDD. However, it might be helpful to begin treatment in people as soon as they begin to have symptoms. Teaching and encouraging healthy and realistic attitudes about body image also might help prevent the development or worsening of BDD. Finally, providing the person with an understanding and supportive environment might help decrease the severity of the symptoms and help him or her better cope with the disorder.

Bigorexia

"Bigorexia," © 2008 by Matthew Tiemeyer (http://menshealth.about.com/cs/ menonly/a/bigorexia.htm). Used with permission of About, Inc., which can be found online at www.about.com. All rights reserved.

Reverse Anorexia

Being preoccupied with muscle development may involve a disturbance in body image similar to anorexia. Bigorexia (muscular dysmorphia) is now affecting hundreds of thousands of men. For some men muscle development is such a complete preoccupation that they will miss important events, continue training through pain or broken bones, and even lose their job rather than interrupt their physical development schedule. Curiously, these same men are not in love with their bodies. Despite a well-developed physique, they are unlikely to show it off and will shy away from situations that expose their bodies.

Muscle Dysmorphia

The term "muscle dysmorphia" was coined in 1997 to describe this new form of disorder. Other people refer to the condition as "reverse anorexia," and now more commonly "bigorexia."

The causes are not known, but two key ideas revolve around bigorexia as a form of obsessive-compulsive behavior and secondly, the effect of the media putting the same type of pressure on men to conform to an ideal shape as has been the case with women for years.

The Main Characteristic Of Bigorexia

The main characteristic of bigorexia is the thought that no matter how hard you try your body is never muscular enough. The condition is recognized as more common with men, although some women body builders have also been reported with similar symptoms. Most men with bigorexia are weight lifters, but this does not mean that most weight lifters are bigorexic. Compared to normal weightlifters, who report spending up to 40 minutes a day thinking about body development, men with bigorexia report being preoccupied five or more hours a day thinking their bodies are under-developed.

With the increase in gymnasium provisions and attendance, there is some speculation that this alone accounts for increased awareness of physical imperfection in men and a quest to attain the perfect body.

> ♣ **It's A Fact!!**
> Conservative estimates put bigorexia as affecting hundreds of thousands of men.
>
> Source: © 2008 by Matthew Tiemeyer.

Typical Features Of Bigorexia

Bigorexia And Mirror Checking

Bigorexic men check themselves up to 12 times a day. This compares to roughly three times a day with other weight lifters. Important social events like birthdays, meeting friends, keeping appointments, etc. are overlooked because they interrupt the training schedule. Working hours may be seen as too long, and some men have lost their jobs because they spend too long training during break periods.

Bigorexia And Measuring Up

Bigorexic men constantly compare their own physique with that of other men. Invariably their perceptions are incorrect. Even when observing men of equal physique, they will judge themselves as smaller.

Bigorexia And Drugs

The use of anabolic steroids is common amongst bigorexics. Men continue using steroids despite experiencing side effects such as increased

---

♣ It's A Fact!!

Diet And Bigorexia

Very strict diets are important. Bigorexics will rarely eat at another person's house or at a restaurant because they are unable to control the dietary balance or know exactly what has gone into food preparation. It has been known for men to develop eating disorders such as bulimia.

Source: © 2008 by Matthew Tiemeyer.

---

aggression, acne, breast enlargement, impotence, baldness, and testicular shrinkage.

Bigorexia And Body Fat

Men with bigorexia typically worry about the percentage of body fat they carry rather than being overweight.

Psychological Factors And Bigorexia

Unlike many body builders who enjoy the opportunity to show their physique in public, bigorexics do not. Many will hide away for days at a time because of embarrassment about their body shape. Research undertaken by H.G. Pope and others in 2000 found that one man avoided sex with his wife in case it used up energy he could apply to bodybuilding.

Typically, men with bigorexia have low self-esteem. Many report having been teased at school about their physique leading to a focus on "making good." However, the attempt to catch up is never achieved and results in a poor sense of self and feelings of emptiness. Studies by R. Olivardia and others in 2000 also found that 29 per cent of men with bigorexia had a history of anxiety disorder, and 59 per cent exhibited some other form of mood disorder.

Treatment Options For Bigorexia

At this time, no systematic studies have been produced to compare the effectiveness of one treatment over another, either individually or in combination. A particular problem with the condition is that, rather like anorexics, men rarely see themselves as having a problem and are unlikely to come forward for treatment. The condition itself occurs partly as a response to feelings of depression and lack of self-esteem, so coming forward for treatment is admitting defeat.

Where men have come forward, a combination of educational and psychotherapeutic techniques has begun to show promising results. Cognitive-behavioral techniques place an emphasis on identifying and changing patterns of thinking towards more realistic and achievable goals. Future treatment packages may well be informed by such approaches, but more systematic studies are now required.

Part Three

Health Consequences Of Eating Disorders And Co-Occurring Concerns

Chapter 23

Medical And Psychological Complications Of Eating Disorders

Medical Problems

If not stopped, starving, stuffing, and purging can lead to irreversible physical damage and even death. Eating disorders can affect every cell, tissue, and organ in the body. The following is a partial list of the medical dangers associated with anorexia nervosa, bulimia, and binge eating disorder.

- Irregular heartbeat, cardiac arrest, death.

- Kidney damage, renal failure, death.

- Liver damage (made worse by substance abuse), death.

- Loss of muscle mass. Broomstick arms and legs.

- Permanent loss of bone mass; fractures and lifelong problems caused by fragile bones and joints. Osteopenia, osteoporosis, and dowager's hump.

- Destruction of teeth, rupture of esophagus, damage to lining of stomach; gastritis, gastric distress including bloat and distension.

- Disruption of menstrual cycle, infertility.

- Delayed growth and permanently stunted growth due to under-nutrition. Even after recovery and weight restoration, person may not catch up to expected normal height.

- Weakened immune system.

- Icy hands and feet.

- Swollen glands in neck; stones in salivary duct, "chipmunk cheeks."

- Excess hair on face, arms, and body. Long, downy lanugo hair that may be an emaciated body's attempt to be warm.

- Dry, blotchy skin that has an unhealthy gray or yellow cast.

- Anemia, malnutrition. Disruption of body's fluid/mineral balance (electrolyte imbalance, loss of potassium; can be fatal).

- Fainting spells, seizures, sleep disruption, bad dreams, and mental fuzziness.

- Low blood sugar (hypoglycemia), including shakiness, anxiety, restlessness, and a pervasive itchy sensation all over the body.

- Anal and bladder incontinence, urinary tract infections, vaginal prolapse, and other problems related to weak and damaged pelvic floor muscles. Some problems may be related to chronic constipation, which is commonly found in people with anorexia nervosa. Structural damage and atrophy of pelvic floor muscles can be caused by low estrogen levels, excessive exercise, and inadequate nutrition. Surgery may be necessary to repair the damage.

- Because of changes in the brain associated with under-nourishment, binge eating, and purging, the person does not, and perhaps cannot, weigh priorities, make judgments, and make choices that are logical and rational for normal people. Recovery, once the process has begun, requires time for the brain to readjust, chemically and physically, to normal and healthy patterns of eating. This is a combined physical/psychological problem.

If binge eating disorder leads to obesity, add the following:

- Increased risk of cardiovascular disease.

- Increased risk of bowel, breast, and reproductive cancers.

- Increased risk of diabetes.

- Arthritic damage to joints.

Dieting Risk

In one study, researchers asked women to reduce their caloric intake by 50%. After 15 weeks, the activity of their natural killer cells (a part of the immune system that combats viruses) fell 20%. (*Health* magazine, 1999)

Psychological Problems

As painful as the medical consequences of an eating disorder are, the psychological agony can be worse. It is a sad irony that the person who develops an eating disorder often begins with a diet, believing that weight loss will lead to improved self-esteem, self-confidence, and happiness. The cruel reality is that persistent under-eating, binge eating, and purging have the opposite effect. Eating disordered individuals typically struggle with one or more of the following complications:

- Depression that can lead to self-harm and suicide.

- Person feels out of control and helpless to do anything about problems.

- Anxiety, self-doubt.

- Guilt and shame, feelings of failure.

- Hyper-vigilance. Thinks other people are watching and waiting to confront or interfere.

- Fear of discovery.

- Obsessive thoughts and preoccupations.

- Compulsive behaviors. Rituals dictate most activities.

- Feelings of alienation and loneliness. "I don't fit in anywhere."

- Feels hopeless and helpless. Cannot figure out how to make things better. May give up and sink into despair, fatalism, or suicidal depression.

- Because of changes in the brain associated with under-nourishment, binge eating, and purging, the person does not, and perhaps cannot, weigh priorities, make judgments, and make choices that are logical and rational for normal people. Recovery, once the process is begun, requires time for the brain to readjust, chemically and physically, to normal and healthy patterns of eating. This is a combined physical/psychological problem.

Related Problems

Eating disorders bring pain and suffering not only to the people who have them but also to their families, friends, and romantic partners. Co-workers, and even casual acquaintances, can be affected too. These problems include the following:

- Disruption of family. Blame, fights over food, weight, treatment, and so forth.

- Family members struggle with guilt, worry, anxiety, and frustration. Nothing they do seems to make things better.

- Friendships and romantic relationships are damaged or destroyed. The

♣ It's A Fact!!
A Note About Exercise-Induced Disruption Of Menstrual Periods And Infertility

Women with reproductive problems related to excessive exercise may be able to correct those problems by eating more calories. A 2001 study at University of Pittsburgh looked at whether amenorrhea and infertility are caused by exercise stress or expenditure of high levels of energy. "The findings show that it is [lack of] energy consumption during exercise that causes reproductive dysfunction," said Dr. Judy Cameron, one of the researchers. When the study created exercise conditions for monkeys that approximated human marathon training, the animals experienced reproductive impairments. When they were given more to eat, those impairments disappeared. It is logical to think the results in humans would be the same.

person with the eating disorder is, or becomes, emotionally cool and withdrawn, crabby and cranky, minimally or not at all interested in sex, and secretive and controlling, often in a passive/aggressive manner.

• If person binges and purges while driving (yes, some people do that), auto accidents may be the result of distraction.

• If person is a student or athlete, teachers, coaches, and trainers may experience the same worry and frustration that plagues family members.

Chapter 24

What Is Malnutrition?

What are hunger and malnutrition?

We all feel hungry at times. Hunger is the way the body signals that it needs to eat. Once a person is able to eat enough food to satisfy the body's needs, he or she stops being hungry. Teens can feel hungry a lot because their rapidly growing and developing bodies demand extra food.

People with malnutrition lack the nutrients necessary for their bodies to grow and stay healthy. Someone can be malnourished for a long or short period of time, and the condition may be mild or severe. Malnutrition can affect a person's physical and mental health. People who are suffering from malnutrition are more likely to get sick; in very severe cases, they may even die from its effects.

Kids who are malnourished don't grow as tall as they should (a condition referred to as stunted growth), and they are underweight as well. (People can also become underweight because they have an illness, and some are underweight because of their genes.)

About This Chapter: Information in this chapter is from "Hunger and Malnutrition," October 2006, reprinted with permission from www.kidshealth.org. Copyright © 2006 The Nemours Foundation. This information was provided by KidsHealth, one of the largest resources online for medically reviewed health information written for parents, kids, and teens. For more articles like this one, visit www.KidsHealth.org, or www.TeensHealth.org.

What causes hunger and malnutrition?

People suffer from hunger because they don't get enough food, and not getting enough food over the long term can lead to malnutrition. But someone can become malnourished for reasons that have nothing to do with hunger.

People who have plenty to eat may still be malnourished if they don't eat food that provides the right nutrients, vitamins, and minerals.

Some people become malnourished because they have a disease or condition that prevents them from digesting or absorbing their food properly. For example, someone with celiac disease has intestinal problems that are triggered by a protein called gluten, which is found in wheat, rye, barley, and oats. Celiac disease can interfere with the intestine's ability to absorb nutrients, which may result in nutritional deficiencies.

People with cystic fibrosis have trouble absorbing nutrients because the disease affects the pancreas, an organ that normally produces chemical substances called enzymes that are necessary for digesting food. People who are lactose intolerant have difficulty digesting milk and some other dairy products. By avoiding dairy products, they are at higher risk of malnutrition because milk and dairy products provide 75% of the calcium in America's food supply.

If you don't get enough of one specific nutrient, that's a form of malnutrition (although it doesn't mean you will necessarily become seriously ill). The most common form of malnutrition in the world is iron deficiency. The World Health Organization (WHO) estimates that as many as 4 to 5 billion people—up to 80% of all people in the world—don't have enough iron in their diets. Iron comes from foods like red meat, egg yolks, and fortified flour, bread, and cereals.

Who is at risk for hunger and malnutrition?

No matter what country they live in, poor people are most likely to suffer from hunger and malnutrition. In poor countries, natural disasters—such as the severe droughts that African countries often experience—can contribute to malnutrition because they make it hard for people to get the food that they need.

In the United States, food manufacturers fortify some common foods with vitamins and minerals to prevent certain nutritional deficiencies. For example, the addition of iodine to salt helps prevent some thyroid gland problems, the folic acid that's added to foods can help prevent certain birth defects, and added iron can help prevent iron-deficiency anemia.

Malnutrition affects people of every age, although infants, children, and adolescents may suffer the most because many nutrients are critical for growth. Older people may develop malnutrition because aging, illness, and other factors can sometimes lead to a poor appetite, so they may not eat enough.

Alcohol can interfere with nutrient absorption, so alcoholics may not benefit from the vitamins and minerals they consume. People who abuse drugs or alcohol may also be malnourished or underweight because they don't eat properly.

♣ **It's A Fact!!**
If you know someone with anorexia, bulimia, or another eating disorder, they're also at risk of malnutrition.

Source: The Nemours Foundation.

If you're on a special diet, you need to be careful about eating balanced meals and a variety of foods to get the right nutrients. Vegetarians and vegans need to make sure they get enough protein and vitamins like B12.

What happens to someone who is malnourished?

Malnutrition harms people both physically and mentally. The more malnourished someone is—in other words, the more nutrients they're missing—the more likely it is that person will have physical problems. (People who are only slightly to moderately malnourished may show no outward physical signs at all.)

The signs and symptoms of malnutrition depend on which nutritional deficiencies a person has, although they can include:

• fatigue and low energy

• dizziness

- poor immune function (which can cause the body to have trouble fighting off infections)

- dry, scaly skin

- swollen and bleeding gums

- decaying teeth

- slowed reaction times and trouble paying attention

- underweight

- poor growth

- muscle weakness

- bloated stomach

- bones that break easily

- problems with organ function

♣ **It's A Fact!!**
Students who are malnourished often have trouble keeping up in school.

Source: The Nemours Foundation.

When a pregnant woman is malnourished, her child may weigh less at birth and have a smaller chance of survival.

Vitamin A deficiency is the biggest cause of preventable blindness in the developing world. Children in developing countries who have a severe vitamin A deficiency as a result of malnutrition have a greater chance of getting sick or of dying from infections such as diarrhea and measles.

Iodine deficiency, another form of malnutrition, can cause mental retardation, delayed development, and even blindness in severe cases. Iron deficiency can cause a person to be less active and less able to concentrate.

What can doctors do?

Fortunately, many of the harmful effects of malnutrition can be reversed, especially if a person is only mildly or briefly malnourished. If you or your parents think you aren't getting enough of the right nutrients, you can seek advice from your doctor, who may look for signs of malnutrition in several ways. He or she will ask about how you are feeling, do a physical exam, and probably ask about the types and amounts of food in your diet.

When checking for malnutrition, a doctor may do one of several things:

- Look at a person's height and weight or body mass index (BMI) to get an idea of whether their weight is in the healthy range for their height and age

- Use blood tests to check for abnormalities

- Take X-rays or other types of images to look for signs of malnutrition in organs and bones

- Check for diseases or conditions that might be the underlying cause of malnutrition

To correct problems related to malnutrition, a doctor or dietitian would recommend specific changes in the types and quantities of foods that a person eats. Sometimes he or she will prescribe dietary supplements, such as vitamins and minerals. Other treatment may be necessary for people who are found to have a specific disease or condition causing their malnutrition.

Few teens in the United States and other developed nations suffer from serious malnutrition like that seen in Third World countries. Over time, even people who are very finicky eaters usually will get enough calories and nutrients to develop a healthy body. But if you're worried that you're not eating right or you're not feeling as well as you should, talk about your concerns with your parents, your doctor, or another trusted adult.

Chapter 25

Anorexia Nervosa And Osteoporosis

Defining Osteoporosis

Osteoporosis is a disease marked by reduced bone strength leading to an increased risk of fractures, or broken bones. Bone strength has two main features: bone mass (amount of bone) and bone quality. Osteoporosis is the major underlying cause of fractures in postmenopausal women and the elderly. Fractures occur most often in bones of the hip, spine, and wrist, but any bone can be affected. Some fractures can be permanently disabling, especially when they occur in the hip.

Osteoporosis is often called a "silent disease" because it usually progresses without any symptoms until a fracture occurs or one or more vertebrae (bones in the spine) collapse. Collapsed vertebrae may first be felt or seen when a person develops severe back pain, loss of height, or spine malformations such as a stooped or hunched posture. Bones affected by osteoporosis may become so fragile that fractures occur spontaneously or as the result of minor bumps, falls, or normal stresses and strains such as bending, lifting, or even coughing.

Many people think that osteoporosis is a natural and unavoidable part of aging. However, medical experts now believe that osteoporosis is largely

About This Chapter: Information in this chapter is excerpted from "Osteoporosis," National Institute of Arthritis and Musculoskeletal and Skin Diseases, National Institutes of Health, April 2007.

preventable. Furthermore, people who already have osteoporosis can take steps to prevent or slow further progress of the disease and reduce their risk of future fractures.

✤ It's A Fact!!

Although osteoporosis was once viewed primarily as a disease of old age, it is now recognized as a disease that can stem from less-than-optimal bone growth during childhood and adolescence, as well as from bone loss later in life.

Source: Excerpted from "Osteoporosis," National Institute of Arthritis and Musculoskeletal and Skin Diseases.

The Occurrence And Impact Of Osteoporosis

In the United States today, an estimated 10 million people over age 50 have osteoporosis, and almost 34 million have low bone mass that puts them at increased risk for developing the disease. Four out of five people who have osteoporosis are women, but about 2 million men in the U.S. also have the disease, and 14 million more have low bone mass that puts them at risk for it. One in two women and as many as one in four men over age 50 will have an osteoporosis-related fracture in their lifetime. Osteoporosis can strike at any age, although the risk of developing the disease increases as you get older. In the future, more people will be at risk of developing osteoporosis because people are living longer, and the number of elderly people in the population is increasing.

Osteoporosis affects women and men of all races and ethnic groups. It is most common in non-Hispanic white women and Asian women. African American women have a lower risk of developing osteoporosis, but they are still at significant risk. For Hispanic and Native American women the data are not clear. Among men, osteoporosis is more common in non-Hispanic whites and Asians than in men of other ethnic or racial groups.

Bone Basics

Bone is a living tissue that supports our muscles, protects vital internal organs, and stores most of the body's calcium. It consists mainly of a framework of tough, elastic fibers of a protein called collagen and crystals of calcium phosphate mineral that harden and strengthen the framework. The combination of collagen and calcium phosphate makes bones strong yet flexible to hold up under stress.

Bone also contains living cells, including some that nourish the tissue and others that control the process known as bone remodeling. Throughout life, our bones are constantly being renewed by means of this remodeling process, in which old bone is removed (bone resorption) and replaced by new bone (bone formation). Bone remodeling is carried out through the coordinated actions of bone-removing cells called osteoclasts and bone-forming cells called osteoblasts.

During childhood and the teenage years, new bone is added to the skeleton faster than old bone is removed, or resorbed. As a result, bones grow in both size and strength. After you stop growing taller, bone formation continues at a faster pace than resorption until around the early 20s, when women and men reach their peak bone mass, or maximum amount of bone. Peak bone mass is influenced by various genetic and external, or environmental, factors, including whether you are male or female (your sex), hormones, nutrition, and physical activity. Genetic factors may determine as much as 50 to 90 percent of bone mass, while environmental factors account for the remaining 10 to 50 percent. This means you have some control over your peak bone mass.

After your early 20s, your bone mass may remain stable or decrease very gradually for a period of years, depending on a variety of lifestyle factors such as diet and physical activity. Starting in midlife, both men and women experience an age-related decline in bone mass. Women lose bone rapidly in the first 4 to 8 years after menopause (the completion of a full year without a menstrual period), which usually occurs between ages 45 and 55. By age 65, men and women tend to be losing bone tissue at the same rate, and this more gradual bone loss continues throughout life.

Causes Of Osteoporosis

A major cause of osteoporosis is less-than-optimal bone growth during childhood and adolescence, resulting in failure to reach optimal peak bone mass. Thus, peak bone mass attained early in life is one of the most important factors affecting your risk of osteoporosis in later years. People who start out with greater reserves of bone (higher peak bone mass) are less likely to develop osteoporosis when bone loss occurs as a result of aging, menopause, or other factors. Other causes of osteoporosis are bone loss due to a greater-than-expected rate of bone resorption, a decreased rate of bone formation, or both.

Deterioration of bone quality, which reflects the internal structure, or "architecture," of bone as well as other factors, is also thought to contribute to decreased bone strength and increased fracture risk. Scientists do not yet clearly understand all the factors that affect bone quality and the relationship between these factors and the risk of osteoporosis and fractures. However, this is an active area of research.

A major contributor to bone loss in women during later life is the reduction in estrogen production that occurs with menopause. Estrogen is a sex hormone that plays a critical role in building and maintaining bone. Decreased estrogen, whether due to natural menopause, surgical removal of the ovaries, or chemotherapy or radiation treatments for cancer, can lead to bone loss and eventually osteoporosis. After menopause, the rate of bone loss speeds up as the amount of estrogen produced by a woman's ovaries drops dramatically. Bone loss is most rapid in the first few years after menopause but continues into the postmenopausal years.

In men, sex hormone levels also decline after middle age, but the decline is more gradual. These declines probably also contribute to bone loss in men after around age 50.

♣ It's A Fact!!

Some causes of osteoporosis include alcoholism, anorexia nervosa, abnormally low levels of sex hormones, hyperthyroidism, kidney disease, and certain gastrointestinal disorders. Sometimes osteoporosis results from a combination of causes.

Source: Excerpted from "Osteoporosis," National Institute of Arthritis and Musculoskeletal and Skin Diseases.

Osteoporosis can also result from bone loss that may accompany a wide range of disease conditions, eating disorders, and certain medications and medical treatments. For instance, osteoporosis may be caused by long-term use of some anti-seizure medications (anticonvulsants) and glucocorticoid medications such as prednisone and cortisone. Glucocorticoids are anti-inflammatory drugs used to treat many diseases, including rheumatoid arthritis, lupus, asthma, and Crohn disease.

Risk Factors For Osteoporosis

Factors that are linked to the development of osteoporosis or contribute to an individual's likelihood of developing the disease are called risk factors. Many people with osteoporosis have several risk factors for the disease, but others who develop osteoporosis have no identified risk factors. There are some risk factors that you cannot change and others that you can or may be able to change.

Risk Factors You Cannot Change

- **Sex:** Your chances of developing osteoporosis are greater if you are a woman. Women have lower peak bone mass and smaller bones than men. They also lose bone more rapidly than men in middle age because of the dramatic reduction in estrogen levels that occurs with menopause.

- **Age:** The older you are, the greater your risk of osteoporosis. Bone loss builds up over time and your bones become weaker as you age.

- **Body Size:** Slender, thin-boned women are at greater risk, as are, surprisingly, taller women.

- **Race:** Caucasian (white) and Asian women are at highest risk. African American and Hispanic women have a lower but significant risk. Among men, Caucasians are at higher risk than others. These differences in risk can be explained in part, though not entirely, by differences in peak bone mass among these groups.

- **Family History:** Susceptibility to osteoporosis and fractures appears to be, in part, hereditary. People whose parents have a history of fractures also tend to have reduced bone mass and an increased risk for fractures.

Risk Factors You Can Or May Be Able To Change

- **Sex Hormone Deficiencies:** The most common manifestation of estrogen deficiency in pre-menopausal women is amenorrhea, which is the abnormal absence of menstrual periods. Missed or irregular periods can be caused by various factors, including hormonal disorders, as well as extreme levels of physical activity combined with restricted calorie intake—for example, in female marathon runners, ballet dancers, and women who spend a great deal of time and energy working out at the gym. Low estrogen levels in women after menopause and low testosterone levels in men also increase the risk of osteoporosis. Lower-than-normal estrogen levels in men may also play a role. Low testosterone and estrogen levels are often a cause of osteoporosis in men being treated with certain medications for prostate cancer.

- **Diet:** From childhood into old age, a diet low in calcium and vitamin D can increase your risk of osteoporosis and fractures. Excessive dieting or inadequate caloric intake can also be bad for bone health. People who are very thin and do not have much body fat to cushion falls have an increased risk of fracture.

- **Certain Medical Conditions:** In addition to sex hormone problems and eating disorders, other medical conditions, including a variety of genetic, endocrine, gastrointestinal, blood, and rheumatic disorders, are associated with an increased risk for osteoporosis. Late onset of puberty and early menopause reduce lifetime estrogen exposure in women and also increase the risk of osteoporosis.

- **Medications:** Long-term use of certain medications, including glucocorticoids and some anticonvulsants, leads to bone loss and increased

---

♣ It's A Fact!!

Anorexia nervosa, for example, is an eating disorder that leads to abnormally low body weight, malnutrition, amenorrhea, and other effects on the body that adversely affect bone health.

Source: Excerpted from "Osteoporosis," National Institute of Arthritis and Musculoskeletal and Skin Diseases.

risk of osteoporosis. Other drugs that may lead to bone loss include anti-clotting drugs, such as heparin; drugs that suppress the immune system, such as cyclosporine; and drugs used to treat prostate cancer.

- **An Inactive Lifestyle Or Extended Bed Rest:** Low levels of physical activity and prolonged periods of inactivity can contribute to an increased rate of bone loss. They also leave you in poor physical condition, which can increase your risk of falling and breaking a bone.

- **Excessive Use Of Alcohol:** Chronic heavy drinking is a significant risk factor for osteoporosis.

- **Smoking:** Most studies indicate that smoking is a risk factor for osteoporosis and fracture, although the exact reasons for the harmful effects of tobacco use on bone health are still unclear.

Diagnosing Osteoporosis

Diagnosing osteoporosis involves several steps, starting with a physical exam and a careful medical history, blood and urine tests, and possibly a bone mineral density assessment. When recording information about your medical history, your doctor will ask questions to find out whether you have risk factors for osteoporosis and fractures. The doctor may ask about any fractures you have had, your lifestyle (including diet, exercise habits, and whether you smoke), current or past health problems and medications that could contribute to low bone mass and increased fracture risk, your family history of osteoporosis and other diseases, and, for women, your menstrual history. The doctor will also do a physical exam that should include checking for loss of height and changes in posture and may also include checking your balance and gait (the way you walk).

If you have back pain or have experienced a loss in height or a change in posture, the doctor may request an x-ray of your spine to look for spinal fractures or malformations due to osteoporosis. However, x-rays cannot necessarily detect osteoporosis. The results of laboratory tests of blood and urine samples can help your doctor identify conditions that may be contributing to bone loss, such as hormonal problems or vitamin D deficiency. If the results of your physical exam, medical history, x-rays, or laboratory tests indicate that you may have osteoporosis or that you have significant risk factors for the disease, your doctor may recommend a bone density test.

Mineral is what gives hardness to bones, and the density of mineral in the bones is an important determinant of bone strength. Bone mineral density (BMD) testing can be used to definitively diagnose osteoporosis, detect low bone mass before osteoporosis develops, and help predict your risk of future fractures. In general, the lower your bone density, the higher your risk for fracture. The results of a bone density test will help guide decisions about starting therapy to prevent or treat osteoporosis. BMD testing may also be used to monitor the effectiveness of ongoing therapy.

The most widely recognized test for measuring bone mineral density is a quick, painless, noninvasive technology known as dual-energy x-ray absorptiometry (DXA). This technique, which uses low levels of x-rays, involves passing a scanner over your body while you are lying on a cushioned table. DXA can be used to determine BMD of the entire skeleton and at various sites that are prone to fracture, such as the hip, spine, or wrist. Bone density measurement by DXA at the hip and spine is generally considered the most reliable way to diagnose osteoporosis and predict fracture risk.

The doctor will compare your BMD test results to the average bone density of young, healthy people and to the average bone density of other people of your age, sex, and race. For both women and men, the diagnosis of osteoporosis using DXA measurements of BMD is currently based on a number called a T-score. Your T-score represents the extent to which your bone density differs from the average bone density of young, healthy people. If you are diagnosed with osteoporosis or very low bone density, or if your bone density is below a certain level and you have other risk factors for fractures, the doctor will talk with you about options for treatment or prevention of osteoporosis.

Treating Osteoporosis

The primary goal in treating people with osteoporosis is preventing fractures. A comprehensive treatment program includes a focus on proper nutrition, exercise, and prevention of falls that may result in fractures. Your doctor may also prescribe one of several medications that have been shown to slow or stop bone loss or build new bone, increase bone density, and reduce fracture risk. If you take medication to prevent or treat osteoporosis, it is still essential that you obtain the recommended amounts of calcium and vitamin

D. Exercising and maintaining other aspects of a healthy lifestyle are also important.

Medical specialists who treat osteoporosis include family physicians, internists, endocrinologists, geriatricians, gynecologists, orthopedic surgeons, rheumatologists, and physiatrists (doctors specializing in physical medicine and rehabilitation). Physical and occupational therapists and nurses may also participate in the care of people with osteoporosis.

Nutrition

A healthy, balanced diet that includes plenty of fruits and vegetables; enough calories; and adequate calcium, vitamin D, and vitamin K is essential for minimizing bone loss and maintaining overall health. Calcium and vitamin D are especially important for bone health. Calcium is the most important nutrient for preventing osteoporosis and for reaching peak bone mass. For healthy postmenopausal women who are not consuming enough calcium (1,200 mg per day) in their diet, calcium and vitamin D supplements help to preserve bone mass and prevent hip fracture. Calcium is also needed for the heart, muscles, and nerves to work properly and for blood to clot normally. We take in calcium from our diet and lose it from the body mainly through urine, feces, and sweat. The body depends on dietary calcium to build healthy new bone and avoid excessive loss of calcium from bone to meet other needs.

Many people in the U.S. consume much less than the recommended amount of calcium in their diets. Good sources of calcium include low-fat dairy products; dark green leafy vegetables, including broccoli, bok choy, collards, and turnip greens; sardines and salmon with bones; soy beans, tofu, and other soy products; and calcium-fortified foods such as orange juice, cereals, and breads. If you have trouble getting enough calcium in your diet, you may need to take a calcium supplement such as calcium carbonate, calcium phosphate, or calcium citrate. Your daily calcium intake should not exceed 2,500 milligrams, because too much calcium can cause problems such as kidney stones. Calcium coming from food sources provides better protection from kidney stones. Anyone who has had a kidney stone should increase their dietary calcium and decrease the amount from supplements as well as increase fluid intake.

Vitamin D is required for proper absorption of calcium from the intestine. It is made in the skin after exposure to sunlight. Fifteen minutes in the sun every day without sunscreen and with some of your skin exposed is enough to meet the body's needs for vitamin D. Only a few foods naturally contain significant amounts of vitamin D, including fatty fish and fish oils. Foods fortified with vitamin D, such as milk and cereals, are a major dietary source of vitamin D. Although many people obtain enough vitamin D naturally, studies show that vitamin D production decreases in older adults, in people who are housebound, and during the winter—especially in northern latitudes.

Lifestyle

In addition to a healthy diet, a healthy lifestyle is important for optimizing bone health. You should avoid smoking. It is also important to recognize that some prescription medications can cause bone loss or increase your risk of falling and breaking a bone. Talk to your doctor if you have concerns about any medications you are taking.

Exercise

Exercise is an important part of an osteoporosis treatment program. Physical activity is needed to build and maintain bone throughout adulthood, and complete bed rest leads to serious bone loss. The evidence suggests that the most beneficial physical activities for bone health include strength training or resistance training. Exercise can help maintain or even modestly increase bone density in adulthood, and, together with adequate calcium and vitamin D intake, can help minimize age-related bone loss in older people. Exercise of various sorts has other important benefits for people with osteoporosis. It can reduce your risk of falling by increasing muscle mass and strength and improving coordination and balance.

Although exercise is beneficial for people with osteoporosis, it should not put any sudden or excessive strain on your bones. If you have osteoporosis, you should avoid high-impact exercise. To help ensure against fractures, a physical therapist or rehabilitation medicine specialist can recommend specific exercises to strengthen and support your back, teach you safe ways of moving and carrying out daily activities, and recommend an exercise program that is tailored to your circumstances. Other trained exercise specialists, such as exercise physiologists, may also be able to help you develop a safe and effective exercise program.

Preventing Osteoporosis

Preventing osteoporosis is a lifelong endeavor. To reach optimal peak bone mass and minimize loss of bone as you get older, there are several factors you should consider. Addressing all of these factors is the best way to optimize bone health throughout life.

Calcium

An inadequate supply of calcium over a lifetime is thought to play a significant role in the development of osteoporosis. Many published studies show that low calcium intakes are associated with low bone mass, rapid bone loss, and high fracture rates. National surveys suggest that the average calcium intake of individuals is far below the levels recommended for optimal bone health. Individuals who consume adequate amounts of calcium and vitamin D throughout life are more likely to achieve optimal skeletal mass early in life and are less likely to lose bone later in life.

Calcium needs change during your lifetime. The body's demand for calcium is greater during childhood and adolescence, when the skeleton is growing rapidly, and in women during pregnancy and breastfeeding. Postmenopausal women and older men also need to consume more calcium. Increased calcium requirements in older people may be related to vitamin D deficiencies that reduce intestinal absorption of calcium. Also, as you age, your body becomes less efficient at absorbing calcium and other nutrients. Older adults are also more likely to have chronic medical problems and to use medications that may impair

♣ **It's A Fact!!**
Adolescence is the most critical period for building bone mass that helps protect against osteoporosis later in life. Yet studies show that in the U.S., among children aged 9 to 19, few meet the recommended levels.

Source: Excerpted from "Osteoporosis," National Institute of Arthritis and Musculoskeletal and Skin Diseases.

calcium absorption. Calcium and vitamin D supplements may help slow bone loss and prevent hip fracture.

Vitamin D

Vitamin D plays an important role in calcium absorption and bone health. It is made in the skin after exposure to sunlight and can also be obtained through the diet. Although many people are able to obtain enough vitamin D naturally, vitamin D production decreases in the elderly, in people who are housebound or do not get enough sun, and in some people with chronic neurological or gastrointestinal diseases. These individuals and others at risk for vitamin D deficiency may require vitamin D supplementation.

Overall Nutrition

A healthy, balanced diet that includes lots of fruits and vegetables and enough calories is also important for lifelong bone health.

Exercise

Like muscle, bone is living tissue that responds to exercise by becoming stronger. There is good evidence that physical activity early in life contributes to higher peak bone mass. (However, remember that excessive exercise can be bad for bone health.) The best exercise for building and maintaining bone mass is weight-bearing exercise—exercise that you do on your feet and that forces you to work against gravity. Weight-bearing exercises include jogging, aerobics, hiking, walking, stair climbing, weight training, tennis, and dancing. High-impact exercises may provide the most benefit. Bicycling and swimming are not weight-bearing exercises, but they have other health benefits. Exercise machines that provide some degree of weight-bearing exercise include treadmills, stair-climbing machines, ski machines, and exercise bicycles.

Strength training to build and maintain muscle mass and exercises that help with coordination and balance are also important. Experts recommend 30 minutes or more of moderate physical activity on most (preferably all) days of the week, including a mix of weight-bearing exercises, strength training (two or three times a week), and balance training.

♣ It's A Fact!!
The Anorexia Nervosa-Osteoporosis Link

Anorexia nervosa has significant physical consequences. Affected individuals can experience nutritional and hormonal problems that negatively impact bone density. Low body weight in females causes the body to stop producing estrogen, resulting in a condition known as amenorrhea, or absent menstrual periods. Low estrogen levels contribute to significant losses in bone density.

In addition, individuals with anorexia often produce excessive amounts of the adrenal hormone cortisol, which is known to trigger bone loss. Other problems, such as a decrease in the production of growth hormone and other growth factors, low body weight (apart from the estrogen loss it causes), calcium deficiency, and malnutrition, contribute to bone loss in girls and women with anorexia. Weight loss, restricted dietary intake, and testosterone deficiency may be responsible for the low bone density found in males with the disorder.

Studies suggest that low bone mass (osteopenia) is common in people with anorexia and that it occurs early in the course of the disease. Girls with anorexia are less likely to reach their peak bone density and therefore may be at increased risk for osteoporosis and fracture throughout life.

Source: Excerpted from "Conditions and Behaviors that Increase Osteoporosis Risk," National Institute of Arthritis and Musculoskeletal and Skin Diseases, National Institutes of Health, June 2005.

Smoking

Smoking is bad for your bones and for your heart and lungs. Women who smoke have lower levels of estrogen compared to nonsmokers and frequently go through menopause earlier.

Alcohol

People who drink heavily are more prone to bone loss and fractures because of poor nutrition and harmful effects on calcium balance and hormonal factors. Drinking too much also increases the risk of falling, which is likely to increase fracture risk.

Medications That Cause Bone Loss

The long-term use of glucocorticoids can lead to a loss of bone density and fractures. Other forms of drug therapy that can cause bone loss include long-term treatment with certain anti-seizure drugs, such as phenytoin (Dilantin) and barbiturates; some drugs used to treat endometriosis; excessive use of aluminum-containing antacids; certain cancer treatments; and excessive thyroid hormone. It is important to discuss the use of these drugs with your doctor and not to stop or alter your medication dose on your own.

Prevention Medications

Various medications are available for the prevention, as well as treatment, of osteoporosis.

Chapter 26

Eating Disorders And Oral Health

The oral effects of an eating disorder are hard to hide from a dental professional. Telltale signs appear early in the mouth, and despite the secretive nature of the disease, a dental professional may be the first to know and encourage a patient to get help. The most common eating disorders that cause problems in the mouth are bulimia nervosa and anorexia nervosa. Although there are other types of eating disorders, these tend to cause the most damage to the teeth and mouth.

Bulimia And Oral Health

Bulimia is an eating disorder that involves eating more food at one time than you think you should, called binge eating, and then trying to get rid of that food by purging— self induced vomiting, use of laxatives, fasting, diuretics, diet pills, or over exercising. Bulimia is dangerous to your overall health and especially harmful to your teeth:

• When repeated vomiting is used to purge food from the body, the strong acids in the digestive system erode tooth enamel and weaken fillings, and teeth become worn and translucent.

• Your mouth, throat, and salivary glands become swollen and tender.

About This Chapter: Information in this chapter is from "Eating Disorders and Oral Health," © 2007 Colorado Department of Public Health and Environment. Reprinted with permission.

• Repeatedly vomiting can cause sores in the corners of the mouth and bad breath.

Anorexia And Oral Health

Anorexia is a psychological dis-order that involves a distortion of body image, an intense fear of weight gain, and the desire to be thinner. Anorexia often involves self-induced starvation, purging, and over ex-ercising—the same as bulimia.

♣ **It's A Fact!!**
About 1% of female adolescents have anorexia, and 4% of college-aged women have bulimia, according to Anorexia Nervosa and Related Eating Disorders Inc.

Anorexia nervosa may produce some of the same oral symptoms as bu-limia.

The Dental Professional

• May encourage you to seek professional help for the eating disorder.

• May create a mouth guard that covers the teeth to help protect them from further erosion by stomach acid.

• Restore damaged teeth, but not until after you get treatment for the eating disorder.

• Provide you with fluoride treatments to help protect your teeth.

✔ **Quick Tip**

In order to neutralize the effects of stomach acid on your teeth, you should:

• Immediately after purging, do not brush, but rinse the mouth with bak-ing soda mixed in water, or sugar-free, alcohol-free mouth rinse, or with plain water if nothing else is available.

• Brush and floss daily.

Chapter 27

Diabetes And Eating Disorders

Diabetes

What is diabetes?

Diabetes means that your blood sugar is too high. Your blood always has some sugar in it because the body uses sugar for energy; it is the fuel that keeps you going. But too much sugar in the blood is not good for your health.

Your body changes most of the food you eat into sugar. Your blood takes the sugar to the cells throughout your body. The sugar needs insulin to get into the body's cells. Insulin is a hormone made in the pancreas, an organ near the stomach. The pancreas releases insulin into the blood. Insulin helps the sugar from food get into body cells. If your body does not make enough insulin or the insulin does not work right, the sugar cannot get into the cells, so it stays in the blood. This makes your blood sugar level high, causing you to have diabetes.

If not controlled, diabetes can lead to blindness, heart disease, stroke, kidney failure, amputations (having a toe or foot removed, for example), and nerve damage. In women, diabetes can cause problems during pregnancy and make it more likely that your baby will be born with birth defects.

About This Chapter: This chapter begins with text excerpted from "Diabetes," National Women's Health Information Center, U.S. Department of Health and Human Services, Office on Women's Health, June 2006. Additional text from ANRED: Anorexia Nervosa and Related Eating Disorders, Inc. is cited separately within the chapter.

What are the different types of diabetes?

The three main types of diabetes are:

- **Type 1 Diabetes** is commonly diagnosed in children and young adults, but it is a lifelong condition. If you have this type of diabetes, your body does not make insulin, so you must take insulin every day. Treatment for type 1 diabetes includes taking insulin shots or using an insulin pump, eating healthy, exercising regularly, taking aspirin daily (for some), and controlling blood pressure and cholesterol.

- **Type 2 Diabetes** is the most common type of diabetes—about 9 out of 10 people with diabetes have type 2 diabetes. You can get type 2 diabetes at any age, even during childhood. In type 2 diabetes, your body makes insulin, but the insulin cannot do its job, so sugar is not getting into the cells. Treatment includes taking medicine, eating healthy, exercising regularly, taking aspirin daily (for some), and controlling blood pressure and cholesterol.

> **✤ It's A Fact!!**
> About 20 million Americans have diabetes, about half of whom are women. As many as one third do not know they have diabetes.
>
> Source: National Women's Health Information Center.

- **Gestational (jess-TAY-shun-ul) Diabetes** occurs during pregnancy. This type of diabetes occurs in about 1 in 20 pregnancies. During pregnancy, your body makes hormones that keep insulin from doing its job. To make up for this, your body makes extra insulin. In some women this extra insulin is not enough, so they get gestational diabetes. Gestational diabetes usually goes away when the pregnancy is over. Women who have had gestational diabetes are more likely to develop type 2 diabetes later in life.

Who gets diabetes?

Type 1 diabetes occurs at about the same rate in men and women, but it is more common in Whites than in minorities.

Type 2 diabetes is more common in older people, mainly in people who are overweight. It is more common in African Americans, Hispanic Americans/Latinos, and American Indians.

What causes diabetes?

Type 1 And Type 2 Diabetes: The exact causes of both types of diabetes are still not known. Type 1 diabetes tends to show up after a person is exposed to a trigger, such as a virus, which can start an attack on the cells in the pancreas that make insulin. There is no one cause for type 2 diabetes, but it seems to run in families, and most people who get type 2 diabetes are overweight.

Gestational Diabetes: Changing hormones and weight gain are part of a healthy pregnancy, but these changes make it hard for your body to keep up with its need for insulin. When that happens, your body does not get the energy it needs from the foods you eat.

Am I at risk for diabetes?

Things that can put you at risk for diabetes include the following:

- Age—being older than 45

- Overweight or obesity

- Family history—having a mother, father, brother, or sister with diabetes

- Race/ethnicity—your family background is African American, American Indian/Alaska Native, Hispanic American/Latino, Asian American/Pacific Islander and Native Hawaiian

- Having a baby with a birth weight more than 9 pounds

- Having diabetes during pregnancy (gestational diabetes)

- High blood pressure—140/90 mm HG or higher. Both numbers are important. If one or both numbers are usually high, you have high blood pressure.

- High cholesterol—total cholesterol over 240 mg/dL

- Inactivity—exercising less than three times a week

- Abnormal results in a prior diabetes test

- Having other health conditions that are linked to problems using insulin, like Polycystic Ovarian Syndrome (PCOS)

- Having a history of heart disease or stroke

What are the signs of diabetes?

- Being very thirsty

- Urinating a lot

- Feeling very hungry

- Feeling very tired

- Losing weight without trying

- Having sores that are slow to heal

- Having dry, itchy skin

- Losing feeling in, or having tingling in the hands or feet

- Having blurry vision

- Having more infections than usual

If you have one or more of these signs, see your doctor.

Is there a cure for diabetes?

There is no cure for diabetes at this time. The National Institutes of Health (NIH) is doing research in hopes of finding cures for both type 1 and type 2 diabetes. Many different approaches to curing diabetes are being studied, and researchers are making progress.

Diabetes And Eating Disorders

"Diabetes and Eating Disorders," Used with permission of ANRED: Anorexia Nervosa and Related Eating Disorders, Inc., http://www.anred.com, © 2008.

Because both diabetes and eating disorders involve attention to body states, weight management, and control of food, some people develop a pattern in which they use the disease to justify or camouflage the disorder.

How many people have both an eating disorder and diabetes?

We are not sure, but the combination is common. Some clinicians think that eating disorders are more common among folks with diabetes than they are in the general population. Research is currently underway to find out if this is so.

Does diabetes cause anorexia nervosa or bulimia?

♣ It's A Fact!!

Because the complications of diabetes and eating disorders can be serious, even fatal, responsible, healthy behavior is essential.

Source: ANRED: Anorexia Nervosa and Related Eating Disorders, Inc.

No, diabetes does not cause eating disorders, but it can set the stage, physically and emotionally, for their development. Once people develop eating disorders, they can hide them in the overall diabetic constellation. This makes treatment, and even diagnosis, difficult. In some of these cases the eating disorder has gone undetected for years, sometimes coming to light only when life-altering complications appear.

What are some of those life-altering complications?

Blindness, kidney disease, impaired circulation, nerve death, and amputation of limbs. Death, of course, is the ultimate life-altering complication.

People who have both diabetes and an eating disorder eat in ways that would make their doctors shudder. Many believe that being fat is far worse than the consequences noted above, which, they rationalize, may never happen; or, if they do, will happen years down the road. Like Scarlett O'Hara, they will worry tomorrow.

Many of these people superstitiously believe they will escape complications. They are wrong.

A study led by researchers at the Joslin Diabetes Center indicates that women with Type 1 diabetes who reported taking less insulin than prescribed had a three-fold increased risk of death and higher rates of disease complications than those who did not skip needed insulin shots. You can read more about the research on the Joslin website (http://www.joslin.org).

What is the main mechanism that connects diabetes and eating disorders?

People who take insulin to control diabetes can misuse it to lose weight. If they reduce the required dosage, blood sugar will rise and spill over into the urine. These folks will lose weight, but the underlying biochemical process is particularly dangerous. Reducing insulin causes body tissues to dissolve and be flushed out in urination. Those tissues can include the heart and other internal organs.

Once diabetics discover that they can manipulate their weight this way, they are reluctant to stop, even if they know about potential consequences, because weight loss is rewarding in our fat-phobic culture. They decide to maintain the weight loss, and that decision can serve as the trigger for a full-blown eating disorder.

What are the similarities between diabetes and eating disorders?

Both demand that people pay close attention to body states, weight management, types and amounts of food consumed, and the timing and content of meals. Both encourage people to embrace some foods as "safe" and "good" and fear others as "dangerous" and "bad."

Control is a central issue in both diabetes and eating disorders. Diabetics may feel guilty, anxious, or out of control if their blood sugar swings more than a few points. Anorexics and bulimics may feel the same way if their weight fluctuates. People with both problems may become consumed with strategies to rigidly control both weight and blood sugar.

Children with diabetes may have parents that they perceive as overprotective and overcontroling. The parents of young people with eating disorders are often described in similar terms. In both kinds of families, over involvement and enmeshment can lead children to rebellion and dramatic, potentially catastrophic, acts of independence.

People with eating disorders are preoccupied with weight, food, and diet. So are folks with diabetes. In fact, the latter can use their diabetes to hide anorexia or bulimia because, after all, they are supposed to be watching what they eat, and they can blame poorly controlled diabetes for alarming weight loss.

Are there any other problems related to a combination of diabetes and eating disorders?

Yes. When people misuse insulin to lose weight, sometimes that weight loss seems to improve diabetes, at least temporarily, by reducing or eliminating the need for insulin. It's interesting to note that starvation was a primary treatment for diabetes before commercial production of supplemental insulin. This weight loss method is not without problems, however. If continued, the person experiences life-threatening organ failure and death.

What kind of treatment should people who have both diabetes and eating disorders have?

Getting them into treatment is the first step. Many of these folks are embarrassed to admit that they have been doing something as unhealthy as deliberately misusing insulin, which is intended to be a life-preserving medication. Often they defiantly hang onto starving and stuffing behaviors in spite of real threats to life and health. Families sometimes collude by denying that anything is wrong.

Nevertheless, it is important to begin treatment early. Eating disorders can be treated, and people do recover from them; but the longer symptoms are ignored, the harder it is to turn them around, and the greater the challenge of reversing the severe effects on one's body.

The best treatment is team treatment. That means that many professionals are involved with the patient, and perhaps with the family as well: a physician to manage the diabetes and the effects of starving and stuffing, a mental health therapist to help define and deal with underlying emotional issues, a family therapist to help the family, and a dietitian to provide nutritional counseling and education.

The first priority is restoration of physical health. For diabetic anorexics, that means weight gain back to healthy levels. For diabetic anorexics and bulimics, the next step is implementation of balanced, varied, and healthy meal plans that provide adequate calories and nutrients. After physical health is stabilized, treatment can focus on the underlying psychological issues, plus of course ongoing attention to the diabetes.

It is important to stop self-induced vomiting because it throws blood sugar into chaos.

Most treatment for eating disorders is outpatient, but if the patient is suicidal, severely depressed, or in any kind of medical danger, hospitalization is appropriate until the crisis has passed. Medication may be used to ease depression and anxiety, but it must be carefully monitored by a physician.

In Summary

Diabetes and eating disorders are a nasty combination with very real potential for catastrophic complications, including death. The good news, however, is that in most cases diabetes can be controlled, and eating disorders can be treated. Many people recover from anorexia nervosa and bulimia, but almost always professional help is required.

✔ Quick Tip

If you are concerned about yourself, arrange right now to talk to your physician. Don't let shame or embarrassment stop you from telling the truth. The doctor has heard your story before. Ask for a referral to a mental health professional who works with people with eating disorders. Contact that person and ask for an evaluation. Then follow up on any treatment recommendations that come from the evaluation. Other people have made this journey successfully. You can too.

Source: ANRED: Anorexia Nervosa and Related Eating Disorders, Inc.

Chapter 28

Eating Disorders And Pregnancy

Pregnancy and motherhood. Professionals recommend that women with eating disorders do their best to resolve the eating disorder related weight and behavior problems before they attempt to get pregnant.

Pregnancy and motherhood require a great amount of physical and psychological strength. During pregnancy, the growing baby receives all its nourishment from the mother's body. When stores of carbohydrates, proteins, fats, vitamins, minerals, and other nutrients are low, a woman's body will drain them to support the growth and development of the baby. If reserves are not sufficiently restored through healthy eating, the mother can become severely malnourished, and this in turn can lead to depression, exhaustion, and many other serious health complications.

The average woman gains between 25–35 pounds during pregnancy. While this amount is required for a healthy pregnancy, for women with eating disorders having to gain this amount can be very frightening. Some women with disordered eating are able to more easily cope with weight gain during pregnancy because they see it as a sacrifice for an important cause. But others may plunge into deep depression as they struggle with the tension between

About This Chapter: Information in this chapter is from "Eating Disorders and Pregnancy: Facts about the Risks," © 2005 National Eating Disorders Association. Reprinted with permission. For additional information, visit www.NationalEatingDisorders.org, or call the toll-free Information and Referral Helpline at 800-931-2237.

the idea of weight gain and their body image issues. Most women with eating disorders fall somewhere between these two extremes.

The Relationship Between Specific Eating Disorders And Pregnancy

Women with anorexia nervosa are underweight and may not gain enough weight during pregnancy. They risk having a baby with abnormally low birth weight and related health problems. Women with bulimia nervosa who continue to purge may suffer dehydration, chemical imbalances, or even cardiac irregularities. Pregnancy heightens these health risks. Women who are overweight due to binge eating are at greater risk of developing high blood pressure, gestational diabetes, and overgrown babies.

Risks For The Mother: Poor nutrition, dehydration, cardiac irregularities, gestational diabetes, severe depression during pregnancy, premature births, labor complications, difficulties nursing, post-partum depression.

Risks For The Baby: Poor development, premature birth, low birth weight for age, respiratory distress, other perinatal complications, feeding difficulties.

Professionals recommend that women with eating disorders do their best to resolve the eating disorder related weight and behavior problems before they attempt to get pregnant. It is important to consult with your physician, counselors, and/or registered dietitian before attempting to get pregnant. Women with eating disorders who become pregnant are advised to seek specialized medical and psychological help. Pregnant women with eating disorders should inform their obstetricians about these problems and may require "high risk" obstetrical care.

☞ Remember!!
Eat healthy, well-balanced meals and maintain a healthy weight for several months before conceiving and throughout pregnancy to protect the health of yourself and your baby.

What If I Become Pregnant While Struggling With An Eating Disorder?

Though having an eating disorder may decrease the chances of pregnancy, sometimes women with anorexia or bulimia do become pregnant. When this happens, steps should be taken to protect the health of the mother and the baby. Professionals can address the specific needs related to pregnancy and disordered eating only if you are willing to be completely honest with them about your struggles.

If you are pregnant and struggling with disordered eating:

• Be honest with your prenatal health provider regarding past or present struggles with an eating disorder or disordered eating.

• Extra appointments with your prenatal health provider may be necessary to more closely track the growth and development of your baby.

• Consult a nutritionist with expertise in eating disorders before or immediately after becoming pregnant. Work with the nutritionist throughout the pregnancy to create a plan for healthy eating and weight gain. Continue to see her post-partum. She can help you return to a normal weight through healthy means.

• Individual counseling during and after pregnancy can help you cope with your concerns and fears regarding food, weight gain, body image, and the new role of mothering.

• Attend a support group for people with eating disorders.

• If your doctor approves, attend a prenatal exercise class. It can help you practice healthy limits to exercising.

• Other classes on pregnancy, childbirth, child development, and parenting skills can also be helpful in preparing to become a mother.

• Allow your prenatal health provider to weigh you. This information is essential to track the health of your baby. If you would prefer not to monitor your weight gain, ask your doctor about standing on the scale backwards.

- Under certain circumstances, for example if you suffer from severe depression or obsessive-compulsive problems, you may require medications for these conditions even during pregnancy.

The skills and support of a multidisciplinary team of health care providers and of family and friends can help you deliver a healthy baby and protect yourself.

Chapter 29

Eating Disorders And Obesity: How Are They Related?

Eating disorders and obesity are usually seen as very different problems but actually share many similarities. In fact, eating disorders, obesity, and other weight-related disorders may overlap as teens move from one problem, such as unhealthy dieting, to another, such as obesity.

Eating disorders and obesity are part of a range of weight-related problems. These problems include anorexia nervosa, bulimia nervosa, anorexic and bulimic behaviors, unhealthy dieting practices, binge eating disorder, and obesity. Adolescents may suffer from more than one disorder or may progress from one problem to another at varying degrees of severity. It is important to understand this range of weight-related problems in order to avoid causing one disorder, such as bulimia, while trying to prevent another, such as obesity.

Body dissatisfaction and unhealthy dieting practices are linked to the development of eating disorders, obesity, and other problems. High numbers of adolescents are reporting that they are dissatisfied with their bodies and are trying to lose weight in unhealthy ways, including skipping meals, fasting, and using tobacco. A smaller number of teens are even resorting to more extreme methods such as self-induced vomiting, diet pills, and laxative use.

About This Chapter: National Women's Health Information Center, U.S. Department of Health and Human Services, Office on Women's Health, 2008.

These attitudes and behaviors place teens at a greater risk for eating disorders, obesity, poor nutrition, growth impairments, and emotional problems such as depression. Research shows, for example, that overweight teens are more concerned about their weight, more dissatisfied with their bodies, and more likely to diet than their normal-weight peers.

Binge eating is common among people with eating disorders and people who are obese. People with bulimia binge eat and then purge by vomiting, using laxatives, or other means. Binge eating that is not followed by purging may also be considered an eating disorder and can lead to weight gain. More than one-third of obese individuals in weight-loss treatment programs report difficulties with binge eating. This type of eating behavior contributes to feelings of shame, loneliness, poor self-esteem, and depression. Conversely, these kinds of feelings can cause binge eating problems. A person may binge or overeat for emotional reasons, including stress, depression, and anxiety.

Depression, anxiety, and other mood disorders are associated with both eating disorders and obesity. Adolescents who are depressed may be at an increased risk of becoming obese. One recent study found that depressed adolescents were two times more likely to become obese at the one-year follow-up than teens that did not suffer from depression. In addition, many people with eating disorders suffer from clinical depression, anxiety, personality or substance abuse disorders, or in some cases, obsessive-compulsive disorder. Therefore, a mental health professional may need to be involved in treating an adolescent who is obese or suffers from an eating disorder or other weight-related problem.

The environment may contribute to both eating disorders and obesity. The mass media, family, and peers may be sending children and adolescents mixed messages about food and weight that encourage disordered eating. Today's society idealizes thinness and stigmatizes fatness, yet high-calorie foods are widely available and heavily advertised. At the same time, levels of physical activity are at record lows as television and computers replace more active leisure activities, travel by automobile has replaced walking, and many communities lack space for walking and recreation.

Health Risks

Eating disorders may lead to the following:

• Stunted growth

• Delayed menstruation

• Damage to vital organs such as the heart and brain

• Nutritional deficiencies, including starvation

• Cardiac arrest

• Emotional problems such as depression and anxiety

Obesity increases the risk for the following:

• High blood pressure

• Stroke

• Cardiovascular disease

• Gallbladder disease

• Diabetes

• Respiratory problems

• Arthritis

• Cancer

• Emotional problems such as depression and anxiety

Did You Know...

• In American high schools, 30 percent of girls and 16 percent of boys suffer from disordered eating, including bingeing, vomiting, fasting, laxative and diet pill use, and compulsive exercise.

• Childhood obesity has more than tripled in the last 30 years. By the year 2000, 15 percent of children and adolescents ages 6 to 19 were obese.

• Studies suggest that about 70 percent of overweight adolescents will become obese adults.

- A personal or family history of obesity is a risk factor for later development of bulimia.

- The average child in the U.S. watches 10,000 television advertisements for food each year, 95% of which are for foods in one of four categories: sugared cereals, candy, fast foods, and soft drinks.

The Diet Trap

- The risk for obesity may be 324 percent greater for adolescent girls who describe themselves as dieters than girls who do not diet.

- Up to one in four 11-year-old girls have already tried to diet at least once.

- Children who diet may actually end up gaining more weight in the long term than children who do not diet. This is because dieting may cause a cycle of restrictive eating, followed by overeating or binge eating.

- People who are obese, or at risk of becoming obese, are more likely to use unhealthy weight loss practices, such as vomiting and using diet pills or laxatives.

- Disordered eating and dieting have been linked to serious risk-taking behaviors such as drug, alcohol and tobacco use, delinquency, unprotected sexual activity, dating violence, and suicide attempts.

♣ It's A Fact!!

The potential consequences of body dissatisfaction and unhealthy weight control behaviors are of considerable public health significance because these negative cognitions and behaviors are associated with the development of both eating disorders and obesity.

—Dianne Neumark-Sztainer, Ph.D., M.P.H., R.D.,
Division of Epidemiology, University of Minnesota School of Public Health

Chapter 30

Co-Occurring Disorders: Anxiety Disorders And Eating Disorders

Almost everyone is unhappy with his or her weight, body shape, or other aspect of his or her appearance at some point. Individuals may take steps to eat healthier, try a new diet, or start an exercise plan to improve their appearance. However, some people may have eating and exercising habits that go way beyond normal. They may fast or severely restrict their caloric intake, exercise for hours on end each day, or take other actions to prevent weight gain. They may have an intense fear of gaining weight or becoming fat, even though they are underweight. These people may be suffering from an eating disorder—a category of medical conditions that commonly co-occur with anxiety disorders.

What is an anxiety disorder?

Anxiety disorders are a unique group of illnesses that fill people's lives with persistent, excessive, and unreasonable anxiety, worry, and fear. They include generalized anxiety disorder (GAD), obsessive-compulsive disorder (OCD), panic disorder, posttraumatic stress disorder (PTSD), social anxiety disorder (SAD), and specific phobias. Although anxiety disorders are serious medical conditions, they are treatable.

About This Chapter: Information in this chapter is from "Anxiety and Eating Disorders," © 2007 Anxiety Disorders Association of America (www.adaa.org). Reprinted with permission.

♣ **It's A Fact!!**

For people with anxiety disorders, having a co-occurring eating disorder may make their symptoms worse and recovery more difficult. This makes it essential to be treated for both disorders.

What is an eating disorder?

According to the National Mental Health Information Center, an eating disorder is an emotional and physical problem that is associated with an obsession with food, body weight, or body shape. Often, a person with an eating disorder diets, exercises, and/or eats excessively. These behaviors can have serious health consequences and can even be life threatening. The three most common types of eating disorders are anorexia, bulimia, and binge eating. Symptoms of each include:

Anorexia Nervosa

- Refusal to maintain body weight at or above a minimally normal weight for age and height

- Intense fear of gaining weight or becoming fat, even though underweight

- Disturbance in the way in which one's body weight or shape is experienced, undue influence of body weight or shape on self-evaluation, or denial of the seriousness of the current low body weight

- Infrequent or absent menstrual periods (more specifically, the absence of at least three consecutive menstrual cycles) in females who have reached puberty

People with this disorder see themselves as overweight even though they are dangerously thin. The process of eating becomes an obsession. Unusual eating habits develop, such as avoiding food and meals, picking out a few foods and eating these in small quantities, or carefully weighing and portioning food. People with anorexia may repeatedly check their body weight, and many engage in other techniques to control their weight, such as intense and compulsive exercise, or purging by means of vomiting and abuse of laxatives, enemas, and diuretics. Individuals with anorexia nervosa who regularly engage in binge eating or purging behavior are considered to have the binge eating/purging type of anorexia nervosa.

Bulimia Nervosa

- Recurrent episodes of binge eating, characterized by eating an excessive amount of food within a discrete period of time and by a sense of lack of control over eating during the episode

- Recurrent inappropriate compensatory behavior in order to prevent weight gain, such as self-induced vomiting or misuse of laxatives, diuretics, enemas, or other medications (purging), fasting, or excessive exercise

- The binge eating and inappropriate compensatory behaviors both occur, on average, at least twice a week for three months

- Self-evaluation is unduly influenced by body shape and weight

Because purging or other compensatory behavior follows the binge eating episodes, people with bulimia usually weigh within the normal range for their age and height. However, like individuals with anorexia, they may fear gaining weight, desire to lose weight, and feel intensely dissatisfied with their bodies. People with bulimia often perform the behaviors in secrecy, feeling disgusted and ashamed when they binge, yet relieved once they purge.

Binge Eating Disorder

- Recurrent episodes of binge eating, characterized by eating an excessive amount of food within a discrete period of time and by a sense of lack of control over eating during the episode

- The binge eating episodes are associated with at least three of the following: eating much more rapidly than normal; eating until feeling uncomfortably full; eating large amounts of food when not feeling physically hungry; eating alone because of being embarrassed by how much one is eating; feeling disgusted with oneself, depressed, or very guilty after overeating

- Marked distress about the binge eating behavior

- The binge eating occurs, on average, at least two days a week for six months

- The binge eating is not associated with the regular use of inappropriate compensatory behaviors (for example, purging, fasting, excessive exercise)

People with binge eating disorder experience frequent episodes of out-of-control eating, with the same kinds of binge eating symptoms as those with bulimia. The main difference is that individuals with binge eating disorder do not purge their bodies of excess calories. Therefore, many with the disorder are overweight for their age and height. Feelings of self-disgust and shame associated with this illness can lead to bingeing again, creating a cycle of binge eating.

What differences are there between men and women who have eating disorders?

First it is important to note that while eating disorders are more common in women, men also can suffer from these disorders. It is estimated that about ten percent of people who suffer from anorexia or bulimia are men,

---

♣ It's A Fact!!
How often do anxiety and eating disorders occur together, and which occurs first?

A major study conducted by University of Pittsburgh researchers in 2004 found two-thirds of people with eating disorders suffer from an anxiety disorder at some point in their lives. It also found that a significant number of these people— 42 percent— developed an anxiety disorder during childhood, well before the onset of their eating disorder. Other studies have also found that anxiety disorders usually precede development of an eating disorder. Some researchers, including those from the 2004 study, noted that early diagnosis and treatment of an anxiety disorder might provide some preventative effect against eating disorders, although this is an area that requires further study.

but the proportion of men with an eating disorder may be even higher, especially among people with binge eating disorder. While most of the underlying psychological factors that lead to an eating disorder are the same for men and women, men with eating disorders can have some added difficulties. They may be less likely to report their symptoms because they think eating disorders are a "woman's disease"—some may think it reflects negatively on their masculinity or are worried about people questioning their sexual orientation. Additionally, men may be less likely to seek help because they don't feel comfortable being the only man (or one of the few) participating in a support group and treatment program for eating disorders, which is often the case. However, it is just as important for men to seek treatment as women, and men are generally thought to respond to the same types of treatment for eating disorders as women.

Are there specific anxiety disorders that are more often associated with eating disorders?

Although people with eating disorders can suffer from any of the anxiety disorders and vice versa, specific ones are associated with the co-occurrence of eating disorders. These include:

- Obsessive-Compulsive Disorder (OCD): OCD is one of the most common anxiety disorders to co-occur with eating disorders. In fact, the disorders share many of the same features. Women with anorexia may suffer from obsessions with exercise, dieting, and food. They often develop compulsive rituals such as weighing every bit of food, cutting food into tiny pieces, repeated checking of weight, or mirror checking. There are also similar characteristics between bulimia and OCD. Like the compulsions in OCD, binges are difficult to resist and hard to control. While binges provide some immediate relief to the sufferer, like the compulsions characteristic of OCD, this relief is short-lived and temporary. While similar, eating disorders and OCD also have differences, such as a wider variety of symptoms in OCD and different treatment considerations.

- Posttraumatic Stress Disorder (PTSD): In the National Women's Study of over 3,000 women in the community who were questioned about their history of aggravated and sexual assault, PTSD, bulimia, and binge eating disorder, higher rates of sexual and aggravated assault were found in women with bulimia compared to women without bulimia. The study also found that women with bulimia had higher rates of PTSD compared to those without bulimia. The odds of developing bulimia are greater for women with PTSD, even if the trauma resulting in the PTSD was not assault.

- **Social Anxiety Disorder (SAD):** SAD, along with OCD, has been found to be among the most common anxiety disorder to co-exist with eating disorders in many studies.

- **Panic Disorder:** Panic disorder, unlike many of the other anxiety disorders, has been found in many studies to follow the onset of an eating disorder.

Why do these disorders occur together so frequently?

More research is needed to determine why this is the case. Many scientists believe a childhood anxiety disorder may contribute to increased vulnerability to a later eating disorder, or that eating disorders and anxiety disorders share common biological/genetic and/or environmental causes. In both OCD and eating disorders, for instance, levels of the neurotransmitter serotonin (which plays a role in regulating mood, sleep, appetite, and other important body functions) are abnormal. These and other possible factors are areas that are being explored further.

What complications can arise from having both disorders?

People with both disorders may suffer more severe anxiety symptoms and have a more difficult recovery than those with an anxiety disorder alone. Moreover, having an eating disorder can have serious physical consequences and risks that are not normally present with an anxiety disorder alone, some of which may be life threatening. Because of the potentially dangerous effects of an eating disorder, it is crucial for people with both disorders to pursue treatment.

Can these disorders be treated together?

Yes. The same types of therapies used to treat anxiety disorders may be used to treat eating disorders, and the disorders can often be treated at the same time (by one professional or as part of a treatment team). Recovery from one disorder does not ensure recovery from the other disorder, which is why it is necessary to seek help for both. Treatment options for both include:

- **Psychological Treatment (Psychotherapy):** Cognitive-behavioral therapy (CBT) is a type of therapy in which individuals learn to identify, challenge, and gain control over unwanted behaviors and develop more accurate and helpful beliefs. These therapies have been demonstrated to be effective in both anxiety and eating disorders. Interpersonal therapy is another type of psychotherapy that may be effective for eating disorders. Psychological treatments are sometimes provided in an individual format and sometimes in a group. Family therapy is a type of treatment that uses strategies to reduce the level of distress within the family that may either contribute to, or result from, the ill person's symptoms. It also provides psycho education to family members about an illness.

- **Medication:** Antidepressants, such as selective serotonin reuptake inhibitors (SSRIs), may be used to treat both anxiety disorders and eating disorders. Other medications may also be helpful for certain disorders. The choice of medication should be discussed carefully between doctor and patient and will always depend on individual circumstances.

- **Self-Help/Other Treatment Groups:** Individuals with similar needs or experiences meet, and meetings are facilitated by a consumer, layperson, or survivor. It is suggested that self-help groups be used in addition to one of the treatments above.

Treatment for eating disorders also includes nutritional management and nutritional counseling. Sometimes, people experiencing severe symptoms of an eating disorder may require hospitalization to help restore them to a safe and healthy weight.

Chapter 31

The Link Between Eating Disorders And Substance Abuse

"Food for Thought—Substance Abuse and Eating Disorders," the first comprehensive examination of the link between substance abuse and eating disorders, reveals that up to one-half of individuals with eating disorders abuse alcohol or illicit drugs, compared to nine percent of the general population.

Conversely, up to 35 percent of alcohol or illicit drug abusers have eating disorders compared to three percent of the general population. The 73-page report by The National Center on Addiction and Substance Abuse (CASA) at Columbia University was released by CASA president and former U.S. Secretary of Health, Education, and Welfare, Joseph A. Califano, Jr.

"For many young women, eating disorders like anorexia and bulimia, are joined at the hip with smoking, binge drinking, and illicit drug use," said Califano.

"This lethal link between substance abuse and eating disorders sends a signal to parents, teachers, and health professionals—where you see the smoke of eating disorders, look for the fire of substance abuse and vice versa."

The exhaustive report finds anorexia nervosa and bulimia nervosa as the eating disorders most commonly linked to substance abuse; and for the first time, identifies the shared risk factors and shared characteristics of both afflictions. The report lists caffeine, tobacco, alcohol, diuretics, laxatives, emetics, amphetamines, cocaine, and heroin as substances used to suppress appetite, increase metabolism, purge unwanted calories, and self-medicate negative emotions.

The report found that because health professionals often overlook the link between substance abuse and eating disorders, treatment options are virtually nonexistent for these co-occurring conditions.

"The public health community, parents, and policy makers must educate our children about healthy body images from a very young age, and treatment and prevention programs must address the common co-occurrence of substance abuse and eating disorders," stated Susan Foster, vice president and director of policy research and analysis at CASA, who spearheaded the project.

"Advertisers put children at greater risk of developing an eating disorder through the portrayal of unrealistic body images," noted Mr. Califano. "The average American woman is 5'4" tall and weighs approximately 140 pounds, but the average model that purportedly epitomizes our standard of beauty is 5'11" tall and weighs 117 pounds." The report found that women's magazines contain more than ten times more ads and articles related to weight loss than men's magazines, which is the same gender ratio reported for eating disorders.

The report finds that while only 15 percent of girls are overweight, 40 percent of girls in grades one through five and 62 percent of teenage girls are trying to lose weight. These girls are especially vulnerable to eating disorders and related substance abuse problems.

Other notable findings include:

- Middle school girls (10–14 year olds) who diet more than once a week are nearly four times likelier to become smokers.

- 12.6 percent of female high school students take diet pills, powders, or liquids to control their weight without a doctor's advice.

- Bulimic women who are alcohol dependent report a higher rate of suicide attempts, anxiety, personality and conduct disorders, and other drug dependence than bulimic women who are not alcohol dependent.

♣ It's A Fact!!
Girls with eating disorder symptoms are almost four times likelier to use inhalants and cocaine.

- Hispanic girls are slightly more likely than Caucasian girls and significantly more likely than African-American girls to report having fasted for 24 hours or more and having vomited or taken laxatives to lose weight.

- As many as one million men and boys suffer from an eating disorder; gay and bisexual males are at increased risk of such disorders.

Shared Risk Factors

- Occur in times of transition or stress

- Common brain chemistry

- Common family history

- Low self-esteem, depression, anxiety, impulsivity

- History of sexual or physical abuse

- Unhealthy parental behaviors and low monitoring of children's activities

- Unhealthy peer norms and social pressures

- Susceptibility to messages from advertising and entertainment media

Shared Characteristics

- Obsessive preoccupation, craving, compulsive behavior, secretiveness, rituals

- Experience mood altering effects, social isolation

- Linked to other psychiatric disorders, suicide

- Difficult to treat, life threatening
- Chronic diseases with high relapse rates
- Require intensive therapy

The National Center on Addiction and Substance Abuse (CASA) at Columbia University is the only national organization that brings together under one roof all the professional disciplines needed to study and combat all types of substance abuse as they affect all aspects of society.

Chapter 32

Self-Harm And Eating Disorders

Self-Harm

What is self-harm?

Self-harm refers to the deliberate, direct destruction of body tissue that results in tissue damage. When someone engages in self-harm, they may have a variety of intentions; these are discussed below. However, the person's intention is not to kill themselves. You may have heard self-harm referred to as "para suicide," "self-mutilation," "self-injury," "self-abuse," "cutting," "self-inflicted violence," and so on.

How common is self-harm?

Self-harm is not well understood and has not yet been extensively studied. The rates of self-harm revealed through research vary tremendously depending on how researchers pose their questions about this behavior. One widely cited estimate of the incidence of impulsive self-injury is that it occurs in at least one person per 1,000 annually. A recent study of psychiatric outpatients found that 33% reported engaging in self-harm in the previous three

About This Chapter: This chapter begins with "Self-Harm," by Laura E. Gibson, Ph.D. Reprinted from the National Center for Posttraumatic Stress Disorders, United States Department of Veterans Affairs (www.ncptsd.va.gov), May 2007. Additional text from Gürze Books, under the heading "Eating Disorders and Self-Harm," is cited separately within the chapter.

months. A recent study of college undergraduates asked study participants about specific self-harm behaviors and found alarmingly high rates. Although the high rates may have been due in part to the broad spectrum of self-harm behaviors that were assessed (for example, severe scratching and interfering with the healing of wounds were included), the numbers are certainly cause for concern:

- Eighteen percent reported having harmed themselves more than ten times in the past.

- Ten percent reported having harmed themselves more than 100 times in the past.

- Thirty-eight percent endorsed a history of deliberate self-harm.

- The most frequently reported self-harm behaviors were needle sticking, skin cutting, and scratching, endorsed by 16%, 15%, and 14% of the participants, respectively.

It is important to note that research on self-harm is still in the early stages, and these rates may change as researchers begin to utilize more consistent definitions of self-harm and more studies are completed.

Who engages in self-harm?

Only a handful of empirical studies have examined self-harm in a systematic, sound manner.

While some people may engage in self-harm a few times and then stop, others engage in it frequently and have great difficulty stopping the behavior. Several studies have found that individuals who engage in self-harm report unusually high rates of histories of the following:

- Childhood sexual abuse

- Childhood physical abuse

- Emotional neglect

- Insecure attachment

♣ It's A Fact!!
Self-harm appears to be more common in females than in males, and it tends to begin in adolescence or early adulthood.

Source: National Center for Posttraumatic Stress Disorders, United States Department of Veterans Affairs.

• Prolonged separation from caregivers

At least two studies have attempted to determine whether particular characteristics of childhood sexual abuse place individuals at greater risk for engaging in self-harm as adults. Both studies reported that more severe, more frequent, or a longer duration of sexual abuse was associated with an increased risk of engaging in self-harm in one's adult years.

Also, individuals who self-harm appear to have higher rates of the following psychological problems:

• High levels of dissociation

• Borderline personality disorder

• Substance abuse disorders

• Posttraumatic stress disorder

• Intermittent explosive disorder

• Antisocial personality

• Eating disorders

Why do people engage in self-harm?

While there are many theories about why individuals harm themselves, the answer to this question varies from individual to individual.

The following are some reasons why people engage in self-harm:

• To distract themselves from emotional pain by causing physical pain

• To punish themselves

• To relieve tension

• To feel real by feeling pain or seeing evidence of injury

• To feel numb, zoned out, calm, or at peace

• To experience euphoric feelings (associated with release of endorphins)

• To communicate their pain, anger, or other emotions to others

• To nurture themselves (through the process of healing the wounds)

Eating Disorders And Self-Harm

From "Eating Disorders and Self-Harm: A Chaotic Intersection" by Randy A. Sansone, MD, John L. Levitt, PhD & Lori A. Sansone, MD. Eating Disorders Review, *May/June 2003. © 2003 Gürze Books. Reprinted with permission.*

There is clear empirical evidence that a subgroup of individuals with eating disorders (ED) engage in self-harm behavior (SHB). Individually these disorders are difficult to treat; in combination they represent a chaotic intersection. SHB ranges from various non-lethal forms of self-injury to genuine suicide attempts. Some examples of non-lethal self-injury include hitting, burning, scratching, or cutting oneself; pulling out one's hair and eyelashes; purposefully precipitating harmful "accidents," and participating in physically abusive relationships.

SHB may also manifest as overt eating disorder symptoms, such as abusing laxatives, inducing vomiting, or exercising excessively with the expressed or primary intent to experience pain or cause self-injury. Therefore, when assessing ED symptoms, it is essential to determine the intent or function of the symptoms (for example, food, body, and weight issues versus purposeful self-harm).

The Prevalence Of SHB Among Eating Disorders Patients

The prevalence of non-lethal self-injury among ED patients is approximately 25%, regardless of the type of eating disorder or the treatment setting (Eating Disorders 2002; 10:205). As for suicide attempts, the prevalence rates appear to vary, depending on the ED diagnostic subgroup and study setting. The prevalence of suicide attempts is lowest among outpatients with anorexia nervosa (16%). Prevalence rates are higher for bulimic individuals treated as outpatients (23%) and inpatients (39%). The highest rates of suicide attempts are reported among bulimic individuals who have co-morbid alcohol abuse (54%) (*Eating Disorders* 2002; 10:205).

Variables that contribute to BPD include temperament, traumatic triggering events, family-of-origin dysfunction (for example, inconsistent treatment by a caretaker, a negative family environment, or "bi-parental failure"), and various biological abnormalities, including possible aberrations in serotonin levels. Because BPD is frequently associated with a history of abuse

---

♣ It's A Fact!!
Causes Of Self-Harm Behavior (SHB)
Among Those With Eating Disorders (ED)

The precise etiology of SHB among those with ED is unknown, but it is suspected to be complex, with many underlying causes. It is also known to vary between individuals. About 25% of self-harming individuals with ED appear to meet the criteria for borderline personality disorder.

Source: "Eating Disorders and Self-Harm: A Chaotic Intersection," by Randy A. Sansone, MD, John L. Levitt, PhD & Lori A. Sansone, MD. *Eating Disorders Review*, May/June 2003. © 2003 Gürze Books. Reprinted with permission.

---

during childhood (for example, sexual, physical, and emotional abuse and witnessing violence), it is difficult to ascertain if associated biological findings are the causes of and/or outcomes of early developmental trauma. However, early violation of body boundaries appears to foster dissociative defenses in young victims, as well as a separation of body self and psychological self ("You can hurt my body, but not me"). These processes appear to subsequently lower the threshold for SHB in adulthood.

Multi-Impulsive Bulimia

A related construct, multi-impulsive bulimia, also involves impulsive SHB (for example, suicide attempts), in addition to other forms of impulsivity such as substance abuse and sexual promiscuity. Compared with BPD, considerably less is known about multi-impulsive bulimia in terms of etiology. It may be that this syndrome is actually made up of a subset of individuals with BPD.

Assessment

When assessing an individual with suspected SHB and an eating disorder, it is crucial to explore in depth not only ED symptoms, but also the presence of concomitant SHB. These may include: (1) past suicide attempts; (2) repetitive, ongoing, non-lethal self-harm behavior; and (3) ED symptoms that do not appear to be related to concerns about food, body, and/or weight. An example of the latter could include self-injury equivalents such as inducing vomiting without food in one's stomach.

Although proven thresholds for various symptoms have not been established, an ongoing pattern of SHB is the conceptual benchmark. Several instruments to help detect and measure self-harm are now available to clinicians, including the Self-Harm Inventory (*J Clin Psychol* 1998; 54:973), the Self-Injury Survey (1994; Providence, RI), and the Impulsive and Self-Harm Questionnaire (*Dissert Abstr Int* 1997; 58:4469).

Conclusions

Patients with SHB constitute a substantial minority of individuals with eating disorders. While our understanding of the causes for SHB in this population remain somewhat elusive, it is likely that this phenomenon has many causes. Assessment of all ED patients should include clinical inquiry into the presence of SHB. In addition, formal measures of SHB are available.

Treatment approaches need to be individualized and consist of a combination of psychotherapeutic strategies and medications. A reduction in SHB is a reasonable expectation, but a full and sustained remission is less likely to occur in the short term. Whether full remission occurs with longer follow-up periods is unknown. Clearly, these patients remain complex enigmas in our clinical realms.

Part Four

Prevention, Diagnosis, And Treatment Of Eating Disorders

Chapter 33

Are You At Risk? An Eating Disorder Self-Assessment

The following questionnaire can help you decide if you have an eating disorder, or if you are at risk of developing one.

True or False: Even though people tell me I'm thin, I feel fat.

True or False: I get anxious if I can't exercise.

True or False: (Female) My menstrual periods are irregular or absent. (Male) My sex drive is not as strong as it used to be.

True or False: I worry about what I will eat.

True or False: If I gain weight, I get anxious and depressed.

True or False: I would rather eat by myself than with family or friends.

True or False: Other people talk about the way I eat.

True or False: I get anxious when people urge me to eat.

True or False: I don't talk much about my fear of being fat because no one understands how I feel.

About This Chapter: "Are You at Risk? Take a Self-Test," used with permission of ANRED: Anorexia Nervosa and Related Eating Disorders, Inc., http://www.anred.com, © 2008.

True or False: I enjoy cooking for others, but I usually don't eat what I've cooked.

True or False: I have a secret stash of food.

True or False: When I eat, I'm afraid I won't be able to stop.

True or False: I lie about what I eat.

True or False: I don't like to be bothered or interrupted when I'm eating.

True or False: If I were thinner, I would like myself better.

True or False: I like to read recipes, cookbooks, calorie charts, and books about dieting and exercise.

True or False: I have missed work or school because of my weight or eating habits.

True or False: I tend to be depressed and irritable.

True or False: I feel guilty when I eat.

True or False: I avoid some people because they bug me about the way I eat.

True or False: When I eat, I feel bloated and fat.

True or False: My eating habits and fear of food interfere with friendships or romantic relationships.

True or False: I binge eat.

True or False: I do strange things with my food (cut it into tiny pieces, eat it in special ways, eat it on special dishes with special utensils, make patterns on my plate with it, secretly throw it away, give it to the dog, hide it, spit it out before I swallow, etc.)

True or False: I get anxious when people watch me eat.

True or False: I am hardly ever satisfied with myself.

True or False: I vomit or take laxatives to control my weight.

True or False: I want to be thinner than my friends.

True or False: I have said or thought, "I would rather die than be fat."

True or False: I have stolen food, laxatives, or diet pills from stores or from other people.

True or False: I have fasted to lose weight.

True or False: In romantic moments, I cannot let myself go because I am worried about my fat and flab.

True or False: I have noticed one or more of the following: cold hands and feet, dry skin, thinning hair, fragile nails, swollen glands in my neck, dental cavities, dizziness, weakness, fainting, rapid or irregular heartbeat.

Discussion And Scoring

As strange as it seems in our thin-obsessed society, none of the above behaviors is normal or healthy. Because of unhealthy demands for unrealistic thinness, most women—and a lot of men—will answer "True" to a few of the above items. But remember, the more items you have answered "True," the more serious your situation may be. Please consult with your physician or a qualified mental health counselor to prevent medical and psychological problems. You could show the person this questionnaire and the items you have answered as "True" as a way to begin the conversation. We know this is hard, and we appreciate your courage as you take the first step by calling today to make an appointment with your physician or counselor.

♣ **It's A Fact!!**

People do recover from eating disorders, but almost all of those who do, need professional help to get back on track.

Chapter 34

Signs And Symptoms Of Eating Disorders

Because everyone today seems concerned about weight, and because most people diet at least once in a while, it is hard to tell what is normal behavior and what is a problem that may escalate to threaten life and happiness. No one person will show all of the characteristics listed below, but people with eating disorders will manifest several.

In addition, the early stages of an eating disorder can be difficult to define. When does normative dieting become a health and emotional problem? When does weight loss cross the line and become pathological? Answering these questions is hard, especially when the person has not yet lost enough weight to qualify for a clinical diagnosis. Nevertheless, the questions are important. The sooner an eating disorder is treated, the easier it is for the person to recover.

Food Behaviors

The person skips meals, takes only tiny portions, will not eat in front of other people, eats in ritualistic ways, and mixes strange food combinations. May chew mouthfuls of food but spits them out before swallowing. Shops for groceries and cooks for the entire household, but will not eat the tasty

About This Chapter: "Eating Disorders Warning Signs," used with permission of ANRED: Anorexia Nervosa and Related Eating Disorders, Inc., http://www.anred.com, © 2008.

meals. Always has an excuse not to eat—is not hungry, just ate with a friend, is feeling ill, is upset, and so forth.

Becomes "disgusted" with former favorite foods like red meat and desserts. Will eat only a few "safe" foods. Boasts about how healthy the meals s/he does consume are. Becomes a "vegetarian" but will not eat the necessary fats, oils, whole grains, and the denser fruits and veggies (such as sweet potatoes and avocados) required for health and total nutrition by true vegetarianism. Chooses primarily low-fat items with low levels of necessary nutrients, foods such as lettuce, tomatoes, sprouts, and so forth.

> **♣ It's A Fact!!**
> If warning signs and symptoms are allowed to persist until they become entrenched behaviors, the person may struggle for years before s/he can turn the problem around.

Usually has a diet soda in hand. Drastically reduces or completely eliminates fat intake. Reads food labels religiously. If s/he breaks self-imposed rigid discipline and eats normal or large portions, excuses self from the table to vomit and get rid of the calories.

Or, in contrast to the above, the person gorges, usually in secret, emptying cupboards and refrigerator. May also buy special high-calorie binge food. Is panicked about weight gain and will purge to get rid of the calories. May leave clues that suggest discovery is desired—empty boxes, cans, and food packages; foul smelling bathrooms; running water to cover sounds of vomiting; excessive use of mouthwash and breath mints; and in some cases, containers of vomit poorly hidden that invite discovery.

Sometimes the person uses laxatives, diet pills, water pills, or "natural" products from health food stores to promote weight loss. May abuse alcohol or street drugs, sometimes to deaden appetite, sometimes to escape emotional pain, and usually in hopes of feeling better, at least temporarily.

Appearance And Body Image Behaviors

The person loses, or tries to lose, weight. Has frantic fears of weight gain and obesity. Wears baggy clothes, sometimes in layers, to hide fat or emaciation.

If too thin, will wear layers of clothing to stay warm. Obsesses about clothing size. Complains that s/he is fat even though others truthfully say this is not so. S/he will not believe them.

Spends lots of time inspecting self in the mirror and usually finds something to criticize. Detests all or specific parts of the body, especially belly, thighs, and buttocks. Insists s/he cannot feel good about self unless s/he is thin, and s/he is never thin enough to satisfy her/himself.

Exercise Behaviors

The person exercises excessively and compulsively. May tire easily, keeping up a harsh regimen only through sheer will power. As time passes, athletic performance suffers. Even so, s/he refuses to change excessively demanding routines.

May develop strange eating patterns, supposedly to enhance athletic performance. May consume sports drinks and supplements, but total calories are less than what an active lifestyle requires.

Up to five percent of high school girls and seven percent of middle-school girls have tried steroids in attempts to get bigger and stronger in sports and also to reduce body fat and control weight. Some say they don't mind gaining weight as long as it's muscle weight, not fat. Male abuse of steroids is also well documented. (Statistics provided by Charles Yesalis, professor of health and human development at Pennsylvania State University, 2005. Some studies show that steroid use in young people is even higher.)

Thoughts And Beliefs

In spite of average or above-average intelligence, the person thinks in magical and simplistic ways, for example, "If I am thinner, I will feel better about myself." S/he loses the ability to think logically, evaluate reality objectively, and admit and correct undesirable consequences of choices and actions.

Becomes irrational and denies that anything is wrong. Argues with people who try to help, and then withdraws, sulks, or throws a tantrum. Wanting to be special, s/he becomes competitive. Strives to be the best, the smallest, the thinnest, and so forth.

Has trouble concentrating. Obsesses about food and weight and holds to rigid, perfectionistic standards for self and others.

Is envious of thin people in general and thinner people in particular. Seeks to emulate them.

Not all, but a subset of people with eating disorders think they do not deserve to eat or enjoy tasty food. They starve, stuff, or purge in deliberate attempts to punish themselves. They may also cut their flesh or otherwise hurt themselves. Some want to become increasingly debilitated, even to suffer the indignities of tube feedings and IVs, and eventually to weaken and die. They see this not as a cry for help or attention, or an attempt to control their lives, but as well-deserved punishment for misperceived flaws and misdeeds. Their extreme self-hatred must be dealt with in therapy if they are to recover.

Feelings

Has trouble talking about feelings, especially anger. Denies anger, saying something like, "Everything is OK. I am just tired and stressed." Escapes stress by turning to binge food, exercise, or anorexic rituals.

Becomes moody, irritable, cross, snappish, and touchy. Responds to confrontation and even low-intensity interactions with tears, tantrums, or withdrawal. Feels s/he does not fit in and therefore avoids friends and activities. Withdraws into self and feelings, becoming socially isolated.

Feels inadequate, fearful of not measuring up. Frequently experiences depression, anxiety, guilt, loneliness, and at times overwhelming emptiness, meaninglessness, hopelessness, and despair.

Some of these emotional problems are the natural consequences of undernutrition. Even normal, healthy people who find themselves trapped in famine situations become depressed, anxious, moody, and irritable when they cannot find enough food to satisfy physiological needs. (Google <Keyes study starvation> for details.)

Self-Harm And Self-Injury

In some people the above-mentioned feelings are overwhelming; they are too many and too strong to be endured. To cope, to release the pain, to escape it, to distract and anesthetize themselves, some people hurt their bodies. They cut their flesh or burn it. They bang their heads or swallow foreign objects. They report that while they are engaged in self-harm, they experience peace, tranquility, and calm—a sense of being grounded after feeling tossed about by chaos and misery—at least for a while, until stress and tension mount again.

In some cases, past trauma (especially sexual abuse) has been so devastating that all feelings have been numbed. Then the person self-injures in order to feel something, anything.

In spite of appearances, the person who self-injures is not consciously trying to commit suicide. Neither is s/he "only" seeking attention. Self-harm is frequently a symptom of borderline personality disorder, a problem that often co-exists with an eating disorder. Treatment is available and can be combined with treatment for an eating disorder. Evaluation by a mental health care provider is essential. Since people who hurt themselves can inadvertently create a medical crisis, sooner is better than later.

Social Behaviors

Tries to please everyone and withdraws when this is not possible. Tries to take care of others when s/he is the person who needs care. May present self as needy and dependent or conversely as fiercely independent and rejecting of all attempts to help.

Person tries to control what and where the family eats. To the dismay of others, s/he consistently selects low-fat, low-sugar non-threatening—and unappealing—foods and restaurants that provide these "safe" items.

♣ It's A Fact!!
Anorexics tend to avoid sexual activity. Bulimics may engage in casual or even promiscuous sex.

Relationships tend to be either superficial or dependent. Person craves true intimacy but at the same time is terrified of it. As in all other areas of life, anorexics tend to be rigidly controlling while bulimics have problems with lack of impulse control that can lead to rash and regrettable decisions about sex, money, stealing, commitments, careers, and all forms of social risk taking.

Other Behaviors

Eating disorders frequently occur in combination with other problems. All of the following deserve professional attention in their own right. When they appear in the company of an eating disorder, the need for professional attention is even more urgent to prevent harm or death:

- Alcohol abuse

- Abuse of prescription medications (including insulin, Ritalin, and pain killers)

- Abuse of recreational drugs (speed, cocaine, steroids, diet pills, so-called club drugs, etc.)

- Abuse of laxatives and diuretics (water pills)

- Physical, emotional, or sexual abuse

- Threats of suicide or suicide attempts

- Cutting, burning, hair pulling or other self-harm behaviors

- Rage attacks

- Placing oneself in dangerous situations

- Homicidal threats or attempts

- Stealing and other criminal acts

- Any other behaviors that can logically be expected to bring harm to self or others

♣ It's A Fact!!

A relatively recent development in eating disorders pathology is the use of illegal steroids by both males and females to help build muscle and improve shape. About 12 percent of adolescent boys and 8 percent of adolescent girls report using such a substance in the past year. About 4.7 percent of the boys and 1.6 percent of the girls say they use supplements to enhance their appearance once or more a week. These adolescents say they want to be toned and firm, like people in movies, TV or magazines, and they are willing to risk the health consequences of steroid abuse to achieve that look. In this study, nearly as many boys as girls had body-image concerns. (Field, Austin, Camargo, et al, *Pediatrics*, August 1, 2005)

Steroids, of course, have serious side effects including severe acne; smaller breasts in women; smaller genitalia in men; deeper, more masculine voices in women; irregular or absent menstrual periods; impaired fertility; excess facial hair; excess body hair; depression; paranoia; and out-of-proportion anger ("roid rage"). Steroids can stunt the height of growing adolescents and lead to premature heart attacks, strokes, liver tumors, kidney failure, and serious psychiatric problems. In addition, because steroids are often injected, users risk contracting or transmitting human immunodeficiency virus (HIV) and hepatitis.

Chapter 35

Body Image And Self-Esteem

I'm fat. I'm too skinny. I'd be happy if I were taller, shorter, had curly hair, straight hair, a smaller nose, bigger muscles, longer legs.

Do any of these statements sound familiar? Are you used to putting yourself down? If so, you're not alone. As a teen, you're going through a ton of changes in your body. And as your body changes, so does your image of yourself. Lots of people have trouble adjusting, and this can affect their self-esteem.

Why Are Self-Esteem And Body Image Important?

Self-esteem is all about how much people value themselves, the pride they feel in themselves, and how worthwhile they feel. Self-esteem is important because feeling good about yourself can affect how you act. A person who has high self-esteem will make friends easily, is more in control of his or her behavior, and will enjoy life more.

Body image is how a person feels about his or her own physical appearance.

About This Chapter: "Body Image And Self-Esteem," April 2006, reprinted with permission from www.kidshealth.org. Copyright © 2006 The Nemours Foundation. This information was provided by KidsHealth, one of the largest resources online for medically reviewed health information written for parents, kids, and teens. For more articles like this one, visit www.KidsHealth.org, or www.TeensHealth.org.

For many people, especially people in their early teens, body image can be closely linked to self-esteem. That's because as kids develop into teens, they care more about how others see them.

What Influences A Person's Self-Esteem?

Puberty

Some teens struggle with their self-esteem when they begin puberty because the body goes through many changes. These changes, combined with a natural desire to feel accepted, mean it can be tempting for people to compare themselves to others. They may compare themselves to the people around them or to actors and celebs they see on TV, in movies, or in magazines.

But it's impossible to compare ourselves to others because the changes that come with puberty are different for everyone. Some people start developing early; others are late bloomers. Some get a temporary layer of fat to prepare for a growth spurt, others fill out permanently, and others feel like they stay skinny no matter how much they eat. It all depends on how our genes have programmed our bodies to act.

The changes that come with puberty can affect how both girls and guys feel about themselves. Some girls may feel uncomfortable or embarrassed about their maturing bodies. Others may wish that they were developing faster. Girls may feel pressure to be thin, but guys may feel like they don't look big or muscular enough.

Outside Influences

It's not just development that affect self-esteem, though. Lots of other factors (like media images of skinny girls and bulked-up guys) can affect a person's body image too.

Family life can sometimes influence a person's self-esteem. Some parents spend more time criticizing their children and the way they look than praising them. This criticism may reduce a person's ability to develop good self-esteem.

People may also experience negative comments and hurtful teasing about the way they look from classmates and peers. Sometimes racial and ethnic prejudice is the source of such comments. Although these comments often come from ignorance on the part of the person who makes them, sometimes they can affect a person's body image and self-esteem.

Healthy Self-Esteem

If you have a positive body image, you probably like and accept yourself the way you are. This healthy attitude allows you to explore other aspects of growing up, such as developing good friendships, growing more independent from your parents, and challenging yourself physically and mentally. Developing these parts of yourself can help boost your self-esteem.

A positive, optimistic attitude can help people develop strong self-esteem. For example, saying, "Hey, I'm human," instead of "Wow, I'm such a loser," when you've made a mistake. Or not blaming others when things don't go as expected.

> ## ♣ It's A Fact!! Resilience
>
> People who believe in themselves are better able to recognize mistakes, learn from them, and bounce back from disappointment. This skill is called resilience.
>
> Source: The Nemours Foundation.

Knowing what makes you happy and how to meet your goals can help you feel capable, strong, and in control of your life. A positive attitude and a healthy lifestyle (such as exercising and eating right) are a great combination for building good self-esteem.

Tips For Improving Your Body Image

Some people think they need to change how they look or act to feel good about themselves. But actually all you need to do is change the way you see your body and how you think about yourself.

The first thing to do is recognize that your body is your own, no matter what shape, size, or color it comes in. If you are very worried about your weight or size, check with your doctor to verify that things are OK. But it is no one's business but your own what your body is like—ultimately, you have to be happy with yourself.

Next, identify which aspects of your appearance you can realistically change and which you can't. Everyone (even the most perfect-seeming celeb) has things about themselves that they can't change and need to accept—like their height, for example, or their shoe size.

If there are things about yourself that you want to change and can (such as how fit you are), do this by making goals for yourself. For example, if you want to get fit, make a plan to exercise every day and eat nutritious foods. Then keep track of your progress until you reach your goal. Meeting a challenge you set for yourself is a great way to boost self-esteem.

When you hear negative comments coming from within yourself, tell yourself to stop. Try building your self-esteem by giving yourself three compliments every day. While you're at it, every evening list three things in your day that really gave you pleasure. It can be anything from the way the sun felt on your face, the sound of your favorite band, or the way someone laughed at your jokes. By focusing on the good things you do and the positive aspects of your life, you can change how you feel about yourself.

Where Can I Go If I Need Help?

Sometimes low self-esteem and body image problems are too much to handle alone. A few teens may become depressed, lose interest in activities or friends—and even hurt themselves or resort to alcohol or drug abuse. If you're feeling this way, it can help to talk to a parent, coach, religious leader, guidance counselor, therapist, or an adult friend. A trusted adult—someone who supports you and doesn't bring you down—can help you put your body image in perspective and give you positive feedback about your body, your skills, and your abilities.

If you can't turn to anyone you know, call a teen crisis hotline (check the yellow pages under social services). The most important thing is to get help if you feel like your body image and self-esteem are affecting your life.

Chapter 36

A Guy's Guide To Body Image

Al's friend Rachel invited him to go to the lake for the day with her family. Rachel thought Al was fun to be around—plus he was cute. Rachel really hoped he'd say yes.

Al turned Rachel down. He liked Rachel, too, but was self-conscious about taking off his T-shirt. He worried that her family and others at the lake would see what he saw when he looked in the mirror—a scrawny excuse for a man. Al hadn't gone to the pool in more than a year because he was so self-conscious about his appearance.

The Truth About Guys

Many people think of guys as being carefree when it comes to their appearance. But the reality is that a lot of guys spend plenty of time in front of the mirror. It's a fact— some guys care just as much as girls do about their appearance.

You may hear a lot about being a tough guy, but how often do you hear that being a guy is tough? Guys might think that they shouldn't worry about how they look, but body image can be a real problem for them. Unlike girls, guys are less likely to talk to friends and relatives about their bodies and how they're developing. Without support from friends and family, they may develop a negative self-image. The good news is that self-image and body image can be changed.

Why Is Body Image Important?

Body image is a person's opinions, thoughts, and feelings about his or her own body and physical appearance. Having a positive body image means feeling pretty satisfied with the way you look, appreciating your body for its capabilities, and accepting its imperfections. Body image is part of someone's total self-image. So how a guy feels about his body can affect how he feels about himself. If he gets too focused on not liking the way he looks, a guy's self-esteem can take a hit and his confidence can slide. (The same thing can happen to girls, too.)

How Puberty Affects Body Image

Although body image is just one part of our self-image, during the teen years, and especially during puberty, it can be easy for a guy's whole self-image to be based on how his body looks. That's because our bodies are changing so much during this time that they can become the main focus of our attention.

A change in your body can be tough to deal with emotionally—mainly because, well, your body is yours and you have become used to it.

Some guys don't feel comfortable in their changing bodies and can feel as if they don't know who they are anymore. Being the only guy whose voice is changing or who's growing body hair (or the only guy who isn't) can also make some guys feel self-conscious for a while.

Some guys go into puberty not feeling too satisfied with their body or appearance to begin with. They may have wrestled with body image even before puberty started (for example, battles with weight or dissatisfaction with height). For them, puberty may add to their insecurities.

It Could Be In Your Genes

It can be tough to balance what you expect to happen to your body with what actually does happen. Lots of guys can have high expectations for puberty, thinking they'll develop quickly or in a certain way.

The best way to approach your own growth and development is to not assume you'll be a certain way. Look at everyone in your family—uncles, grandfathers, and even female relatives—to get an idea of the kinds of options your genes may have in store for you.

♣ It's A Fact!!
When Body Worries Go Too Far

It's normal for a guy to have a few minor complaints about his looks, but a focus that's too intense can signal a problem. Body dysmorphic disorder is a mental health condition in which people are so preoccupied with what they believe are defects in the way they look that they spend hours of time and attention every day checking, fixing, or hiding appearance flaws. This body image disorder interferes with a person's ability to function or be happy and requires a professional's help.

Source: The Nemours Foundation.

When Everyone Else Seems Bigger

Not everyone's body changes at the same time or even at the same pace. It can be tough if all of your friends have already matured physically and are taller and more muscular. Most guys eventually catch up in terms of growth, although some will always be taller or more muscular than others—it's in their genes.

It's natural to observe friends and classmates and notice the different ways they're growing and developing. Guys often compare themselves with other guys in certain settings, and one of the most common is the locker room. Whether at a local gym or getting ready for a game at school, time in the locker room can be daunting for any guy.

✔ **Quick Tip**

Big Bullies

Sometimes if people haven't caught up physically, bigger kids may tease them. Often, the guys who put others down do it because they aren't comfortable with their bodies. Putting someone else down makes them feel more powerful. A simple and effective way to deal with annoying guys like this is to be comfortable with who you are and get in touch with your strengths. Use humor and wit to combat a bully—he won't know what hit him.

Source: The Nemours Foundation.

Try to keep in mind in these situations that you aren't alone if you feel you don't "measure up." Many guys feel exactly the same way about their own bodies—even those whose physiques you envy. Just knowing that almost everyone else will go through the same thing can make all the difference.

You could try talking to a trusted male adult—maybe a coach, a doctor, a teacher, or your dad. Chances are they went through similar experiences and had some of the same feelings and apprehensions when their bodies were changing.

Picture Perfect?

Guys put enough pressure on themselves, but what about the pressure society puts on them to be perfect?

It used to be that only girls felt the pressure of picture-perfect images, but these days the media emphasis on men's looks creates a sense of pressure for guys, too. And sometimes (actually many times) that "as advertised" body is just not attainable. The men you see in those pictures may not even be real. Magazines and ad agencies often alter photographs of models, either by airbrushing the facial and muscular features, or by putting a good-looking face on someone else's buff body.

Building A Better Body Image

So in the face of all the pressure society places on guys—and guys place on themselves—what can you do to fuel a positive body image? Here are some ideas:

- **Recognize your strengths.** Different physical attributes and body types are good for different things—and sometimes the things you did well as a kid can change during puberty. What does your body do well? Maybe your speed, flexibility, strength, or coordination leads you to excel at a certain sport. Or perhaps you have non-sports skills, like drawing, painting, singing, playing a musical instrument, writing, or acting. Just exploring talents that you feel good about can help your self-esteem and how you think of yourself.

- **A good body doesn't always translate into athletic success.** Too often, the way guys see their body image is closely associated with their performance on a sports field or in the gym. The upside to this is that if you're good at a team sport, you might have a pretty good view of your body. But what if you don't like team sports or you got cut from a team you really wanted to make? In these cases, it helps to look at individual accomplishments.

  If you don't like team sports, that's OK. Try finding another form of physical activity that really gets you going. Depending on your interests and where you live, that may be mountain biking, rock climbing, dancing, yoga, or even jogging. This will help you stay in shape and help you to appreciate skills you may not have realized you had in a team environment.

  If you like team sports but didn't make a particular team, don't let it get you down. Use this as an opportunity to discover what you're good at, not to lament what you aren't best at. Maybe try out for another team—so soccer wasn't for you, but maybe cross-country running will be.

  If none of these appeal to you, continue to practice the sport you were cut from and try again next year. The people around you probably won't remember that you didn't make the team—not being picked was a much bigger deal to you than it was to them.

- **Look into starting a strength-training program.** Exercise can help you look good and feel good about yourself. Good physiques don't just happen—they take hard work, regular workouts, and a healthy diet.

There's no need to work out obsessively. A healthy routine can be as simple as exercising 20 minutes to 1 hour three days a week. Another benefit to working out properly is that it can boost your mood—lifting weights can lift your spirits.

- **Don't trash your body—respect it.** To help improve your view of your body, take care of it. Smoking and other things you know to be harmful will take a toll after a while. Treating yourself well over time results in a healthier, stronger body—and that contributes to a better body image. Practicing good grooming habits—regular showering; taking care of your teeth, hair, and skin; wearing clean clothes, etc.—also can help you build a positive body image.

- **Be yourself.** Your body is just one part of who you are—along with your talent for comedy, a quick wit, or all the other things that make you unique. Your talents, skills, and beliefs are just as much a part of you as the casing they come in. So try not to let minor imperfections take over.

While it's important to have a positive body image, getting too focused on body image and appearance can cause a guy to overlook the other positive parts of himself. If you're like most guys who take care of their bodies and wear clothes that look good, you probably look great to others. You just might not be aware of that if you're too busy being self-critical.

Chapter 37

How Can I Improve My Self-Esteem?

Steve's mind wanders as he does his homework. "I'm never going to do well on this history test," he thinks. "My dad's right, I'm just like him—I'll never amount to much." Distracted, he looks down and thinks how skinny his legs are. "Ugh," he says to himself. "I bet the football coach won't even let me try out when he sees what a wimp I am."

Julio is studying for the same history test as Steve, and he's also not too fond of the subject. But that's where the similarity ends. Julio has a completely different outlook. He's more likely to think, "OK, history again, what a pain. Thank goodness I'm acing the subject I really love—math." And when Julio thinks about the way he looks, it's also a lot more positive. Although he is shorter and skinnier than Steve, Julio is less likely to blame or criticize his body and more likely to think, "I may be skinny, but I can really run. I'd be a good addition to the football team."

We all have a mental picture of who we are, how we look, what we're good at, and what our weaknesses might be. We develop this picture over time, starting when we're very young kids. The term self-image is used to refer to a person's mental picture of himself or herself. A lot of our self-image

About This Chapter: "How Can I Improve My Self-Esteem?" April 2006, reprinted with permission from www.kidshealth.org. Copyright © 2006 The Nemours Foundation. This information was provided by KidsHealth, one of the largest resources online for medically reviewed health information written for parents, kids, and teens. For more articles like this one, visit www.KidsHealth.org, or www.TeensHealth.org.

is based on interactions we have with other people and our life experiences. This mental picture (our self-image) contributes to our self-esteem.

Self-esteem is all about how much we feel valued, loved, accepted, and thought well of by others—and how much we value, love, and accept ourselves. People with healthy self-esteem are able to feel good about themselves, appreciate their own worth, and take pride in their abilities, skills, and accomplishments. People with low self-esteem may feel as if no one will like them or accept them or that they can't do well in anything.

We all experience problems with self-esteem at certain times in our lives—especially during our teens when we're figuring out who we are and where we fit in the world. The good news is that, because everyone's self-image changes over time, self-esteem is not fixed for life. So if you feel that your self-esteem isn't all it could be, you can improve it.

Self-Esteem Problems

Before a person can overcome self-esteem problems and build healthy self-esteem, it helps to know what might cause those problems in the first place. Two things in particular—how others see or treat us and how we see ourselves—can have a big impact on our self-esteem.

Parents, teachers, and other authority figures influence the ideas we develop about ourselves—particularly when we are little kids. If parents spend more time criticizing than praising a child, it can be harder for a kid to develop good self-esteem. Because teens are still forming their own values and beliefs, it's easy to build self-image around what a parent, coach, or other person says.

Obviously, self-esteem can be damaged when someone whose acceptance is important (like a parent or teacher) constantly puts you down. But criticism doesn't have to come from other people. Like Steve in the story above, some teens also have an "inner critic," a voice inside that seems to find fault with everything they do. And, like Steve, people sometimes unintentionally model their inner voice after a critical parent or someone else whose opinion is important to them.

Over time, listening to a negative inner voice can harm a person's self-esteem just as much as if the criticism were coming from another person.

Some people get so used to their inner critic being there that they don't even notice when they're putting themselves down.

Unrealistic expectations can also affect a person's self-esteem. People have an image of who they want to be (or who they think they should be). Everyone's image of the ideal person is different. For example, some people admire athletic skills and others admire academic abilities. People who see themselves as having the qualities they admire—such as the ability to make friends easily—usually have high self-esteem.

People who don't see themselves as having the qualities they admire may develop low self-esteem. Unfortunately, people who have low self-esteem often do have the qualities they admire. They just can't see that they do because their self-image is trained that way.

Why Is Self-Esteem Important?

How we feel about ourselves can influence how we live our lives. People who feel that they are likable and lovable (in other words people with good self-esteem) have better relationships. They are more likely to ask for help and support from friends and family when they need it. People who believe they can accomplish goals and solve problems are more likely to do well in school. Having good self-esteem allows you to accept yourself and live life to the fullest.

✔ Quick Tip
Retrain Your Inner Critic

Because it comes from inside you, you can take back control over that inner voice that puts you down or tells you not to bother trying something because you're sure to fail. Decide that your inner voice will only give you constructive feedback from now on.

Source: The Nemours Foundation.

Steps To Improving Self-Esteem

If you want to improve your self-esteem, here are some steps to start empowering yourself:

- **Try to stop thinking negative thoughts about yourself.** If you're used to focusing on your shortcomings, start thinking about positive aspects of yourself that outweigh them. When you catch yourself being too critical, counter it by saying something positive about yourself. Each day, write down three things about yourself that make you happy.

- **Aim for accomplishments rather than perfection.** Some people become paralyzed by perfection. Instead of holding yourself back with thoughts like, "I won't audition for the play until I lose ten pounds," think about what you're good at and what you enjoy, and go for it.

- **View mistakes as learning opportunities.** Accept that you will make mistakes because everyone does. Mistakes are part of learning. Remind yourself that a person's talents are constantly developing, and everyone excels at different things—it's what makes people interesting.

- **Try new things.** Experiment with different activities that will help you get in touch with your talents. Then take pride in new skills you develop.

- **Recognize what you can change and what you can't.** If you realize that you're unhappy with something about yourself that you can change, then start today. If it's something you can't change (like your height), then start to work toward loving yourself the way you are.

- **Set goals.** Think about what you'd like to accomplish, and then make a plan for how to do it. Stick with your plan and keep track of your progress.

- **Take pride in your opinions and ideas.** Don't be afraid to voice them.

- **Make a contribution.** Tutor a classmate who's having trouble, help clean up your neighborhood, participate in a walk-a-thon for a good cause, or volunteer your time in some other way. Feeling like you're making a difference and that your help is valued can do wonders to improve self-esteem.

- **Exercise.** You'll relieve stress and be healthier and happier.

- **Have fun.** Ever found yourself thinking stuff like "I'd have more friends if I were thinner"? Enjoy spending time with the people you care about and doing the things you love. Relax and have a good time—and avoid putting your life on hold.

It's never too late to build healthy, positive self-esteem. In some cases where the emotional hurt is deep or long lasting, it can take the help of a mental health professional, like a counselor or therapist. These experts can act as a guide, helping people learn to love themselves and realize what's unique and special about them.

Self-esteem plays a role in almost everything you do. People with high self-esteem do better in school and find it easier to make friends. They tend to have better relationships with peers and adults, feel happier, find it easier to deal with mistakes, disappointments, and failures, and are more likely to stick with something until they succeed. It takes some work, but it's a skill you'll have for life.

✔ Quick Tip
Beware The Perfectionist!

Are you expecting the impossible? It's good to aim high, but your goals for yourself should be within reach. So go ahead and dream about being a star athlete—but set your sights on improving your game in specific ways.

Source: The Nemours Foundation.

Chapter 38

How The Media Influences Risk For Eating Disorders

It's commonly understood that the media bombards people with images of unrealistic beauty, and you may know that these images can be triggering agents for eating disorder behaviors. But what are the differences between advertising and news media? And what can you and I do about the problem? Understanding the issue is motivation to take practical steps to achieve healthy body image (for ourselves and our loved ones).

Advertising In Media Links To Eating Disorders

There is no better example of how advertisers manipulate images for effect (and revenue) than the short film "Evolution" created for Dove's Campaign for Real Beauty (Click on "Evolution" at http://www.dove.us/#/features/videos/videogallery.aspx). It shows a time lapsed account of how a model is transformed into billboard material. It's especially shocking to see the digital enhancement of the woman's face after her hair and makeup work are complete.

The images we see in advertising are not images of real women. They are modifications of those women. And they're associated with success, power,

About This Chapter: Information in this chapter is from "The Media's Influence on Eating Disorders." © 2008 by Matthew Tiemeyer (http://eatingdisorders.about.com/od/riskfactors/a/edmedia.htm). Used with permission of About, Inc., which can be found online at www.about.com. All rights reserved.

wealth, and happiness, supposedly gained by using certain products. This sets us up to believe that we must pursue unrealistic appearance to get things that we want. And when living in healthy, normal ways doesn't produce that appearance, many turn to what is abnormal and unhealthy—eating disorders.

☞ Remember!!

- All media images and messages are constructions. They are not reflections of reality. Advertisements and other media messages have been carefully crafted with intent to send a very specific message.

- Advertisements are created to do one thing: convince you to buy or support a specific product or service.

- To convince you to buy a specific product or service, advertisers will often construct an emotional experience that looks like reality. Remember, you are only seeing what the advertisers want you to see.

- Advertisers create their message based on what they think you will want to see and what they think will affect you and compel you to buy their product. Just because they think their approach will work with people like you doesn't mean it has to work with you as an individual.

- As individuals, we decide how to experience the media messages we encounter. We can choose to use a filter that helps us understand what the advertiser wants us to think or believe and then choose whether we want to think or believe that message. We can choose a filter that protects our self-esteem and body image.

Source: Excerpted from "Tips for Becoming a Critical Viewer of the Media," © 2005 National Eating Disorders Association. Reprinted with permission. For additional information, visit www.NationalEatingDisorders.org, or call the toll-free Information and Referral Helpline at 800-931-2237.

Eating Disorders And News Media

News media coverage of eating disorders is disturbingly sensational. Much of the day of a person with anorexia or bulimia is affected by the disorder, but it may not be obvious to the casual observer. So reporters and editors pick out the most dramatic "highlights" of the eating problem and bring them front and center. You can almost see the furrowed brow of the commentator as she says lines like these (cue the horror-film music): *Katie just wanted to lose a little weight. But this time, she was on a path to self-destruction and personal torment.*

And we lean in and watch more. And advertisers see the ratings and pay more money so that we can see more of the same. Meanwhile, those with eating disorders see the pictures of bony limbs and protruding ribs and consider it "thinspiration"—a trigger to engage in more disordered eating.

So the media can have a negative effect on promoting images that push healthy people toward eating disorders, and they also have a negative effect in the way they report on those who do develop eating disorders. There's nothing against media outlets making money, and producers and other executives don't necessarily intend to do harm. But this double blow to women is especially damaging.

Eating Disorders And Magazines

You know what kinds of images you see on the covers of magazines at your supermarket. The images of women outnumber men by a huge margin. These attention-grabbing photos are often digitally edited to shift facial features and change body structure to evoke a certain response in those who see them.

For those with eating and body-related disorders, especially anorexia and body dysmorphic disorder (in which a person has a very inaccurate view of his or her body, usually focused on one or two body parts), these magazines are common fuel for negative thinking. Perhaps this is because the images are still shots that can be examined slowly and repeatedly.

Amazingly, the waiting rooms of counseling offices and medical practitioners often have a large supply of these very magazines. There is a need to raise awareness in this area. If we can't set a good example, who can?

What Can You Do About The Media's Influence On Eating Disorders?

"The media" has no face and no name, and it's easy to think that we are powerless to do anything about these issues. But we can.

✔ **Quick Tip**

To help promote healthier body image messages in the media, you can:

• Talk back to the TV when you see an ad or hear a message that makes you feel bad about yourself or your body by promoting only thin body ideals.

• Write a letter to an advertiser you think is sending positive, inspiring messages that recognize and celebrate the natural diversity of human body shapes and sizes. Compliment their courage to send positive, affirming messages.

• Make a list of companies who consistently send negative body image messages and make a conscious effort to avoid buying their products. Write them a letter explaining why you are using your "buying power" to protest their messages. Tear out the pages of your magazines that contain advertisements or articles that glorify thinness or degrade people of larger sizes. Enjoy your magazine without negative media messages about your body.

• Talk to your friends about media messages and the way they make you feel. Ask yourself, are you inadvertently reinforcing negative media messages through the ways you talk to yourself (and the mirror) and the comments you make to your friends?

Source: Excerpted from "Tips for Becoming a Critical Viewer of the Media," © 2005 National Eating Disorders Association. Reprinted with permission. For additional information, visit www.NationalEatingDisorders.org, or call the toll-free Information and Referral Helpline at 800-931-2237.

• It's our responsibility to cultivate a better perspective on body image and eating disorders in our own circles of influence. Those who produce media images are people, and the more people we challenge (gently and firmly) in their encouragement of the images, the more people will be influenced to think differently.

• If that isn't direct enough for you, partner with the National Eating Disorders Association and become a media watchdog. You can get information about negative media influences to an organization that has the voice to be heard with advertisers.

- Support positive media campaigns like Dove's Campaign for Real Beauty, mentioned above. It provides a number of resources designed to help build self-esteem, particularly in young girls. It's true that Dove also has the goal of appealing to a certain group of women who might then be encouraged to buy Dove's products, but I believe the advertisements celebrate genuine beauty (not artificial appearances) and are positive influences. What kind of advertising would you rather see?

Standing Firm For Something Better

Research on the causes of eating disorders is growing rapidly, and it's clear that there are many contributors. The news media are only one source of problems, and we must acknowledge that any comprehensive effort to curb eating disorders must include education on family dynamics, abuse, triggering comments, and many other factors. The media is unique, though, in that it's everywhere. It's in our homes, in our cars, on the streets, and in grocery stores. Challenging media can interrupt the constant pressure to be perfect and create a place for women (and men) to breathe.

Chapter 39

Helping A Friend Or Loved One Who May Have An Eating Disorder

First, understand that eating disorders are serious medical and psychological problems. They are not just fads, phases, or trivial eccentricities. If your friend or loved one had cancer, you would do everything you could to get her/him the finest professional care available. Eating disorders require that same level of treatment. In fact we sometimes refer to them as "soul cancer" because they so effectively destroy a person's body, mind, self-esteem, and relationships with friends and family. They deserve and require professional evaluation, diagnosis, and treatment.

Eating disorders cripple the mind and heart with growing tumors of body dissatisfaction, perfectionism, and an overarching need for control. You cannot fix those things. That is a job for physicians, psychologists, and other mental health therapists who have been trained to work with these desperately needy, yet stubborn and defiant, people who are doing the best they know how to take control of their lives in a world they find scary, lonely, and confusing.

Many factors contribute to the development of an eating disorder. Recovery means much more than replacing dieting, binge eating, and purging with healthy eating. It means identifying the underlying dynamics that have

About This Chapter: Information in this chapter is from "When You Want to Help a Friend or Loved One," used with permission of ANRED: Anorexia Nervosa and Related Eating Disorders, Inc., http://www.anred.com, © 2008.

brought the person to disordered eating in the first place and then resolving them. The process requires skill, sensitivity, and training; in other words, it's a job for medical and mental health professionals.

Does that mean there is nothing you can do to help? No. There is much you can do. You can be a friend, a partner, a sibling—someone who cares—and there is great value in the support and encouragement that you can provide in that role. What you cannot be is a trained clinician, and trained clinicians are what are required for recovery from an eating disorder. Therefore, your primary focus should be to encourage the person to talk things over with a physician or counselor. If, after an evaluation, ongoing treatment is advised, encourage the person to begin it, and stick with it, until the problem is resolved.

Your biggest problem will be convincing the person to do this. Nothing will change until s/he admits s/he has a problem and accepts help. At first s/he will deny there is a problem. S/he will fear weight gain and resist it mightily. S/he will be ashamed and not want to admit what s/he is doing. S/he has used the eating disorder to protect, hide, comfort, and empower her/himself. In the beginning, at least, s/he will not want to give it up. S/he sees asking for help as some kind of shameful admission of inadequacy and entering treatment as loss of control. Arriving at a new and healthier perspective is her/his first challenge on the road to recovery.

Here are some suggestions to help you talk to an unhappy, and defiant, person.

If Your Friend Is Younger Than 18

Tell a trusted adult—parent, teacher, coach, pastor, school nurse, school counselor, etc.—about your concern. If you don't, you may unwittingly help your friend avoid the treatment s/he needs to get better.

Consider telling your friend's parents, even though it would be hard, why you are concerned. S/he may be hiding unhealthy behaviors from them, and they deserve to know so they can arrange help and treatment. If you cannot bear to do this yourself, ask your parents, or perhaps the school nurse, for help.

A word about secrets: The person with the eating disorder may have told you about it and asked you to not tell anyone. Please understand that while most secrets deserve respect, some do not. For example, if a friend swore you to secrecy and then disclosed plans to commit suicide, you would be ethically bound to report those plans to someone who could intervene. Remember that in some respects an eating disorder could be considered a slow form of suicide. The best course of action is to tell a resource person what's going on so that your friend can be helped.

If The Person Is Older Than 18

Recognize the boundaries. Legally the person is now an adult and can refuse treatment if s/he is not ready to change. Nevertheless, reach out. Tell her/him that you are concerned. Be gentle. Suggest that there has to be a better way to deal with life than starving and stuffing. Encourage professional help, but expect resistance and denial. You can lead a horse to water, but you can't make it drink—even when it is thirsty—if it is determined to follow its own path.

✔ **Quick Tip**

A Note For Boyfriends And Girlfriends

If you are in love with someone with an eating disorder, by all means provide whatever support you can, but we suggest you postpone making a binding commitment until s/he is recovered. People with eating disorders can be physically and emotionally attractive. Their vulnerability and fragility can appeal to a partner's instincts to protect and help. This can be a trap.

Some people never do recover from an eating disorder. Don't link your life to a person with problems unless you are willing to put up with them for the rest of your life—or theirs. It might come to that. It is far wiser to wait until you can see that your life partner will be able to hold up her/his end of the commitment contract.

The kind of change required for recovery is extremely difficult. Kindness and love, as beautiful as they are, will not by themselves heal your beloved. S/he needs professional treatment too.

Some Things To Do

- Talk to the person when you are calm, not when you are frustrated or emotional. Be kind. Underneath the denial and bravado, the person is probably ashamed and fears criticism and rejection.

- Mention evidence you have heard or seen that suggests disordered eating. Don't dwell on appearance or weight. Instead talk about health, relationships (withdrawal?), and mood.

- Realize that the person will not change until s/he wants to.

- Provide information.

- Be supportive and caring. Be a good listener and don't give advice unless you are asked to do so. Even then be prepared to have it ignored.

- Continue to suggest professional help. Don't pester, but don't give up either.

- Ask: "Is doing what you are doing really working to get you what you want?"

- Talk about the advantages of recovery and a normal life.

- Agree that recovery is hard, but emphasize that many people have done it.

- If s/he is frightened to see a counselor, offer to go with her the first time.

- Realize that recovery is the person's responsibility, not yours.

- Resist guilt. Do the best you can and then be gentle with yourself.

Some Things Not To Do

- Never nag, plead, beg, bribe, threaten, or manipulate. These things don't work.

- Avoid power struggles. You will lose.

- Never criticize or shame. These tactics are cruel, and the person will withdraw.

- Don't pry. Respect privacy.

- Don't be a food monitor. You will create resentment and distance in the relationship.

- Don't try to control. The person will withdraw and ultimately outwit you.

- Don't waste time trying to reassure your friend that s/he is not fat. S/he will not be convinced.

- Don't get involved in endless conversations about weight, food, and calories. That just makes matters worse.

- Don't give advice unless asked.

- Don't expect the person to follow your advice even if s/he asked for it.

- Don't say, "You are too thin." S/he will secretly celebrate.

- Don't say, "It's good you have gained weight." S/he will lose it.

- Don't let the person always decide when, what, and where you will eat. She should not control everything, every time.

- Don't ignore stolen food and evidence of purging. Insist on responsibility.

- Don't overestimate what you can accomplish.

Discussion

Information by itself is never enough to change behavior. Something else is needed.

So what is that magic something? Well, first of all, it isn't magic. It is usually a long and difficult process that begins with the realization that starving and stuffing will never work to increase self-confidence, happiness, and satisfaction with oneself and one's life.

People with eating disorders aren't crazy, irrational, stupid, or dumb. Even if they can't, or won't, express themselves directly, they want to feel better about themselves. They also want to accomplish something, or get something, or avoid something, and because they don't know how to do so in forthright ways, or because they are too frightened or inexperienced to know how to attack their problems directly, they resort to working symbolically via food, weight, and eating. In addition, even though they want us to think they are strong and can handle anything, folks who use food and diets to try to work out other problems are emotionally fragile and easily hurt.

Confrontation and nagging create power struggles. You want the person to do things your way. S/he does not want to be manipulated or controlled. Even when you are right, your approach invites the person to rebel and stubbornly resist taking your good advice. As one person put it, "Even though I'm healthier now, I feel like I've lost and you've won. I hate it!"

Making changes, even minor ones, is hard, and giving up entrenched habits like starving, binge eating, and purging is overwhelming. That's why physicians and mental health therapists should be involved in the process. Friends and family members, as loving and filled with good intentions as they may be, don't have the training and experience to shepherd a person through the usually lengthy, and always hard journey, from eating disorder to health.

And lastly, be aware of your limits and keep your expectations reasonable. You can be a resource person who provides friendship, support, and encouragement, but you cannot control her or make him change before s/he is ready.

A Note To Boyfriends And Other Pragmatists

Sometimes people with eating disorders ask their friends and partners to "be there for me." Most men, and some women, think that means finding an answer or solving the problem. Almost always, however, the person who asks really means, "Just listen and be supportive." This is very hard to do when the person is in medical danger—but it is all that you can do—which underscores the necessity of professional treatment focused on preserving life, resolving underlying issues, and changing behavior.

☞ **Remember!!**

Don't forget to have fun with your friend or loved one. A movie, shopping trip, or a day at an amusement park can give the person a glimpse of some of the benefits of living and acting like normal people do. Don't spoil the event with lots of talk about food and weight.

✔ Quick Tip
A Note To Young Friends

Don't promise to keep secrets about your friend's self-destructive behavior. If you have already promised not to tell her/his parents,
break that promise, and do it now. Yes, your friend will be
angry, but you just might prevent a tragedy, and in
so doing, spare yourself a lifetime of guilt.

In Conclusion

When all is said and done, each of us must be responsible for the choices
we make. We can support one another, encourage mature and rational thinking, provide information, and offer advice, but eventually each individual
must decide what to do and how to do it. To live with honor and integrity
takes courage. You cannot provide that for another person, just yourself.

To protect your own mental and physical health, you may find it necessary to take a break from the person you care about. Tell her/him that it's too
frustrating and heartbreaking to watch the continuing self-abuse and rejection of your best advice and counsel. You might add that when s/he is ready
to get help and make healthy changes, you will be back with support and
encouragement.

Life is not a TV show where some compassionate parent, friend, lover,
pastor, counselor, or doctor says just the right thing so that the victim/suf-
ferer sees the light and makes a 180-degree turn before the last commercial.
Life is complicated and messy. We don't have maps or scripts to follow, but
we do have multiple opportunities to choose wisdom and integrity over blind
adherence to destructive patterns. Best wishes as you continue your journey.

Chapter 40

How Are Eating Disorders Diagnosed?

Diagnosis

The first step towards a diagnosis is to admit the existence of an eating disorder. Often, the patient needs to be compelled by a parent or others to see a doctor because the patient may deny and resist the problem. Some patients may even self-diagnose their condition as an allergy to carbohydrates, because after being on a restricted diet, eating carbohydrates can produce gastrointestinal problems, dizziness, weakness, and palpitations. This may lead such people to restrict carbohydrates even more severely.

It is often extremely difficult for parents as well as the patient to admit that a problem is present. For example, because food is such an intrinsic part of the mother-child relationship, a child's eating disorder might seem like a terrible parental failure. Parents may have their own emotional issues with weight gain and loss and perceive no problem with having a "thin" child.

Interview Tests

It is recommended that a supportive companion be present during part of the initial medical interview to offer additional information on the patient's eating history and to help offset any resistance or denial the patient may express.

About This Chapter: Information in this chapter is from "Eating Disorders," © 2008 A.D.A.M., Inc. Reprinted with permission.

Various questionnaires are available for assessing patients. The Eating Disorders Examination (EDE), which is an interview of the patient by the doctor, and the self-reported Eating Disorders Examination-Questionnaire (EDE-Q) are both considered valid tests for assessing eating disorder diagnosis and determining specific features of the individual's condition (such as vomiting or laxative use).

Another test is called the SCOFF questionnaire. It is proving to be very reliable in accurately identifying both very young and adult patients who meet the full criteria for anorexia or bulimia nervosa. (It may not be as accurate in people who do not meet the full criteria.)

Diagnosing Bulimia Nervosa

In spite of the prevalence of bulimia, in one study only 30% of midwest family doctors had ever diagnosed bulimia in a patient. Younger and female doctors are more likely to detect bulimia. A doctor should make a diagnosis of bulimia if there are at least two bulimic episodes per week for three months. Because people with bulimia tend to have complications with their teeth and gums, dentists could play a crucial role in identifying and diagnosing bulimia.

♣ It's A Fact!!

SCOFF Questionnaire

Do you make yourself **Sick** because you feel uncomfortably full?

Do you worry you have lost **Control** over how much you eat?

Have you recently lost more than **One** stone's worth of weight (14 pounds) in a three-month period?

Do you believe yourself to be **Fat** when others say you are too thin?

Would you say that **Food** dominates your life?

Answering yes to two of these questions is a strong indicator of an eating disorder.

Diagnosing Anorexia Nervosa

Generally, an observation of physical symptoms and a personal history will quickly confirm the diagnosis of anorexia. The standard criteria for diagnosing anorexia nervosa are:

• The patient's refusal to maintain a body weight normal for age and height

• Intense fear of becoming fat even though underweight

• A distorted self-image that results in diminished self-confidence

• Denial of the seriousness of emaciation and starvation

• The loss of menstrual function for at least three months

The doctor then categorizes the anorexia further:

• Restricting (severe dieting only)

• Anorexia bulimia (binge-purge behavior)

Because the disorder rarely shows up in men, doctors may not be on the lookout for it in male patients, even if they show classic symptoms of anorexia. Doctors should be very aware of these symptoms in anyone, particularly in athletes and dancers.

Diagnosing Complications Of Eating Disorders

Once a diagnosis is made, doctors should immediately check for any serious complications of starvation. They should also rule out other medical disorders that might be causing the anorexia. Tests should include:

• A complete blood count

• Tests for electrolyte imbalances (low potassium levels mean the disorder is more likely to be accompanied by the binge-purge syndrome)

• Test for protein levels

• An electrocardiogram and a chest x-ray

• Tests for liver, kidney, and thyroid problems

• A bone density test

Chapter 41

Treatment For Eating Disorders

Treatment

Patients with eating disorders typically require a treatment team consisting of a primary care physician, dietitian, and a mental health professional knowledgeable about eating disorders. The multidisciplinary membership of the Academy for Eating Disorders reflects the consensus view that treatment must often involve clinicians from different health disciplines including psychologists, psychotherapists, physicians, dietitians, and nurses.

Research on the treatment of eating disorders is exploring how different treatments can be helpful for different types of eating disorders. The American Psychiatric Association has published a set of practice guidelines for the treatment of patients with eating disorders (American Psychiatric Association, Practice Guidelines for Eating Disorders, *American Journal of Psychiatry*, 2000).

There is general agreement that good treatment often requires a spectrum of treatment options. These options can range from basic educational interventions designed to teach nutritional and symptom management

✔ **Quick Tip**

Psychotherapy

Psychotherapy can be used to help individuals overcome low self-esteem and address distorted thought and behavior patterns. Psychotherapy is a form of behavioral therapy that focuses on the individual's emotional and psychological well-being. Forms of psychotherapy include psychodynamic, cognitive, family, and group therapy.

- **Psychodynamic therapy** is a general name for approaches that attempt to get the individual to surface his or her true feelings and then to understand those feelings. This therapy focuses on the basic assumption that everyone has an unconscious mind (sometimes called the subconscious) and that feelings held in the unconscious mind are often too painful to be faced. Psychodynamic therapy helps the individual to deal with subconscious feelings.

- **Cognitive therapy** focuses on changing negative thoughts and behaviors and recognizing what triggers them. Cognitive therapy may focus on weight restoration with meal planning, assistance with developing regular eating patterns, and discouraging the use of dieting. This type of behavioral therapy provides a structured, safe, and supportive environment to discuss the foods the individual fears most.

- **Family therapy** is important for patients who live at home because family dynamics play an important role in eating disorders. Parents and siblings can be deeply affected by the presence of an eating disorder within the family and need an outlet to understand the disease and recovery process. Family therapy provides a meeting place to communicate concerns and needs between the family and the patient.

- **Group therapy**, when the individual is ready, can be an important source for peer support. Goals of group therapy typically include the following: (1) exploring underlying emotional conflicts that may be expressed by eating behaviors, (2) sharing problem solving and effective coping strategies, (3) developing realistic weight goals and a healthy relationship with food, and (4) improving interpersonal communications. These groups often focus on exploring the roots and influences of negative body image on the individual and work towards body acceptance.

Source: Excerpted from "How Is It Treated?" www.drugdigest.org, © 2007. All rights reserved.

techniques to long-term residential treatment (living away from home in treatment centers).

Most individuals with eating disorders are treated on an outpatient basis after a comprehensive evaluation. Individuals with medical complications due to severe weight loss or due to the effects of binge eating and purging may require hospitalization. Other individuals, for whom outpatient therapy has not been effective, may benefit from day hospital treatment, hospitalization, or residential placement.

Treatment is usually conducted in the least restrictive setting that can provide adequate safety for the individual. Many patients with eating disorders also have depression, anxiety disorders, drug and/or alcohol use disorders and other psychiatric problems requiring treatment along with the eating disorder.

Initial Assessment

The initial assessment of individuals with eating disorders involves a thorough review of the patient's history, current symptoms, physical status, weight control measures, and other psychiatric issues or disorders such as depression, anxiety, substance abuse, or personality issues. Consultation with a physician and a registered dietitian is often recommended. The initial assessment is the first step in establishing a diagnosis and treatment plan.

Outpatient Treatment

Outpatient treatment for an eating disorder often involves a coordinated team effort between the patient, a psychotherapist, a physician, and a dietitian (yet, many patients are treated by their pediatrician or physician with or without a mental health professional's involvement).

Similarly, many patients are seen and helped by generalist mental health clinicians without specialist involvement. Not all individuals, then, will receive a multidisciplinary approach, but the qualified clinician should have access to all of these resources.

Psychotherapy

There are several different types of outpatient psychotherapies with demonstrated effectiveness in patients with eating disorders. These include cognitive-behavioral therapy, interpersonal psychotherapy, family therapy, and behavioral therapy. Some of these therapies may be relatively short-term (for example, four months), but other psychotherapies may last years.

It is very difficult to predict who will respond to short-term treatments versus longer-term treatments. Other therapies, which some clinicians and patients have found to be useful, include feminist therapies, psychodynamic psychotherapies, and various types of group therapy.

✔ Quick Tip

Before You Choose A Dietitian

When an eating disorder is present, treatment from a dietitian can sound scary. After all, this is the person who is going to work with you to change your eating patterns, which are very important to you. Clearly, a dietitian will need to be someone you can trust.

First, make sure that any dietitian you interview is registered. A registered dietitian is certified by the American Dietetic Association after training in physiology, chemistry, and biochemistry, as well as food science and food preparation.

Here are some questions you can ask a registered dietitian to help you establish trust for a long-term recovery:

Experience

What is your experience with eating disorders? And what is your success rate in establishing good eating patterns in those who have my eating disorder?

These are the biggest questions. Working with eating disorders requires special knowledge and a long-term perspective, regardless of how long you will be meeting face-to-face.

Philosophy

What is your stance on intuitive eating?

Opinions among dietitians vary. Some are more apt to provide you with rigorous food plans to help change your current habits. Others are more interested in helping you learn to listen to what your body is saying—a concept called

Psychopharmacology

Psychiatric medications have a demonstrated role in the treatment of patients with eating disorders. Most of the research to date has involved antidepressant medications such as fluoxetine (for example Prozac®), although some clinicians and patients have found that other types of medications may also be effective.

---

intuitive eating. Your choice of a dietitian will depend in part on whether you want strict accountability, a developing sense of what your body is saying, or both.

Procedures

How often will we meet? What will our appointments be like?

Does the dietitian take an approach with you that is comfortable? What is your sense of what it will be like to work long-term with him or her? Are your concerns heard and valued?

What will I have to do on my own?

The dietitian won't be with you every step of the way, so you will be doing some kind of monitoring of what you're eating. One common way is to fill out a food log, which will give you and your dietitian perspective on your current eating patterns. There may be other assignments as well.

On Your Way Out

As you leave, check your internal reaction. Did the dietitian seem judgmental? You may feel plenty of judgment in other parts of your life; you don't need it from your dietitian. But if the person seems to be competent, matches up with your desires for recovery, and appears to be a person with whom you can connect well, you're a long way toward finding a dietitian who is good for you.

Source: © 2008 by Matthew Tiemeyer (http://eatingdisorders.about.com/od/seekingprofessionalhelp/bb/choosedietitian.htm). Used with permission of About, Inc., which can be found online at www.about.com. All rights reserved.

Nutritional Counseling

Regular contact with a registered dietitian can be an effective source of support and information for patients who are regaining weight or who are trying to normalize their eating behavior. Dietitians may help patients to gain a fundamental understanding of adequate nutrition and may also conduct dietary counseling, which is a more specific process designed to help patients change the nature of their eating behavior.

Medical Treatment

Patients with eating disorders are subject to a variety of physical and medical concerns. Adequate medical monitoring is a cornerstone of effective outpatient treatment. Individuals with anorexia nervosa may be followed quite closely (for example, weekly or more) because of the significant medical problems that this disorder poses for patients. Individuals with bulimia nervosa should be seen regularly but may not require the intensive medical monitoring often seen in anorexia nervosa. Individuals with binge eating disorder may need medical treatment for a variety of complications of obesity, such as diabetes and hypertension.

Day Hospital Care

Patients for whom outpatient treatment is ineffective may benefit from the increased structure provided by a day hospital treatment program. Generally, these programs are scheduled from three to eight hours a day and provide several structured eating sessions per day, along with various other therapies, including cognitive behavioral therapy, body image therapies, family therapy, and numerous other interventions. Day hospital allows the patient to live at home when they are not in treatment and often continue to work or attend school.

Inpatient Treatment

Inpatient treatment provides a structured and contained environment in which the patient with an eating disorder has access to clinical support 24 hours a day. Many programs are now affiliated with a day hospital program so that patients can "step-up" and "step-down" to the appropriate level of care depending on their clinical needs.

Although eating disorder patients can sometimes be treated on general psychiatric units with individuals experiencing other psychiatric disorders, such an approach often poses problems with monitoring and containing eating disorder symptoms. Therefore, most inpatient programs for eating disordered individuals only treat patients with anorexia nervosa, bulimia nervosa, binge eating disorder, or variants of these disorders.

Residential Care

Residential programs provide a longer-term treatment option for patients who require longer-term treatment. This treatment option generally is reserved for individuals who have been hospitalized on several occasions but have not been able to reach a significant degree of medical or psychological stability.

Questions To Ask When Considering Treatment Options

From "Questions to Ask When Considering Treatment Options," © 2005 National Eating Disorders Association. Reprinted with permission. For additional information, visit www.NationalEatingDisorders.org, or call the toll-free Information and Referral Helpline at 800-931-2237.

There are various approaches to eating disorders treatment. It is important to find an option that is most effective for your needs.

There are many differing approaches to the treatment of eating disorders. No one approach is considered superior for everyone, however, it is important to find an option that is most effective for your needs. The following is a list of questions you might want to ask when contacting eating disorder support services. These questions apply to an individual therapist, treatment facility, other eating disorder support services, or any combination of treatment options.

- What is your experience, and how long have you been treating eating disorders?

- How are you licensed? What are your training credentials? Do you belong to the Academy for Eating Disorders (AED)? *AED is a professional group that offers its members educational trainings every year. This doesn't prove that individuals are up-to-date, but it does increase the chances.*

✔ Quick Tip

Questions To Ask Your Treatment Provider

Once you have chosen a treatment provider, you may want to consider asking these questions in your first meeting. Remember that at any time during treatment, you can raise questions and consult your treatment provider regarding areas of concern.

• What is the diagnosis?

• What treatment plan do you recommend?

• Will you, or someone else, conduct the treatment? If someone else, does that person work for you or would this be a referral? Will you supervise the treatment, or who is the team leader?

• What other professionals will you be collaborating with during the treatment?

• Is a physician an integral part of the team?

• What are the alternative treatments?

• What are the benefits and the risks associated with the recommended treatment? With the alternative treatments?

• What will be the sequence of treatment strategies?

• Are there any physical complications of the eating disorder that need to be treated?

• Are there any associated psychiatric disorders that will need to be treated?

• What role will family members or friends play in treatment?

Source: Excerpted from "Questions to Ask Your Treatment Provider," © 2005 National Eating Disorders Association. Reprinted with permission. For additional information, visit www.NationalEatingDisorders.org, or call the toll-free Information and Referral Helpline at 800-931-2237.

- What is your treatment style? *Please note that there are many different types of treatment styles available. Different approaches to treatment may be more or less appropriate for you dependent upon your individual situation and needs.*

- Do you, or your facility, have a quality improvement program in place or regularly assess the outcome of the treatment provided?

- Are you familiar with either the American Psychological Association (APA) Guidelines or Britain's National Institute of Health and Clinical Excellence (NICE) Criteria for the treatment of eating disorders?

- What kind of evaluation process will be used in recommending a treatment plan?

- What kind of medical information do you need? Will I need a medical evaluation before entering the program?

- What is your appointment availability? Do you offer after-work or early morning appointments? How long do the appointments last? How often will we meet?

- How long will the treatment process take? When will we know it's time to stop treatment?

- Are you reimbursable by my insurance? What if I don't have insurance or mental health benefits under my health care plan? *It is important for you to research your insurance coverage policy and what treatment alternatives are available in order for you and your treatment provider to design a treatment plan that suits your coverage.*

- Ask the facility to send information brochures, treatment plans, treatment prices, etc. The more information the facility is able to send in writing, the better informed you will be.

With a careful search, the provider you select will be helpful. But, if the first time your meeting with him or her is awkward, don't be discouraged. The first few appointments with any treatment provider are often challenging. It takes time to build up trust in someone with whom you are sharing highly personal information. If you continue to feel that you need a different therapeutic environment, you may need to consider other providers.

Chapter 42

Medication For Anorexia Nervosa And Bulimia Nervosa

Anorexia nervosa and bulimia nervosa are associated with altered levels of neurotransmitters, or chemical messengers in the brain. This is particularly true of serotonin levels. It makes sense, then, that medications developed to improve the function of neurotransmitters might be useful in the treatment of eating disorders.

Selective Serotonin Reuptake Inhibitors (SSRIs)

Several different categories of psychiatric medications have been shown to be beneficial, but the most widely studied are the SSRIs (selective serotonin reuptake inhibitors), the first and most famous of which is fluoxetine, or Prozac. Other SSRIs include sertraline (Zoloft), paroxetine (Paxil), fluvoxamine (Luvox), and citalopram/escitalopram (Celexa/Lexapro). All raise the levels of serotonin available in parts of the brain. Venlafaxine (Effexor) is a related drug that raises both serotonin and norepinephrine.

Though popularly dubbed antidepressants, these drugs are used for a wide array of psychiatric diagnoses, including anxiety, phobias, panic attacks,

About This Chapter: Information in this chapter is from "Medication for Anorexia Nervosa and Bulimia Nervosa," by Diane Mickley, MD. *Eating Disorders Review.* © Gürze Books. Reprinted with permission; cited January 2008. Medical Advisor's Note added by David Cooke, M.D., in July 2008.

obsessive-compulsive disorder (OCD), premenstrual dysphoria (PMS), post-traumatic stress disorder (PTSD), and impulse control disorders. Many of these are common additional problems in patients with eating disorders and their families.

Anorexia Nervosa Medications

The initial goal in treating anorexia nervosa is the immediate restoration of normal weight. This is urgent for physical health and is a crucial first step in psychological recovery as well. Because people with anorexia nervosa are often sad and obsessional, it is logical to hope that SSRIs might help. Although they are widely prescribed for this purpose, research studies and the clinical experience of specialists both show that SSRIs do not help low-weight patients recover. Malnutrition appears to preclude their usual benefits.

A common adage holds that food is the medicine for anorexia nervosa. Weight gain alone does often normalize mood in anorexia nervosa, but it can be hard to accomplish and frequently requires hospitalization. Although certain psychiatric medications can cause weight gain in the general population, none has had this effect with malnourished anorexic patients. Recent exciting studies suggest that olanzapine (Zyprexa) and other medications in this class may finally offer a drug that can help some low-weight anorexia nervosa patients. Olanzapine lessens anxiety and obsessional thinking, and some anorexic patients find they feel less paralyzed due to rigid thinking and behavior on this medication.

Olanzapine was originally marketed for schizophrenia, and although anorexia nervosa is not a psychotic illness, there is certainly a delusional quality about feeling fat when you are dangerously starved. Clinicians find that on olanzapine, some people with anorexia nervosa are better able to grasp their situation and engage in treatment. Low-dose, short-term use may facilitate

♣ **It's A Fact!!**
Research over more than a decade has shown that medications can indeed be valuable in the treatment of bulimia nervosa. More recent research has shown some promise for the use of medications in treating anorexia nervosa as well.

that elusive transition from low to healthy weight for some people, speeding the initial steps to recovery and sometimes averting hospitalization.

Once someone with anorexia nervosa has been successful in restoring weight, maintaining those gains is the next hurdle. Unfortunately, immediate relapse is common. Here's where fluoxetine enters the picture. Although this drug does not help anorexia nervosa while the patient's weight is low, after the weight has been regained, fluoxetine may significantly lessen the risk of relapse when used as part of a comprehensive treatment program.

Bulimia Nervosa Medications

The initial goal for bulimia nervosa is also symptom management—in this case, stopping the binge/purge behaviors. Two treatments have been documented by evidence-based scientific studies to have the best short-term success rates. The first is cognitive behavioral therapy (CBT), and the second is high-dose fluoxetine. Results are roughly comparable, with a suggestion that the two together may be better than either one alone. However, since only a quarter of patients achieve symptom remission with these approaches, further treatment is generally needed.

The largest bulimia nervosa treatment trial in the world documented the benefits of high-dose fluoxetine. This led to approval of fluoxetine by the Food and Drug Administration (FDA) specifically for the treatment of bulimia nervosa. Treatment is recommended to begin and continue at a dose of 60 mg. (The dose of 20 mg commonly used for depression was no better than a placebo.) Bulimics benefit from fluoxetine regardless of whether they are depressed. Moreover, if fluoxetine is going to be helpful, the results will be apparent within four weeks. At least one study has shown this to be a successful initial approach when used by primary care providers.

Are other medications in the SSRI category also helpful? Published studies have now shown sertraline to benefit bulimia nervosa at a higher dose range (150 mg). Although clinicians commonly do use other SSRIs for this purpose, the data to assess their benefit and dosage is simply not available. Other classes of antidepressant medications have also been shown to be helpful for the treatment of bulimia nervosa and binge eating disorder.

Topiramate is a totally different category of medication that was developed for treating epilepsy. It is now commonly used for migraine headaches, and it is an exciting new option for patients with bulimia nervosa, binge eating disorder, and simple obesity. Studies in patients with these disorders show binge reduction, reduced preoccupation with eating, and weight loss. Topiramate is used in relatively low doses (100–200 mg) for eating disorders and weight loss. Gradual initial dose increases are required to avoid mental sluggishness. Other side effects are common but generally not serious. Patients who are taking hormones, including oral contraceptives, may also require dose adjustment due to interaction with topiramate. Zonisamide is another promising agent in this class.

Side Effects

None of the medications described above have any potential to be addicting. Often their use can be transitional, for several months to a year or two, while recovery progresses and solidifies. However, since eating disorders frequently occur in patients with depression or anxiety disorders, some of these people will benefit from longer-term use of medication.

What about side-effects? As in all medical care, doctors must weigh the risks of the treatment compared to the risks of the illness. Fortunately, most of the side effects of the medications used for eating disorders are relatively minor, especially compared to the serious dangers of being anorexic or bulimic. The most frequent side effect of olanzapine is significant sedation, especially at the beginning. The SSRIs may have mild initiation side effects including

---

♣ It's A Fact!!

Recently, the news media has focused on whether teenagers respond as well and safely to SSRIs as adults do. A small percent of adolescents (and a few adults) experience akathisia while taking common psychiatric drugs. Akathisia is a kind of motor restlessness, a feeling of "jumping out of your skin," which should be reported to your physician. In addition, concerns have been voiced about an increased risk of suicide among children and teens taking SSRIs, even though overall suicide rates have dropped significantly as SSRI use has become widespread. Government agencies are currently evaluating this question.

nausea, headache, fatigue, or insomnia, and less commonly agitation and over-excitement. These often pass within a week or two, but they may persist and should always be discussed with the physician. More enduring side effects may include vivid dreams, sweating, and a reduction in sexual interest or performance. Medications that leave the body quickly (paroxetine, escitalopram, and venlafaxine) should be tapered off, since sudden discontinuation can produce flu-like symptoms.

The exciting overview is that continuing progress is being made in understanding the biology of anorexia nervosa and bulimia nervosa, as well as how medications can help. Specialists in the field will be aware of the latest developments and the latest information about the uses and benefits of available medications. The best outcome—ideally, complete recovery—is most likely with an up-to-date and experienced eating disorder team working in firm alliance with the patient and family.

Medical Advisor's Note

The latest research data on drug treatment of anorexia nervosa have been disappointing. A carefully designed 2006 study failed to show any benefit from fluoxetine. While some prior studies had reported benefits with the drug, they were poorer quality, and probably less accurate. At this point, the best evidence suggests that antidepressants have minimal, if any, benefit in anorexia nervosa.

Of note, while fluoxetine and other antidepressants do not appear to be effective in anorexia nervosa, they have been confirmed to be quite effective in treatment of bulimia nervosa. This suggests that the two disorders may be less related than once believed.

A number of additional agents, including those mentioned in this article, are actively being studied for use in anorexia nervosa. However, there isn't sufficient good quality evidence at this point to determine whether they are effective or not.

Chapter 43

Eating Disorder Relapse Prevention

The road to recovery is usually long and hard. No one travels it gracefully. There are many slips, trips, and lapses. Those who eventually do recover learn to pick themselves up when they fall, brush off the dust, and keep going. By doing so, they keep temporary lapses from turning into full-blown relapses. Here are things to do when relapse threatens.

Relapse Prevention: Anorexia Nervosa

- It sounds simplistic, but it is true: if no one ever dieted there would be no anorexia nervosa. Instead of dieting, design a meal plan that gives your body all the nutrition it needs for normal growth and health. If you want to work towards a healthy weight, then limit (but don't eliminate) your intake of fatty and sugary foods and refined carbohydrates. Eat lots of whole grains, fruits, vegetables, and enough dairy and protein foods to maintain strong bones and healthy muscles and organs. Also get 30 to 60 minutes of exercise or physical activity three to five days a week. Unless you are working under the supervision of a coach or trainer, anything more rigorous is excessive.

- When you start to get overwhelmed by "feeling fat," instead of dwelling on your appearance, ask yourself how your life would be better if

About This Chapter: "Relapse Prevention," used with permission of ANRED: Anorexia Nervosa and Related Eating Disorders, Inc., http://www.anred.com, © 2008.

you were thinner. What would you have then that you don't have now? Friends? Self-confidence? Love? Control? The admiration of others? Their acceptance? Success and status?

- Then realize that being unhealthfully thin will bring you none of these things, only a fragile illusion of success that has to be constantly reinforced with even more weight loss. All of the items listed in the preceding paragraph are legitimate goals of healthy people, but working to achieve them directly is much more effective than trying to be successful by losing weight. If weight loss brought happiness, then starving Third World children would be ecstatic with joy. They are not. They are miserable and depressed, just like people who have anorexia nervosa.

- Accept that your body shape is determined in part by genetics. Accept that you may never have a totally flat stomach. Even if you are very thin, your internal organs will give your belly a certain roundedness, especially after you eat. That's normal, especially if people in your family tend to store fat in the midsection.

Relapse Prevention: Bulimia Nervosa

- Never ever let yourself get so hungry that the urge to binge is overwhelming. People who recover from bulimia say that they eat regularly. Because they are never ravenous, they have no physical reason to binge eat. Hunger is the most powerful binge trigger there is. It is a recognized fact that the longer one has dieted, and the more severely calories have been restricted, the higher the risk of binge eating.

- Never ever deprive yourself of good-tasting food, even if it has more fat and calories than "safe" diet foods. If you refuse to eat appealing

> ✔ **Quick Tip**
> If you feel yourself slipping back into unhealthy habits, call your therapist and schedule an appointment. Returning to counseling in no way means you have failed. It means only that it's time to reevaluate and fine-tune your recovery plan.

foods that you really want, you will feel deprived and crave them. Then you are vulnerable to bingeing. Remember Adam and Eve in the Garden of Eden? The one food they were not supposed to eat was the one they could not stay away from.

- Until you have achieved some balance and perspective, stay away from temptation. Don't go to all-you-can-eat salad bars. If ice cream is a binge trigger, don't keep it in your freezer. When you want potato salad, for example, or rocky road ice cream, go to a sit-down restaurant and order a single portion, ideally as part of a balanced meal. By doing so, you accomplish three things. You avoid depriving yourself. You avoid the urges to binge created by deprivation, and you also learn how to integrate normal food into a reasonable and healthy meal plan.

- When you do feel powerful urges to binge, postpone the act for thirty minutes. Surely you can wait half an hour. During that time think about what is going on in your life. What stresses are you facing? What is missing right now from your life that you need in order to be happy and avoid the looming binge? Make a list of things you could do instead of binge eating to deal with your situation. If you are truly committed to recovery, at least some of the time you will choose one of these healthier behaviors instead of binge food.

- Take charge of your life. Stop using words like, "I wish," "I want," "I hope," and "I can't." They are weak victim words. Say instead things like, "I choose," even if you are choosing to binge. Say, "I will," even if the thing you will do is vomit. These are words that express responsibility, power, and control. If you can choose to binge, then by implication at some future time you can choose not to binge. If you will vomit, then next week or next month or next year you can choose to say, "I won't vomit" and then choose a healthier and more effective way to deal with whatever is going on in your life.

- If you feel yourself slipping back into unhealthy habits, call your therapist and schedule an appointment. Returning to counseling in no way means you have failed. It means only that it's time to reevaluate and fine-tune your recovery plan.

Relapse Prevention: Binge Eating Disorder

- Same as for bulimia, above.

- If you feel yourself slipping back into unhealthy habits, call your therapist and schedule an appointment. Returning to counseling in no way means you have failed. It means only that it's time to reevaluate and fine-tune your recovery plan.

Relapse Prevention: Everyone

- Nourish yourself physically, emotionally, and spiritually. Accept that everyone has needs, legitimate needs, and you don't need to be ashamed of yours. Learn how to meet your needs in healthy, responsible ways. If you make yourself feel needy, you will be tempted to look for comfort in diet books or the refrigerator. Especially make sure that every day you spend time with friends. In person is best, but phone calls and e-mail are better than nothing.

- Also every day spend time doing things you are good at, things you can take pride in, things that demonstrate your competency and abilities. Allow yourself to enjoy your accomplishments and refuse to listen to the nagging inner voice that insists you could do better if only you tried harder.

- Schedule something to look forward to every day, something that's fun and pleasurable. Watch comedy videos and laugh out loud at outrageous jokes. Play something—a board game, a computer game, a musical instrument, tapes, or CDs. Go outside and enjoy the birds, trees, flowers, and fresh air. If you live in the middle of a big city, go to a park. Make something with your own hands. Figure out how to give yourself a fun break from the daily routine, and then do it.

- Keep tabs on your feelings. Several times during the day, especially in the first stages of recovery, take time out and ask yourself how you feel. If you notice rising stress, anger, anxiety, fear, sadness—and even strong joy—be alert to the possibility that you may try to dull these strong emotions by turning to, or away from, food. Find a better way of dealing with your feelings such as talking them over with a trusted friend.

- The 12-step folks have a useful formula. When they feel on the verge of falling into old behaviors, they say HALT! Then they ask, "Am I too Hungry, too Angry, too Lonely, or too Tired?" All of those states are strong binge triggers. Additional triggers for people with eating disorders seem to be boredom and unstructured time. If you find yourself stressed by any of these feelings, figure out a healthier and more effective way of dealing with them than binge eating or starving.

✔ **Quick Tip**

Do something meaningful every day, something that gives you a sense of having made the world a better place, if only in some small way. If you do this consistently, you will build a sense of your dignity, value, and ability to make a difference in your world.

- If you feel yourself slipping back into unhealthy habits, call your therapist and schedule an appointment. Returning to counseling in no way means you have failed. It means only that it's time to reevaluate and fine-tune your recovery plan.

A Healthy Lifestyle Insulates Against Major Relapse

- **Get at least eight hours of sleep every night,** more if you need it. Sleep deprivation seems to impair the way the human body uses insulin, which can lead to overweight and possible problems with blood sugar.

- **Do thirty to sixty minutes of physical activity every day.** It does not have to be done all at one time, and routine activities such as climbing stairs and yard maintenance count.

- **Nurture supportive relationships** with friends, family members, and romantic partners. Enjoy being with people you like and who like you back.

- **Deliberately make choices.** Don't make the mistake of thinking that you are the victim of forces over which you have no control. As soon as you realize you are making choices, you can decide to choose other possibilities.

- **Do something fun every day.** Let yourself experience pleasure too. When you play and enjoy yourself, you don't have to turn to diet books or binge food for release from daily stress.

- **No smoking.** Anything. Ever.

- **No abuse of prescription drugs or use of recreational drugs.** In addition to hurting your body, these substances impair brain function and muddy your thoughts. If you want to be healthy and free of relapses, you need your wits about you. If you are dependent on alcohol or other drugs, get treatment and get clean. Many people with eating disorders are also chemically dependent.

- **A nutritious breakfast every morning.** Ninety-six percent of everyone who loses weight and keeps it off eats breakfast every day, according to Ann Yelmokas McDermot, a nutrition scientist at Tufts University (USDA Nutrition Research Center).

- **Plus all the things your mother has probably nagged you about:** Wear your seat belt when in a car. No unprotected sex unless you are in a strictly monogamous relationship. Insist on counseling or leave relationships if you are being physically, sexually, or emotionally abused. Also get counseling if you have painful issues in your past that have not been resolved.

Part Five

Healthy Eating And Exercise Plans

Chapter 44

Healthy Eating

Take Charge Of Your Health

Does Your Life Move At A Hectic Pace?

You may feel stressed from school, after-school activities, peer pressure, and family relationships. Your busy schedule may lead you to skip breakfast, buy lunch from vending machines, and grab whatever is in the refrigerator for dinner when you get home.

Where Is The Time To Think About Your Health?

Yet healthy behaviors, like nutritious eating and regular physical activity, may help you meet the challenges of your life. In fact, healthy eating and regular exercise may help you feel energized, learn better, and stay alert in class. These healthy habits may also lower your risk for diseases such as diabetes, asthma, heart disease, and some forms of cancer.

Dieting Is Not The Answer

The best way to lose weight is to eat healthfully and be physically active. It is a good idea to talk with your health care provider if you want to lose weight.

About This Chapter: Information in this chapter is excerpted from "Take Charge of Your Health," Weight-control Information Network, an information service of the National Institute of Diabetes and Digestive and Kidney Diseases, National Institutes of Health, September 2006.

♣ It's A Fact!!

• From 2003 to 2004, approximately 17.4 percent of U.S. teens between the ages of 12 and 19 were overweight.

• Overweight children and teens are at high risk for developing serious diseases. Type 2 diabetes and heart disease were considered adult diseases, but they are now being reported in children and teens.

Many teens turn to unhealthy dieting methods to lose weight, including eating very little, cutting out whole groups of foods (like grain products), skipping meals, and fasting. These methods can leave out important foods you need to grow. Other weight-loss tactics such as smoking, self-induced vomiting, or using diet pills or laxatives can lead to health problems.

What You Can Do

This chapter is designed to help you take small and simple steps to keep a healthy weight. It gives you basic facts about nutrition and offers practical tools that you can use in your everyday life, from reading food labels to selecting how much and what foods to eat.

Healthy Eating

Eating healthfully means getting the right balance of nutrients your body needs to perform every day. You can find out more about your nutritional needs by checking out the 2005 *Dietary Guidelines for Americans*. Published by the U.S. Government, this publication explains how much of each type of food you should eat, along with great information on nutrition and physical

♣ It's A Fact!!

Unhealthy dieting can actually cause you to gain more weight because it often leads to a cycle of eating very little, then overeating or binge eating. Also, unhealthy dieting can put you at greater risk for growth and emotional problems.

activity. The guidelines suggest the number of calories you should eat daily based on your gender, age, and activity level.

According to the guidelines, a healthy eating plan includes the following:

• Fruits and vegetables

• Fat-free or low-fat milk and milk products

• Lean meats, poultry, fish, beans, eggs, and nuts

• Whole grains

In addition, a healthy diet is low in saturated and trans fats, cholesterol, salt, and added sugars.

When it comes to food portions, the *Dietary Guidelines* use the word "servings" to describe a standard amount of food. Serving sizes are measured as "ounce" or "cup equivalents." Listed below are some tips based on the guidelines that can help you develop healthy eating habits for a lifetime.

Eat Fruits And Vegetables Every Day

When consumed as part of a well-balanced and nutritious eating plan, fruits and vegetables can help keep you healthy.

Table 44.1. Fruits and Vegetables

What counts as a serving?	1 serving* equals
Fruits like apples, oranges, bananas, and pears	1 medium fruit
Raw leafy vegetables like romaine lettuce or spinach	1 cup
Cooked or raw vegetables	½ cup
Chopped fruit	½ cup
Dried fruits (raisins or apricots)	¼ cup

*Note: All serving size information is based on *Dietary Guidelines for Americans 2005* (www.health.gov/dietaryguidelines).

You may get your servings from fresh, frozen, dried, and canned fruits and vegetables. Teenagers who are consuming 2,000 calories per day should aim for 2 cups of fruit and 2½ cups of vegetables every day. You may need fewer or more servings depending on your individual calorie needs, which your health care provider can help you determine.

Count Your Calcium

Calcium helps strengthen bones and teeth. This nutrient is very important, since getting enough calcium now can reduce the risk for broken bones later in life. Yet most teens get less than the recommended 1,200 mg of calcium per day. Aim for at least three 1-cup equivalents of low-fat or fat-free calcium-rich foods and beverages each day.

Power Up With Protein

Protein builds and repairs body tissue like muscles and organs. Eating enough protein can help you grow strong and sustain your energy levels. Teens need 5½ one-ounce equivalents of protein-rich foods each day.

Go Whole Grain

Grain foods help give you energy. Whole grain foods like whole wheat bread, brown rice, and oatmeal usually have more nutrients than refined grain products. They give you a feeling of fullness and add bulk to your diet.

Table 44.2. Calcium-Rich Foods

What counts as a serving?	1 cup equivalent equals
Yogurt, low-fat or fat-free	1 cup
Cheddar cheese, low-fat	1½ ounces
American cheese, fat-free	2 ounces
Soy-based beverage (soy milk) with added calcium	1 cup

Table 44.3. Protein Sources

What counts as a serving?	1 ounce equivalent equals
Lean meat, poultry, or fish	1 ounce
Beans (canned or cooked dry beans)	¼ cup
Tofu	¼ cup
Eggs	1
Peanut butter	1 tablespoon
Veggie burger made with soy	A 2½ ounce burger equals 2½ one-ounce equivalents
Nuts/Seeds	½ ounce

Know Your Fats

Fat is also an important nutrient. It helps your body grow and develop, and it is a source of energy as well—it even keeps your skin and hair healthy. But be aware that some fats are better for you than others. Limit your fat intake to 25 to 35 percent of your total calories each day.

Unsaturated fat can be part of a healthy diet—as long as you do not eat too much, since it is still high in calories. Good sources include the following:

- Olive, canola, safflower, sunflower, corn, and soybean oils
- Fish like salmon, trout, tuna, and whitefish
- Nuts like walnuts, almonds, peanuts, and cashews

Limit saturated fat, which can clog your arteries and raise your risk for heart disease. Saturated fat is found primarily in animal products and in a few plant oils like the following:

- Butter

Table 44.4. Whole Grain Sources

What counts as a serving?	1 ounce equivalent equals
Whole grain bread	1 slice
Whole grain pasta (cooked)	½ cup
Brown rice (cooked)	½ cup
Foods made with bulgur (cracked wheat) like tabouli salad	1 cup
Ready-to-eat whole grain breakfast cereals like raisin bran	About 1 cup

Try to get six 1-ounce equivalents of grains every day, with at least three 1-ounce equivalents coming from whole grain sources.

- Full-fat cheese
- Whole milk
- Fatty meats
- Coconut, palm, and palm kernel oils

Limit trans fat, which is also bad for your heart. Trans fat is often found in the following:

- Baked goods like cookies, muffins, and doughnuts
- Snack foods like crackers and chips
- Vegetable shortening
- Stick margarine
- Fried foods

Look for words like "shortening," "partially hydrogenated vegetable oil," or "hydrogenated vegetable oil" in the list of ingredients. These ingredients tell you that the food contains trans fat. Packaged food products are required to list trans fat on their Nutrition Facts.

Replenish Your Body With Iron

Teen boys need iron to support their rapid growth—most boys double their lean body mass between the ages of 10 and 17. Teen girls also need iron to support growth and replace blood lost during menstruation.

To get the iron you need, try eating these foods:

- Fish and shellfish
- Lean beef
- Iron-fortified cereals
- Enriched and whole grain breads
- Cooked dried beans and peas like black beans, kidney beans, black-eyed peas, and chickpeas/garbanzo beans
- Spinach

Control Your Food Portions

The portion sizes that you get away from home at a restaurant, grocery store, or school event may contain more food than you need to eat in one sitting. Research shows that when people are served more food, they eat more food. So, how can you control your food portions? Try these tips:

- When eating out, share your meal, order a half portion, or order an appetizer as a main meal. Be aware that some appetizers are larger than others and can have as many calories as an entree.
- Take at least half of your meal home.
- When eating at home, take one serving out of a package (read the Nutrition Facts to find out how big a serving is) and eat it off a plate instead of eating straight out of a box or bag.
- Avoid eating in front of the TV or while you are busy with other activities. It is easy to lose track of how much you are eating if you eat while doing other things.

- Eat slowly so your brain can get the message that your stomach is full.

- Do not skip meals. Skipping meals may lead you to eat more high-calorie, high-fat foods at your next meal or snack. Eat breakfast every day.

Read Food Labels

When you read a food label, pay special attention to the following:

- **Serving Size:** Check the amount of food in a serving. Do you eat more or less? The "servings per container" line tells you the number of servings in the food package.

- **Calories And Other Nutrients:** Remember, the number of calories and other listed nutrients are for one serving only. Food packages often contain more than one serving.

- **Percent Daily Value:** Look at how much of the recommended daily amount of a nutrient (% DV) is in one serving of food—5 percent DV or less is low and 20 percent DV or more is high. For example, if your breakfast cereal has 25 percent DV for iron, it is high in iron.

Plan Meals And Snacks

You and your family have busy schedules, which can make eating healthfully a challenge. Planning ahead can help. Think about the meals and snacks you would like for the week, including bag lunches to take to school, and help your family make a shopping list. You may even want to go grocery shopping and cook together.

Jumpstart Your Day With Breakfast

Did you know that eating breakfast can help you do better in school? By eating breakfast you can increase your attention span and memory, have more energy, and feel less irritable and restless. A breakfast that is part of a healthy diet can also help you maintain an appropriate weight now and in the future.

Bag It! Pack Your Lunch

Whether you eat lunch from school or pack your own, this meal should provide you with one-third of the day's nutritional needs. A lunch of chips, cookies, candy, or soda just gives you lots of calories but not many nutrients. Instead of buying snacks from vending machines at school, bring food from home. Try packing your lunch with a lean turkey sandwich on whole grain bread, healthy foods like fruits, vegetables, low-fat yogurt, and nuts.

Snack Smart

A healthy snack can contribute to a healthy eating plan and give you the energy boost you need to get through the day. Try these snack ideas, but keep in mind that most of these foods should be eaten in small amounts:

- Fruit—any kind—fresh, canned, dried, or frozen
- Peanut butter on rice cakes or whole-wheat crackers
- Baked potato chips or tortilla chips with salsa
- Veggies with low-fat dip
- String cheese, low-fat cottage cheese, or low-fat yogurt
- Frozen fruit bars, fruit sorbet, or low-fat frozen yogurt
- Vanilla wafers, graham crackers, animal crackers, or fig bars
- Popcorn (air popped or low-fat microwave)

Eat Dinner With Your Family

For many teens, dinner consists of eating on the run, snacking in front of the TV, or nonstop munching from after school to bedtime. Try to eat dinner as a family instead. Believe it or not, when you eat with your family, you are more likely to get more fruits, vegetables, and other foods with the vitamins and minerals your body needs. Family meals also help you reconnect after a busy day. Talk to your family about fitting in at least a few meals together throughout the week.

Limit Fast Food And Choose Wisely

Like many teens, you may eat at fast food restaurants often. If so, you are probably taking in a lot of extra calories from added sugar and fat. Just one value-sized fast food meal of a sandwich, fries, and sweetened soda can have more calories, fat, and added sugar than anyone should eat in an entire day.

The best approach is to limit the amount of fast food you eat. If you do order fast food, try these tips:

- Skip "value-sized" or "super-sized" meals.

- Choose a grilled chicken sandwich or a plain, small burger.

- Use mustard instead of mayonnaise.

- Limit fried foods or remove breading from fried chicken, which can cut half the fat.

- Order garden or grilled chicken salads with light or reduced-calorie dressings.

- Choose water, fat-free, or low-fat milk instead of sweetened soda.

Rethink Your Drinks

Soda and other sugary drinks have replaced milk and water as the drinks of choice for teens and adults alike. Yet these drinks are actually more like desserts because they are high in added sugar and calories. In fact, soda and sugar-laden drinks may contribute to weight problems in kids and teens. Try sticking to water, low-fat milk, or fat-free milk.

Making It Work

Look for chances to move more and eat better at home, at school, and in the community.

It is not easy to maintain a healthy weight in today's environment. Fast food restaurants on every corner, vending machines at schools, and not enough safe places for physical activity can make it difficult to eat healthfully and be active. Busy schedules may also keep families from fixing and eating dinners together.

Understanding your home, school, and community is an important step in changing your eating and activity habits. Your answers to the questions on this checklist can help you identify barriers and ways to change your behavior to support your success.

Home

1. Is the kitchen stocked with fruits, vegetables, low-fat or fat-free milk and milk products, whole-grain items, and other foods you need to eat healthy?

2. Can you get water and low-fat or fat-free milk instead of soda, sweetened tea, and sugary fruit drinks?

3. Do you pack healthy lunches to take to school?

4. Does your family eat dinner together a few times per week?

> ✔ **Quick Tip**
> **What You Can Do At Home**
>
> Talk to your family about making changes that encourage healthy eating. Help your family plan weekly menus and shopping lists. Get involved with shopping and cooking, too.

School

1. Does the cafeteria offer healthy foods such as salads and fruit?

2. Are there vending machines in school where you can buy snacks and drinks like baked chips, fig bars, and bottled water?

Change Occurs Slowly

Old habits are hard to break and new ones, especially those related to eating, can take months to develop and stick with. Here are some tips to help you in the process:

- **Make changes slowly.** Do not expect to change your eating habits overnight. Changing too much too fast can hurt your chances of success.

- **Look at your current eating habits and at ways you can make them healthier.** Use a food journal for four or five days, and write down everything you eat and your emotions. Review your journal to get a picture of your habits. Do you skip breakfast? Are you eating fruits and vegetables every day? Do you eat when you are stressed? Can you substitute physical activity for eating at these times?

- **Set a few realistic goals for yourself.** First, try cutting back the number of sweetened sodas you drink by replacing a couple of them with unsweetened beverages. Once you have reduced your sweetened soda intake, try eliminating these drinks from your diet. Then set a few more goals, like drinking low-fat or fat-free milk and eating more fruits each day.

- **Identify your barriers.** Are there unhealthy snack foods at home that are too tempting? Is the food at your cafeteria too high in fat and added sugars? Do you find it hard to resist drinking several sweetened sodas a day because your friends do it?

- **Get a buddy at school or someone at home to support your new habits.** Ask a friend, sibling, parent, or guardian to help you make changes and stick with your new habits.

> ✔ **Quick Tip**
> **What You Can Do At School**
>
> Form a group of students and ask the principal for healthier food choices in the cafeteria or in vending machines.

- **Know that you can do it.** Stay positive and focused by remembering why you wanted to be healthier—to look, feel, move, and learn better. Accept relapses—if you fail at one of your nutrition goals one day, do not give up. Just try again the next day. Also, share this information with your family. They can support you in adopting healthier behaviors.

Chapter 45

Eating Healthy As A Vegetarian

For much of the world, vegetarianism is largely a matter of economics: Meat costs a lot more than, say, beans or rice, so meat becomes a special-occasion dish (if it's eaten at all). Even where meat is more plentiful, it's still used in moderation, often providing a side note to a meal rather than taking center stage.

In countries like the United States where meat is not as expensive, though, people choose to be vegetarians for reasons other than cost. Parental preferences, religious or other beliefs, and health issues are among the most common reasons for choosing to be a vegetarian. Many people choose a vegetarian diet out of concern over animal rights or the environment. And lots of people have more than one reason for choosing vegetarianism.

Vegetarian And Semi-Vegetarian Diets

Different people follow different forms of vegetarianism. A true vegetarian eats no meat at all, including chicken and fish. A lacto-ovo vegetarian eats dairy products and eggs, but excludes meat, fish, and poultry. It follows, then, that a lacto vegetarian eats dairy products but not eggs, whereas an ovo vegetarian eats eggs but not dairy products.

About This Chapter: "Becoming a Vegetarian," September 2006, reprinted with permission from www.kidshealth.org. Copyright © 2006 The Nemours Foundation. This information was provided by KidsHealth, one of the largest resources online for medically reviewed health information written for parents, kids, and teens. For more articles like this one, visit www.KidsHealth.org, or www.TeensHealth.org.

A stricter form of vegetarianism is veganism (pronounced: vee-gun-izm). Not only are eggs and dairy products excluded from a vegan diet, so are animal products like honey and gelatin.

Some macrobiotic diets fall into the vegan category. Macrobiotic diets restrict not only animal products but also refined and processed foods, foods with preservatives, and foods that contain caffeine or other stimulants.

Following a macrobiotic or vegan diet could lead to nutritional deficiencies in some people. Teens need to be sure their diets include enough nutrients to fuel growth, particularly protein and calcium. If you're interested in following a vegan or macrobiotic diet, it's a good idea to talk to a registered dietitian. He or she can help you design meal plans that include adequate vitamins and minerals.

Some people consider themselves semi-vegetarians and eat fish and maybe a small amount of poultry as part of a diet that's primarily made up of vegetables, fruits, grains, legumes, seeds, and nuts. A pesci-vegetarian eats fish, but not poultry.

Are These Diets OK for Teens?

In the past, choosing not to eat meat or animal-based foods was considered unusual in the United States. Times and attitudes have changed dramatically, however. Vegetarians are still a minority in the United States, but a large and growing one. The American Dietetic Association (ADA) has officially endorsed vegetarianism, stating "appropriately planned vegetarian

✔ Quick Tip
Some foods that appear to be vegetarian aren't. Most cheeses are made using an animal-derived product called rennet. Other ingredients that show up in seemingly vegetarian foods include gelatin, which is made from meat byproducts, and enzymes, which may be animal derived.

Source: Copyright © 2006 The Nemours Foundation.

diets are healthful, are nutritionally adequate, and provide health benefits in the prevention and treatment of certain diseases."

So what does this mean for you? If you're already a vegetarian, or are thinking of becoming one, it means that you're in good company. There are more choices in the supermarket than ever before, and an increasing number of restaurants and schools are providing vegetarian options—way beyond a basic peanut butter and jelly sandwich.

If you're choosing a vegetarian diet, the most important thing you can do is to educate yourself. That's why the ADA says that a vegetarian diet needs to be "appropriately planned." Simply dropping certain foods from your diet isn't the way to go if you're interested in maintaining good health, a high energy level, and strong muscles and bones.

Vegetarians have to be careful to include the following key nutrients that may be lacking in a vegetarian diet:

- Iron
- Calcium
- Protein
- Vitamin D
- Vitamin B12
- Zinc

If meat, fish, dairy products, and/or eggs are not going to be part of your diet, you'll need to know how to get enough of these nutrients, or you may need to take a daily multiple vitamin and mineral supplement.

Here are some suggestions:

Iron

Sea vegetables like nori, wakame, and dulse are very high in iron. Less exotic but still good options are iron-fortified breakfast cereals, legumes (chickpeas, lentils, and baked beans), soybeans and tofu, dried fruit (raisins and figs), pumpkin seeds, broccoli, and blackstrap molasses. Eating these foods along with a food high in vitamin C (citrus fruits and juices, tomatoes, and broccoli) will help you to absorb the iron better.

Girls need to be particularly concerned about getting adequate iron because some iron is lost during menstruation. Some girls who are vegetarians may not get adequate iron from vegetable sources, and they may require a daily supplement. Check with your doctor about your own iron needs.

Calcium

Milk and yogurt are tops if you're eating dairy products— although vegetarians will want to look for yogurt that does not contain the meat by-product gelatin. Tofu, fortified soy milk, calcium-fortified orange juice, green leafy vegetables, and dried figs are also excellent ways for vegetarians (and vegans) to get calcium. Remember that as a teen you're building up your bones for the rest of your life.

Because women have a greater risk for getting osteoporosis (weak bones) as adults, it's particularly important for girls to make sure they get enough calcium. Again, taking a supplement may be necessary to ensure this.

Vitamin D

People need vitamin D to get calcium into our bones. Cow's milk and sunshine are tops on the list for this vitamin. Vegans can try fortified soy milk and fortified breakfast cereals, but they may need a supplement that includes vitamin D, especially during the winter months. Everyone should have some exposure to the sun to help the body produce vitamin D.

Protein

Some people believe that vegetarians must combine incomplete plant proteins in one meal—like red beans and rice—to make the type of complete proteins found in meat. We now know that it's not that complicated. Current recommendations are that vegetarians eat a wide variety of foods during the course of a day. Eggs and dairy products are good sources of protein, but also try nuts, peanut butter, tofu, beans, seeds, soy milk, grains, cereals, and vegetables to get all the protein your body needs.

Vitamin B12

B12 is an essential vitamin found only in animal products, including eggs and dairy. Fortified soy milk and fortified breakfast cereals also have this important vitamin. It's hard to get enough vitamin B12 in your diet if you are vegan, so a supplement may be needed.

Zinc

If you're not eating dairy foods, make sure fortified cereals, dried beans, nuts, and soy products, like tofu and tempeh, are part of your diet so you can meet your daily requirement for this important mineral.

In addition to vitamins and minerals, vegetarians need to keep an eye on their total intake of calories and fat. Vegetarian diets tend to be high in fiber and low in fat and calories. That may be good for people who need to lose weight or lower their cholesterol, but it can be a problem for kids and teens who are still growing and people who are already at a healthy weight.

Diets that are high in fiber tend to be more filling, and as a result strict vegetarians may feel full before they've eaten enough calories to keep their bodies healthy and strong. It's a good idea to let your doctor know that you're a vegetarian so that he or she can keep on eye on your growth and make sure you're still getting adequate amounts of calories and fat.

Getting Some Guidance

If you're thinking about becoming a vegetarian, consider making an appointment to talk with a registered dietitian who can go over lists of foods that would give you the nutrients you need. A dietitian can discuss ways to prevent conditions such as iron-deficiency anemia that you might be at an increased risk for if you stop eating meat.

Also, remember to take a daily standard multivitamin, just in case you miss getting enough vitamins or minerals that day.

Tips For Dining Out

Eating at restaurants can be difficult for vegetarians sometimes, but if you do eat fish, you can usually find something suitable on the menu. If not,

♣ It's A Fact!!

Vegetarianism And Disordered Eating

Whether vegetarian for health, religion, or for ethics, research exists about the benefits of a plant-based diet. Recent research also shows that a growing number of people, especially women in their late teens, are adopting vegetarian and vegan diets in order to lose weight, maintain low body weight, and mask restrictive eating patterns. A study from the University of Minnesota found teen vegetarians are more likely to have eating disorders than non-vegetarians. In this study, vegetarians were more likely to contemplate and attempt suicide, and vegetarian males were noted as an especially high-risk group for unhealthy weight control practices. The research indicated that teens who were already susceptible to emotional difficulties were drawn to vegetarianism as a means to lose weight and fit in, but that vegetarianism itself had no correlation with emotional difficulties. In another study, conducted at California State University-Northridge, researchers found college women who claimed to be vegetarians had a significantly greater risk of developing eating disorders than their meat-eating peers. The overlap between eating disorders and vegetarianism occurs because vegetarianism is a way for men and women to openly control their food choices without attracting negative attention to their behavior. Also, many believe that restricting meat from their diet will lead to weight loss, believes Michelle Morand, founder of The CEDRIC Centre, an eating disorder counseling center in Victoria, British Columbia.

"Family, friends, clinicians, and vegetarians themselves, need to know that the potential exists for vegetarianism and veganism to mask an eating disorder," Morand said. This doesn't mean vegetarianism is the cause of an eating disorder, or that people shouldn't adopt a vegetarian lifestyle, but it may be a way for the individual who is struggling with food and weight issues to justify her or his restrictive eating behaviors. Carol Tickner, R.D. Nutrition Therapist with the Eating Disorders Program in the Capital Region, cites two possibilities for the

opt for salad and an appetizer or two. Even fast-food places sometimes have vegetarian choices, such as bean tacos and burritos, veggie burgers, and soy cheese pizza.

Vegetarians can opt for pasta, along with plenty of vegetables, grains, and fruits. You may also find that the veggie burgers, hot dogs, and chicken substitutes available in your local grocery store taste very much like the real increase in popularity of vegetarianism. "Vegetarianism has been promoted as a healthy way of managing weight. With weight being such a focus in our society, it makes sense to some as a way of managing weight, and health at the same time," she says. "For those teenagers who have disordered eating tendencies, becoming vegetarian can be a way of trying to respond to a changing body, (weight gain due to puberty) in a healthy way versus dieting like their friends." However, this is just dieting for weight loss in another form.

In many ways, beliefs about animal protein in diets versus plant-only diets are similar to the messages we hear about physical appearance in North American culture. In both cases, we are given conflicting messages. In one breath we're admonished not to judge a book by its cover; and in the next, we can never be too rich or too thin. In a similar vein, we say one thing about the humane treatment of animals and treat our pets as mini-humans, but frequently farm animals for food under dreadful conditions. This cultural hypocrisy is increasingly in the media with stories of unsanitary conditions and contamination of foods. And, at this stage in their lives, young adults are acutely aware of societal doubletalk. "Teenagers are searching for meaning and a way of being in the world that expresses their individuality. This is exactly what they are meant to do at this stage in development," says Morand. "They're in the process of individuation, separating from their parents, developing and testing their own value systems, and learning about who they are. By choosing a plant-based diet, they're choosing to exist on the planet in a different way than most of their parents' generation. For many teenagers, becoming a vegetarian may be the first informed adult decision they make.

Source: Excerpted from "Vegetarianism and Disordered Eating." Reprinted with permission. © 2004 National Eating Disorder Information Centre (www.nedic.ca). All rights reserved.

thing. Try the ground meat substitute as a stand-in for beef in foods like tacos and spaghetti sauce.

Regardless of whether you choose a vegetarian way of life, it's always a healthy idea to eat a wide variety of foods and try out new foods when you can.

Chapter 46

A Guide To Eating For Sports

There's a lot more to eating for sports than chowing down on carbs or chugging sports drinks. The good news is that eating to reach your peak performance level likely doesn't require a special diet or supplements. It's all about working the right foods into your fitness plan in the right amounts. Here are some basics.

Eat Extra For Excellence

Teen athletes have unique nutrition needs. Because athletes work out more than their less-active peers, they generally need extra calories to fuel both their sports performance and their growth. Depending on how active they are, teen athletes may need anywhere from 2,000 to 5,000 total calories per day to meet their energy needs.

So what happens if teen athletes don't eat enough? Their bodies are less likely to achieve peak performance and may even break down rather than build up muscles. Athletes who don't take in enough calories every day won't be as fast and as strong as they could be. And extreme calorie restriction could lead to growth problems and other serious health risks for both girls and guys.

About This Chapter: "A Guide to Eating for Sports," July 2005, reprinted with permission from www.kidshealth.org. Copyright © 2005 The Nemours Foundation. This information was provided by KidsHealth, one of the largest resources online for medically reviewed health information written for parents, kids, and teens. For more articles like this one, visit www.KidsHealth.org, or www.TeensHealth.org.

Since teen athletes need extra fuel, it's usually a bad idea for them to diet. Athletes in sports where weight is emphasized—such as wrestling, swimming, dance, or gymnastics—might feel pressure to lose weight, but they need to weigh that choice with the possible negative side effects mentioned above. If a coach, gym teacher, or teammate says that you need to go on a diet, talk to your doctor first or visit a dietitian who specializes in teen athletes. If a health professional you trust agrees that it's safe to diet, he or she can work with you to develop a plan that allows you to perform your best and lose weight.

Eat A Variety Of Foods

You may have heard about "carb loading" before a game. But when it comes to powering your game for the long haul, it's a bad idea to focus on only one type of food. Carbohydrates are an important source of fuel, but they're only one of many foods an athlete needs. It also takes vitamins, minerals, protein, and fats to stay in peak playing shape.

Muscular Minerals And Vital Vitamins

♣ **It's A Fact!!**
Supplements: All Talk And No Action

Your wallet may think a sports bar, powder, or vitamin is special because of the cost (and the hype). But guess what? Your body has no idea that it's eating a supplement and doesn't care where the protein or carbs are coming from—it's just as happy with regular food.

Source: The Nemours Foundation.

Calcium helps build the strong bones that athletes depend on, and iron carries oxygen to muscles. Most teens don't get enough of these minerals, and that's especially true of teen athletes because their needs may be even higher than those of other teens.

To get the iron you need, eat lean red meats (meats with not much fat on them); grains that are fortified with iron; and green, leafy vegetables. Calcium—a must for protecting against stress fractures—is found in dairy foods, such as low-fat milk, yogurt, and cheese.

In addition to calcium and iron, you need a whole bunch of other vitamins and minerals that do everything from help you access energy to keep you from getting sick. Eating a balanced diet, including lots of different fruits and veggies, should provide the vitamins and minerals needed for good health and sports performance.

Protein Power

Athletes need slightly more protein than less-active teens, but most teen athletes get plenty of protein through regular eating. It's a myth that athletes need a huge daily intake of protein to build large, strong muscles. Muscle growth comes from regular training and hard work—not popping a pill. And taking in too much protein can actually harm the body, causing dehydration, calcium loss, and even kidney problems.

Good sources of protein are fish, lean meats and poultry, eggs, dairy, nuts, soy, and peanut butter.

Carb Charge

Carbohydrates provide athletes with an excellent source of fuel. Cutting back on carbs or following low-carb diets isn't a good idea for athletes because restricting carbohydrates can cause a person to feel tired and worn out, which ultimately affects performance.

Nutrition experts advise people to choose whole grains (such as brown rice, oatmeal, sweet potatoes, whole wheat bread, and starchy vegetables like corn and peas) more often than their more processed counterparts like white rice and white bread. That's because whole grains provide both the energy athletes need to perform and the fiber and other nutrients they need to be healthy. Sugary carbs such as candy bars or sodas are less healthy for athletes because they don't contain any of the other nutrients you need. In addition, eating candy bars or other sugary snacks just before practice or competition can give athletes a quick burst of energy and then leave them to "crash" or run out of energy before they've finished working out.

Fat Fuel

Everyone needs a certain amount of fat each day, and this is particularly true for athletes. That's because active muscles quickly burn through carbs and need fats for long-lasting energy. Like carbs, not all fats are created equal. Experts advise athletes to concentrate on healthier fats, such as the unsaturated fat found in most vegetable oils. Choosing when to eat fats is also important for athletes. Fatty foods can slow digestion, so it's a good idea to avoid eating these foods for a few hours before and after exercising.

Shun Supplements

Protein supplements and energy bars don't do a whole lot of good, but they won't really do you much harm either. But other types of supplements can really do some damage.

Anabolic steroids can seriously mess with a person's hormones, causing side effects like testicular shrinkage and baldness in guys and facial hair growth in girls. Steroids can cause mental health problems, including depression and serious mood swings. Some over-the-counter supplements contain hormones that are related to testosterone (such as dehydroepiandrosterone, or DHEA for short). These supplements have similar side effects to anabolic steroids. These and other sports supplements (like creatine, for example) have not been tested in people younger than 18. So the risks of taking them are not yet known.

Salt tablets are another supplement to watch out for. People take them to avoid dehydration, but salt tablets can actually lead a person to become dehydrated. In large amounts, salt can cause nausea, vomiting, cramps, and diarrhea and may damage the lining of the stomach. In general, you are better off drinking fluids in order to maintain hydration. Any salt you lose in sweat can usually be made up in one normal meal after exercise.

Ditch Dehydration

Speaking of dehydration, water is just as important to unlocking your game power as food. When you sweat during exercise, it's easy to become overheated, headachy, and worn out—especially in hot or humid weather. Even mild dehydration can affect an athlete's physical and mental performance.

There's no one-size-fits-all formula for how much water to drink. How much fluid each person needs depends on the individual's age, size, level of physical activity, and environmental temperature.

Experts recommend that athletes drink before and after exercise as well as every 15 to 20 minutes during exercise. In general, most athletes need one to two cups prior to exercise and one-half to one cup every 15 to 20 minutes throughout exercise. Don't wait until you feel thirsty, because thirst is a sign that your body has needed liquids for a while. But don't force yourself to drink more fluids than you may need either. It's hard to run when there's a lot of water sloshing around in your stomach.

If you like the taste of sports drinks better than regular water, then it's OK to drink them. But it's important to know that a sports drink is really no better for you than water unless you are exercising for more than 90 minutes or in really hot weather. The additional carbohydrates and electrolytes may improve performance in these conditions, but otherwise your body will do just as well with water.

Avoid drinking carbonated drinks or juice because they could give you a stomachache while you're competing.

Caffeine

Caffeine is a diuretic, meaning it causes a person to urinate (pee) more. It's not clear whether this causes dehydration or not; but to be safe, it's probably a good idea to stay away from too much caffeine if you'll be exercising in hot weather.

Although some studies have found that caffeine may help with endurance sports performance, it's good to weigh any benefits against potential problems. Too much caffeine can leave an athlete feeling anxious or jittery. It can also cause trouble sleeping. All of these can drag down a person's sports performance. Plus, taking certain medications—including supplements—can make caffeine's side effects seem even worse.

Game Day Eats

Most of your body's energy on game day will come from the foods you've eaten over the past several days. But you can boost your performance even more by paying attention to the food you eat on game day. Strive for a game-day diet rich in carbohydrates, moderate in protein, and low in fat. Here are some guidelines on what to eat and when:

- **Eat a meal two to four hours before the game or event.** Combine a serving of low-fiber fruit or vegetable (such as juice, plums, melons, cherries, or peaches) with a protein and carbohydrate meal (like a turkey or chicken sandwich, cereal and milk, or chicken noodle soup and yogurt).

- **Eat a snack less than two hours before the game.** If you haven't had time to have a pre-game meal, be sure to have a light snack such as crackers, a bagel, or low-fat yogurt.

It's a good idea to avoid eating anything for the hour before you compete or have practice because digestion requires energy—energy that you want to use to win. Also, eating too soon before any kind of activity can leave food in the stomach, making you feel full, bloated, crampy, and sick. Everyone is different, so get to know what works best for you. You may want to experiment with meal timing and how much to eat on practice days so that you are better prepared for game day.

Want to get an eating plan personalized for you? The U.S. government has developed a website, MyPyramid (www.mypyramid.gov), that tells a person how much to eat from different food groups based on age, gender, and activity level.

✔ **Quick Tip**

Carb Recharge

Experts recommend eating carbohydrates and protein after intense activity to replenish energy stores and speed recovery. Prep the body for future events by taking a sports drink or piece of fruit immediately after exercise followed by a balanced meal that includes all the food groups a couple of hours later.

Source: The Nemours Foundation.

Chapter 47

Exercise: How Much And What Kind?

You need to exercise for about 60 minutes every day. Setting aside 60 minutes all at once each day is one way to get in enough exercise. If you wait until the end of the day to squeeze it in, you probably will not exercise enough or at all. If you are not active for 60 minutes straight, it is okay to exercise for 10 or 20 minutes at a time throughout the day.

Different Exercises

No matter what your shape, there is an exercise for you

• Pick exercises you like to do and choose a few different options so you do not get bored.

• Aim to exercise most days of the week.

There are three levels of physical activity. They are as follows:

• **Light:** Not sweating; not breathing hard (slow walking, dancing)

• **Moderate:** Breaking a sweat; can talk but cannot sing (walking fast, dancing)

• **Vigorous:** Sweating, breathing hard, cannot talk or sing (running, swimming laps)

About This Chapter: GirlsHealth.gov, sponsored by the National Women's Health Information Center, U.S. Department of Health and Human Services, August 2007.

No matter what level you are exercising at, the activity can be one of two types.

What Kind Of Exercise Does Your Body Need?

Your exercise should increase your heart rate and move the muscles in your body. Swimming, dancing, skating, playing soccer, or riding a bike are all examples of exercise that does these things.

✔ Quick Tip
If you are not very active right now, start slowly and work your way up to being active every day.

Looking at fitness and your body closer up, your exercise should include something from each of these four basic fitness areas:

- Cardio-respiratory endurance is the same thing as aerobic endurance. It is the ability to exercise your heart and lungs nonstop over certain time periods. When you exercise, your heart beats faster, sending more needed oxygen to your body. If you are not fit, your heart and lungs have to work harder during exercise. Long runs and swims are examples of activities that can help your heart and lungs work better.

- Muscular strength is the ability to move a muscle against resistance. To become stronger, you need to push or pull against resistance, such as your own weight (like in push-ups), using free weights (note: talk to an instructor before using weights), or even pushing the vacuum cleaner. Regular exercise keeps all of your muscles strong and makes it easier to do daily physical tasks.

- Muscular endurance is the ability of a muscle, or a group of muscles, to keep pushing against resistance for a long period. Push-ups are often used to test endurance of arm and shoulder muscles. Aerobic exercise also helps to improve your muscular endurance. Activities such as running increase your heart rate and make your heart muscle stronger.

- Flexibility is the ability to move joints and use muscles as much as they can possibly be used. The sit-and-reach your toes test is a good measure of flexibility of the lower back and backs of the upper legs. When you are flexible, you are able to bend and reach with ease. Being flexible can help prevent injuries like pulled muscles. This is why warming

Table 47.1. Types Of Exercise

Exercise Type	What Is It?	Why Do It?
Resistance exercise (two or more days each week)	Weight-training using weight machines and resistance bands, or doing push-ups	Increases strength and builds muscles
Weight-bearing exercise	Walking, running, hiking, dancing, gymnastics, soccer, and other activities that work bones and muscles against gravity	Makes bones stronger

Table 47.2. Type Of Exercise And The Muscles Worked

Exercise	Muscles Worked
Push-ups	Chest, shoulders, arms, abdominals
Sit-ups	Abdominals
Jumping Jacks	Calves (lower leg), inner/outer thigh, butt
Running	Calves, front/back thigh
Jumping Rope	Calves, thighs, abdominals, shoulders, arms
Swimming	Nearly all major muscles
Dancing	Nearly all major muscles (depending on type of dance)
Walking	Arms, calves, front/back thigh, abdominals
Squats	Calves, front/back thigh, butt
Inline Skating	Inner/outer thigh, butt
Hula Hoop	Lower back, abdominals

up and stretching are so important. If you force your body to move in a way that you are not used to, you risk tearing muscles, as well as ligaments and tendons (other parts of your musculoskeletal system).

Chapter 48

Exercise And Weight Control

Just about everybody seems to be interested in weight control. Some of us weigh just the right amount and others need to gain a few pounds. Most of us "battle the bulge" at some time in our life. Whatever our goals, we should understand and take advantage of the important role of exercise in keeping our weight under control.

Carrying around too much body fat is a major nuisance. Yet excess body fat is common in modern-day living. Few of today's occupations require vigorous physical activity, and much of our leisure time is spent in sedentary pursuits.

Recent estimates indicate that 34 million adults are considered obese (20 percent above desirable weight). Also, there has been an increase in body fat levels in children and youth over the past 20 years. After infancy and early childhood, the earlier the onset of obesity, the greater the likelihood of remaining obese.

Excess body fat has been linked to such health problems as coronary heart disease, high blood pressure, osteoporosis, diabetes, arthritis, and certain forms of cancer. Some evidence now exists showing that obesity has a negative effect on both health and longevity.

About This Chapter: The President's Council on Physical Fitness and Sports, Department of Health and Human Services, October 2004.

Overweight Or Over-Fat?

Overweight and over-fat do not always mean the same thing. Some people are quite muscular and weigh more than the average for their age and height. However, their body composition, the amount of fat versus lean body mass (muscle, bone, organs and tissue), is within a desirable range. This is true for many athletes. Others weigh an average amount yet carry around too much fat.

♣ It's A Fact!!
Exercise is associated with the loss of body fat in both obese and normal weight persons. A regular program of exercise is an important component of any plan to help individuals lose, gain, or maintain their weight.

In our society, however, overweight often implies over-fat because excess weight is commonly distributed as excess fat. The addition of exercise to a weight control program helps control both body weight and body fat levels.

A certain amount of body fat is necessary for everyone. Experts say that percent body fat for women should be about 20 percent, 15 percent for men. Women with more than 30 percent fat and men with more than 25 percent fat are considered obese.

How much of your weight is fat can be assessed by a variety of methods including underwater (hydrostatic) weighing, skin-fold thickness measurements, and circumference measurements. Each requires a specially trained person to administer the test and perform the correct calculations. From the numbers obtained, a body fat percentage is determined. Assessing body composition has an advantage over the standard height-weight tables because it can help distinguish between "overweight" and "over-fat."

An easy self-test you can do is to pinch the thickness of the fat folds at your waist and abdomen. If you can pinch an inch or more of fat (make sure no muscle is included) chances are you have too much body fat.

People who exercise appropriately increase lean body mass while decreasing their overall fat level. Depending on the amount of fat loss, this can result in a loss of inches without a loss of weight, since muscle weighs more than fat. However, with the proper combination of diet and exercise, both body fat and overall weight can be reduced.

Energy Balance: A Weighty Concept

Losing weight, gaining weight, or maintaining your weight depends on the amount of calories you take in and use up during the day, otherwise referred to as energy balance. Learning how to balance energy intake (calories in food) with energy output (calories expended through physical activity) will help you achieve your desired weight.

Although the underlying causes and the treatments of obesity are complex, the concept of energy balance is relatively simple. If you eat more calories than your body needs to perform your day's activities, the extra calories are stored as fat. If you do not take in enough calories to meet your body's energy needs, your body will go to the stored fat to make up the difference. (Exercise helps ensure that stored fat, rather than muscle tissue, is used to meet your energy needs.) If you eat just about the same amount of calories to meet your body's energy needs, your weight will stay the same.

On the average, a person consumes between 800,000 and 900,000 calories each year. An active person needs more calories than a sedentary person, as physically active people require energy above and beyond the day's basic needs. All too often, people who want to lose weight concentrate on counting calorie intake while neglecting calorie output. The most powerful formula is the combination of dietary modification with exercise.

Counting Calories

Each pound of fat your body stores represents 3,500 calories of unused energy. In order to lose one pound, you would have to create a calorie deficit of 3,500 calories by either taking in 3,500 less calories over a period of time than you need or doing 3,500 calories worth of exercise. It is recommended that no more than two pounds (7,000 calories) be lost per week for lasting weight loss.

Adding 15 minutes of moderate exercise, like walking one mile, to your daily schedule will use up 100 extra calories per

♣ It's A Fact!!
By increasing your daily physical activity and decreasing your caloric input, you can lose excess weight in the most efficient and healthful way.

day. (Your body uses approximately 100 calories of energy to walk one mile, depending on your body weight.) Maintaining this schedule would result in an extra 700 calories per week used up, or a loss of about 10 pounds in one year, assuming your food intake stays the same. To look at energy balance another way, just one extra slice of bread or one extra soft drink a day—or any other food that contains approximately 100 calories—can add up to ten extra pounds in a year if the amount of physical activity you do does not increase.

If you already have a lean figure and want to keep it, you should exercise regularly and eat a balanced diet that provides enough calories to make up for the energy you expend. If you wish to gain weight you should exercise regularly and increase the number of calories you consume until you reach your desired weight. Exercise will help ensure that the weight you gain will be lean muscle mass, not extra fat.

The Diet Connection

A balanced diet should be part of any weight control plan. A diet high in complex carbohydrates and moderate in protein and fat will complement an exercise program. It should include enough calories to satisfy your daily nutrient requirements and include the proper number of servings per day from the "basic four food groups": vegetables and fruits (4 servings), breads and cereals (4 servings), milk and milk products (2–4 servings depending on age), and meats and fish (2 servings).

Experts recommend that your daily intake not fall below 1,200 calories unless you are under a doctor's supervision. Also, weekly weight loss should not exceed two pounds.

Remarkable claims have been made for a variety of "crash" diets and diet pills, and some of these very restricted diets do result in noticeable weight loss in a short time. Much of this loss is water, and such a loss is quickly regained when normal food and liquid intake is resumed. These diet plans are often expensive and may be dangerous. Moreover, they

♣ It's A Fact!!
Dieting alone will result in a loss of valuable body tissue such as muscle mass in addition to a loss in fat.

do not emphasize lifestyle changes that will help you maintain your desired weight.

How Many Calories

The estimates for number of calories (energy) used during a physical activity are based on experiments that measure the amount of oxygen consumed during a specific bout of exercise for a certain body weight.

The energy costs of activities that require you to move your own body weight, such as walking or jogging, are greater for heavier people since they have more weight to move. For example, a person weighing 150 pounds would use more calories jogging one mile than a person jogging alongside who weighs 115 pounds. Always check to see what body weight is referred to in caloric expenditure charts you use.

Exercise And Modern Living

One thing is certain. Most people do not get enough exercise in their ordinary routines. All of the advances of modern technology—from electric can openers to power steering—have made life easier, more comfortable, and much less physically demanding. Yet our bodies need activity, especially if they are carrying around too much fat. Satisfying this need requires a definite plan and a commitment. There are two main ways to increase the number of calories you expend. They are as follows:

1. Start a regular exercise program if you do not have one already.

2. Increase the amount of physical activity in your daily routine.

The best way to control your weight is a combination of the above. The sum total of calories used over time will help regulate your weight as well as keep you physically fit.

Active Lifestyles

Before looking at what kind of regular exercise program is best, let's look at how you can increase the amount of physical activity in your daily routine to supplement your exercise program.

Table 48.1. Energy Expenditure Chart

Sedentary Activities	Energy Costs, Calories/Hour*
Lying down or sleeping	90
Sitting quietly	84
Sitting and writing, card playing, etc.	114
Moderate Activities	**(150–350)**
Bicycling (5 mph)	174
Canoeing (2.5 mph)	174
Dancing (ballroom)	210
Golf (two-some, carrying clubs)	324
Horseback riding (sitting to trot)	246
Light housework, cleaning, etc.	246
Swimming (crawl, 20 yards/min)	288
Tennis (recreational doubles)	312
Volleyball (recreational)	264
Walking (2 mph)	198
Vigorous Activities	**More than 350**
Aerobic dancing	546
Basketball (recreational)	450

- Recreational pursuits such as after school sports, inline skating, family outings, dancing, and many other activities provide added exercise. They are fun and can be considered an extra bonus in your weight control campaign.

- Add more "action" to your day. Walk to the store instead of asking for a ride. Walk up the stairs instead of using the elevator; start with one flight of steps and gradually increase.

- Change your attitude toward movement. Instead of considering an extra little walk an annoyance, look upon it as an added fitness boost.

Table 48.1. Energy Expenditure Chart, continued

Vigorous Activities, continued	More than 350
Bicycling (13 mph)	612
Circuit weight training	756
Football (touch, vigorous)	498
Ice skating (9 mph)	384
Racquetball	588
Roller skating (9 mph)	384
Jogging (10-minute mile, 6 mph)	654
Scrubbing floors	440
Swimming (crawl, 45 yards/min)	522
Tennis (recreational singles)	450
Cross country skiing (5 mph)	690

*Hourly estimates based on values calculated for calories burned per minute for a 150-pound (68 kg) person.

Sources: William D. McArdle, Frank I. Katch, Victor L. Katch, *Exercise Physiology: Energy, Nutrition and Human Performance (2nd edition)*, Lea & Febiger, Philadelphia, 1986; Melvin H. Williams, *Nutrition for Fitness and Sport*, William C. Brown Company Publishers, Dubuque, 1983.

Look for opportunities to use your body. Bend, stretch, reach, move, lift, and carry. Timesaving devices and gadgets eliminate drudgery and are a bonus to mankind, but when they substitute too often for physical activity they can demand a high cost in health, vigor, and fitness.

These little bits of action are cumulative in their effects. Alone, each does not burn a huge amount of calories, but when added together they can result in a sizable amount of energy used over the course of the day. They will also help improve your muscle tone and flexibility at the same time.

What Kind Of Exercise?

Although any kind of physical movement requires energy (calories), the type of exercise that uses the most energy is aerobic exercise. The term "aerobic" is derived from the Greek word meaning "with oxygen." Jogging, brisk walking, swimming, biking, cross-country skiing, and aerobic dancing are some popular forms of aerobic exercise.

Aerobic exercises use the body's large muscle groups in continuous, rhythmic, sustained movement and require oxygen for the production of energy. When oxygen is combined with food (which can come from stored fat) energy is produced to power the body's musculature. The longer you move aerobically, the more energy needed and the more calories used. Regular aerobic exercise will improve your cardio-respiratory endurance—the ability of your heart, lungs, blood vessels, and associated tissues to use oxygen to produce energy needed for activity. You will build a healthier body while getting rid of excess body fat.

In addition to the aerobic exercise, supplement your program with muscle strengthening and stretching exercises. The stronger your muscles, the longer you will be able to keep going during aerobic activity, and the less chance of injury.

How Much? How Often?

Experts recommend that you do some form of aerobic exercise at least three times a week for a minimum of 20 continuous minutes. Of course, if that is too much, start with a shorter time span and gradually build up to the minimum. Then gradually progress until you are able to work aerobically for 20–40 minutes. If you need to lose a large amount of weight, you may want to do your aerobic workout five times a week.

It is important to exercise at an intensity vigorous enough to cause your heart rate and breathing to increase. How hard you should exercise depends to a certain degree on your age and is determined by measuring your heart rate in beats per minute.

The heart rate you should maintain is called your target heart rate, and there are several ways you can arrive at this figure. The simplest is to subtract your age from 220 and then calculate 60 to 80 percent of that figure. Beginners should maintain the 60 percent level—more advanced can work up to the 80 percent level. This is just a guide however, and people with any medical limitations should discuss this formula with their physician.

You can do different types of aerobic activities, like walking one day and riding a bike the next. Make sure you choose an activity that can be done regularly and is enjoyable for you. The important thing to remember is not to skip too many days between workouts, or fitness benefits will be lost. If you must lose a few days, gradually work back into your routine.

The Benefits Of Exercise In A Weight Control Program

The benefits of exercise are many—from producing physically fit bodies to providing an outlet for fun and socialization. When added to a weight control program these benefits take on increased significance.

We already have noted that proper exercise can help control weight by burning excess body fat. It also has two other body-trimming advantages: 1) exercise builds muscle tissue, and muscle uses calories up at a faster rate than body fat; and 2) exercise helps reduce inches and a firm, lean body looks slimmer even if your weight remains the same.

Remember, fat does not "turn into" muscle, as is often believed. Fat and muscle are two entirely different substances, and one cannot become the other. However, muscle does use calories at a faster rate than fat, which directly affects your body's metabolic rate or energy requirement. Your basal metabolic rate (BMR) is the amount of energy required to sustain the body's functions at rest, and it depends on your age, sex, body size, genes, and body composition. People with high levels of muscle tend to have higher BMRs and use more calories in the resting stage.

Some studies have even shown that your metabolic rate stays elevated for some time after vigorous exercise, causing you to use even more calories throughout your day. Additional benefits may be seen in how exercise affects appetite. A lean person in good shape may eat more following increased activity, but the regular exercise will burn up the extra calories consumed. On the other hand, vigorous exercise has been reported to suppress appetite, and

✔ Quick Tip

Tips To Get You Started

Hopefully, you are now convinced that in order to successfully manage your weight, you must include exercise in your daily routine. Here are some tips to get you started:

• Check with your doctor first. Since you are carrying around some extra "baggage," it is wise to get your doctor's "OK" before embarking on an exercise program.

• Choose activities that you think you will enjoy. Most people will stick to their exercise program if they are having fun, even though they are working hard.

• Set aside a regular exercise time. Whether this means joining an exercise class or getting up a little earlier every day, make time for this addition to your routine and do not let anything get in your way. Planning ahead will help you get around interruptions in your workout schedule, such as bad weather and vacations.

• Set short-term goals. Do not expect to lose 20 pounds in two weeks. It has taken awhile for you to gain the weight; it will take time to lose it. Keep a record of your progress and tell your friends and family about your achievements.

physical activity can be used as a positive substitute for between meal snacking.

Better Mental Health

The psychological benefits of exercise are equally important to the weight conscious person. Exercise decreases stress and relieves tensions that might otherwise lead to overeating. Exercise builds physical fitness, which in turn builds self-confidence, enhanced self-image, and a positive outlook. When you start to feel good about yourself, you are more likely to want to make other positive changes in your lifestyle that will help keep your weight under control.

• Vary your exercise program. Change exercises or invite friends to join you to make your workout more enjoyable. There is no "best" exercise—just the one that works best for you. It will not be easy, especially at the start; but as you begin to feel better, look better, and enjoy a new zest for life, you will be rewarded many times over for your efforts.

Tips To Keep You Going

• Adopt a specific plan and write it down.

• Keep setting realistic goals as you go along and remind yourself of them often.

• Keep a log to record your progress and make sure to keep it up-to-date.

• Include weight and/or percent body fat measures in your log. Extra pounds can easily creep back.

• Upgrade your fitness program as you progress.

• Enlist the support and company of your family and friends.

• Update others on your successes.

• Avoid injuries by pacing yourself and including a warm-up and cool down period as part of every workout.

• Reward yourself periodically for a job well done.

In addition, exercise can be fun, provide recreation, and offer opportunities for companionship. The exhilaration and emotional release of participating in sports or other activities are a boost to mental and physical health. Pent-up anxieties and frustrations seem to disappear when you are concentrating on returning a serve, sinking a putt, or going that extra mile.

Chapter 49

What Is A Healthy Weight?

Worried About Your Weight?

Some teens have a hard time knowing what a healthy weight is, especially with all the body changes that are taking place. Girls especially may think they need to be thinner even if they are not overweight. If you are worried about your weight, talk to your family doctor. Your doctor can help you find the best way to be at a weight that is healthy for you. This may include having you see an expert in nutrition, called a nutritionist or a dietitian. And remember, weight gains are a normal part of growing up.

If a doctor tells you that you should lose weight, it is best to increase your exercise as the first step. Often that is all teens need to do for weight control because they are rapidly growing and changing. If changing what you eat is also needed, keep eating a variety of foods while cutting down on foods and drinks with extra calories like fats and sugars.

If you need to gain weight, a doctor or nutritionist can help you make a plan that is right for you.

About This Chapter: Information in this chapter is from "What's a Healthy Weight," GirlsHealth.gov, sponsored by the National Women's Health Information Center, U.S. Department of Health and Human Services, July 2007.

Thinking Of Going On A Diet?

Many teens that go on diets do not need to lose weight. Pressure from media images, friends, and sometimes parents, to be very slim may cause you to have a distorted body image. Having a distorted body image is like looking into a funhouse mirror. You see yourself as fatter than you really are.

It can be hard to get the nutrients you need if you eat less than 1,600 calories per day, so do not go below this level unless you are under a doctor's care. You cannot make up for the nutrients you are not getting on such a strict diet by taking a multivitamin.

If you are into sports, taking in fewer calories could hurt your athletic performance. In fact, if you are an athlete, you will need to eat even more healthy grains. Also, never drink less water to lose weight. Skipping meals to lose weight is not a good idea either. You are likely to overeat at the next meal just because you are so hungry, and studies show that people who skip breakfast or other meals tend to have poorer nutrition than those who eat regular meals.

Instead of dieting because your friends are doing it or because you are not as thin as you want to be, first find out from a doctor or nutritionist whether you are carrying too much body fat for your age. With their help, make healthy lifestyle choices to reach a healthy weight. A loss of ½ to 2 pounds a week is usually safe, and losing weight slowly makes it easier to keep off.

What You Should And Should Not Do For Healthy Weight Management

- **Do:** Change your habits to focus on healthy foods and exercise. Overweight or not, regular daily exercise is important to look and feel your best. If you do need to lose weight, stepping up your activity level will help. Exercise increases your lean body tissue, which will help you burn calories more quickly.

- **Don't:** Don't skip meals, eat only bread and water, take diet pills or dietary supplements, or make yourself vomit. You may make it through the end of the week and maybe even lose a pound or two, but you are unlikely to keep the weight off. Forced-vomiting is a sign of an eating disorder called bulimia, which can cause serious health problems.

• **Do:** A healthy diet is one that has balance, variety, and healthy serving sizes. Limit the amount of high-calorie foods that you eat. If high fat foods are among your favorites, balance those foods with fruits and vegetables, which are generally lower in fat and calories.

• **Don't:** Don't deprive yourself of foods you love, because you will be more likely to binge or over eat; and you may gain even more weight.

• **Do:** Try to eat a wide variety of foods to keep from getting bored and to make sure your diet is balanced. Keep portion sizes reasonable so that you can have a dessert once in a while without taking in too many calories.

✔ **Quick Tip**

Healthy Snack Ideas

• Baked potato chips or tortilla chips with salsa
• Pretzels (lightly salted or unsalted)
• Bagels with tomato sauce and low-fat cheese (low-fat version of a pizza)
• Flavored rice cakes (like caramel or apple cinnamon)
• Popcorn (air popped or low-fat microwave)
• Veggies with low fat or fat-free dip
• Low-fat cottage cheese topped with fruit or spread on whole-wheat crackers
• Ice milk, low-fat frozen or regular yogurt (add skim milk, orange, or pineapple juice, and sliced bananas or strawberries to make a low-fat milk shake)
• Frozen fruit bars
• Vanilla wafers, gingersnaps, graham crackers, animal crackers, fig bars, raisins
• Angel food cake topped with strawberries or raspberries and low-fat whipped cream
• String cheese

Source: GirlsHealth.gov.

- **Don't:** Low-calorie diets that allow only a few types of foods can be bad for your health because they do not allow you to get enough vitamins and minerals. Quick weight loss from very low-calorie "starvation diets" can cause serious health problems in teenagers, such as gallstones, hair loss, fatigue, and diarrhea.

- **Do:** Another way to lower your calorie intake is to replace the regular foods you eat with lower-fat options. Try these tips:

  - Switch to one percent or fat-free milk instead of whole milk

---

♣ **It's A Fact!!**

Body Mass Index (BMI)

What is BMI?

BMI is a number calculated from a child's weight and height. BMI is a reliable indicator of body fatness for most children and teens. BMI does not measure body fat directly, but research has shown that BMI correlates to direct measures of body fat, such as underwater weighing and dual energy x-ray absorptiometry (DXA). BMI can be considered an alternative for direct measures of body fat. Additionally, BMI is an inexpensive and easy-to-perform method of screening for weight categories that may lead to health problems.

For children and teens, BMI is age- and sex-specific and is often referred to as BMI-for-age.

What is a BMI percentile?

After BMI is calculated for children and teens, the BMI number is plotted on the Centers for Disease Control and Prevention (CDC) BMI-for-age growth charts (for either girls or boys) to obtain a percentile ranking. Percentiles are the most commonly used indicator to assess the size and growth patterns of individual children in the United States. The percentile indicates the relative position of the child's BMI number among children of the same sex and age. The growth charts show the weight status categories used with children and teens (underweight, healthy weight, at risk of overweight, and overweight).

- Try nonfat or low fat frozen yogurt, or nonfat or low-fat ice cream, instead of regular ice cream

- Have pretzels instead of corn chips or potato chips

- Switch your fries for a small baked potato with a little low-fat sour cream

Remember, low fat does not always mean low calorie. For example, extra sugars may be added to low-fat muffins or desserts to make them taste better, but they may be just as high in calories as the regular kinds.

BMI-for-age weight status categories and the corresponding percentiles are shown in Table 49.1.

How is BMI used with children and teens?

BMI is used as a screening tool to identify possible weight problems for children. CDC and the American Academy of Pediatrics (AAP) recommend the use of BMI to screen for overweight in children beginning at two years old.

For children, BMI is used to screen for overweight, at risk of overweight, or underweight. However, BMI is not a diagnostic tool. For example, a child may have a high BMI for age and sex; but to determine if excess fat is a problem, a health care provider would need to perform further assessments. These assessments might include skin-fold thickness measurements, evaluations of diet, physical activity, family history, and other appropriate health screenings.

Why can't healthy weight ranges be provided for children and teens?

Healthy weight ranges cannot be provided for children and teens for the following reasons:

- Healthy weight ranges change with each month of age for each sex.

- Healthy weight ranges change as height increases.

Source: Excerpted from "About BMI for Children and Teens," Centers for Disease Control and Prevention, May 2007.

Table 49.1. BMI-for-Age Weight Status Categories and Corresponding Percentiles

Weight Status Category	Percentile Range
Underweight	Less than the 5th percentile
Healthy weight	5th percentile to less than the 85th percentile
At risk of overweight	85th to less than the 95th percentile
Overweight	Equal to or greater than the 95th percentile

- **Don't:** Don't believe advertisers trying to sell you miracle foods that burn fat. Foods do not burn fat; they make fat when we eat more than we need. Also, stay away from diets that claim you can lose weight without exercise or say you will lose more than two pounds per week.

Do I Have To Give Up Some Of My Favorite Foods?

Healthy eating does not mean you have to give up all your favorite foods. You can be picky about what you eat and still also eat foods you enjoy.

A nutritionist will tell you to eat an apple or celery sticks if you want a healthy snack. But can you imagine serving celery sticks, tofu kabobs, and rice cakes when "the gang" comes over to watch a video? Even the most health-conscious among us has to admit that there are times when only cookies, chips, crackers, dips, and spreads will do.

Many well-known brands of snack foods are now available in reduced-fat or reduced-sodium versions so that you do not have to be a party pooper. The trick is to find lower calorie, fat, or salt versions of your favorite snacks. Compare the amount that makes up a portion with the amount you normally eat so you can include snack foods in your diet without overdosing on fat and salt.

Healthy Ways To Gain Weight

Have you ever been teased about being too thin? Have ever been called too skinny to the point that it began to worry you? Although most teen girls are concerned about being overweight, some may be worried about being too thin.

If this is your concern, first talk to your parent(s) and your doctor. Also, check your body mass index (BMI) to see if you are underweight for your height. Here are some tips for gaining weight the healthy way:

- **Eat More:** You may think "duh," but many people might not think of this right away. Extra calories above your daily needs can add pounds. Just try to pick foods rich in nutrients, such as complex carbohydrates (whole wheat breads, pasta, or potatoes), milk or other dairy products, or "good fat" (avocado, peanut butter, and olive or canola oil).

- **Increase "Good Fat":** Increasing mono- and polyunsaturated fats, found in foods such as olive oil, canola oil, peanut butter, avocados, and nuts, can be good for you, as well as adding some pounds to your weight.

Chapter 50

How Can I Lose Weight Safely?

Weight loss is a tricky topic. Lots of people are unhappy with their present weight, but most aren't sure how to change it—and many would be better off staying where they are. You may want to look like the models or actors in magazines and on TV, but those goals might not be healthy or realistic for you. Besides, no magical diet or pill will make you look like someone else.

So what should you do about weight control?

Being healthy is really about being at a weight that is right for you. The best way to find out if you are at a healthy weight, or if you need to lose or gain weight, is to talk to a doctor or dietitian who can compare your weight with healthy norms to help you set realistic goals. If it turns out that you can benefit from weight loss, then you can follow a few of the simple suggestions listed below to get started.

Weight management is about long-term success. People who lose weight quickly by crash dieting or other extreme measures usually gain back all (and often more) of the pounds they lost because they haven't permanently changed their habits. Therefore, the best weight-management strategies are those that

About This Chapter: "How Can I Lose Weight Safely?" October 2007, reprinted with permission from www.kidshealth.org. Copyright © 2007 The Nemours Foundation. This information was provided by KidsHealth, one of the largest resources online for medically reviewed health information written for parents, kids, and teens. For more articles like this one, visit www.KidsHealth.org, or www.TeensHealth.org.

you can maintain for a lifetime. That's a long time, so we'll try to keep these suggestions as easy as possible.

Make it a family affair. Ask your mom or dad to lend help and support and to make dietary or lifestyle changes that will benefit the whole family, if possible. Teens who have the support of their families tend to have better results with their weight-management programs. But remember, you should all work together in a friendly and helpful way—making weight loss into a competition is a recipe for disaster.

♣ It's A Fact!!
Skipping Breakfast To Cut Calories?

Guess what—you may end up gaining rather than losing weight. Studies show that teens who don't eat breakfast have a higher body mass index. So make time for breakfast.

Source: The Nemours Foundation.

Watch your drinks. It's amazing how many extra calories can be lurking in the sodas, juices, and other drinks that you take in every day. Simply cutting out a can of soda or one sports drink can save you 150 calories or more each day. Drink water or other sugar-free drinks to quench your thirst and stay away from sugary juices and sodas. Switching from whole to nonfat or low-fat milk is also a good idea.

Start small. Small changes are a lot easier to stick with than drastic ones. Try reducing the size of the portions you eat and giving up regular soda for a week. Once you have that down, start gradually introducing healthier foods and exercise into your life.

Stop eating when you're full. Lots of people eat when they're bored, lonely, or stressed, or keep eating long after they're full out of habit. Try to pay attention as you eat and stop when you're full. Slowing down can help because it takes about 20 minutes for your brain to recognize how much is in your stomach. Sometimes taking a break before going for seconds can keep you from eating another serving.

Avoid eating when you feel upset or bored—try to find something else to do instead (a walk around the block or a trip to the gym are good alternatives).

Many people find it's helpful to keep a diary of what they eat and when. Reviewing the diary later can help them identify the emotions they have when they overeat or whether they have unhealthy habits. A registered dietitian can give you pointers on how to do this.

Eat less more often. Many people find that eating a couple of small snacks throughout the day helps them to make healthy choices at meals. Stick a couple of healthy snacks (carrot sticks, whole-grain pretzels, or a piece of fruit) in your backpack so that you can have one or two snacks during the day. Adding healthy snacks to your three squares and eating smaller portions when you sit down to dinner can help you to cut calories without feeling deprived.

Five a day keep the pounds away. Ditch the junk food and dig out the fruits and veggies. Five servings of fruits and veggies aren't just a good idea to help you lose weight—they'll help keep your heart and the rest of your body healthy. Other suggestions for eating well: replace white bread with whole wheat, trade your sugary sodas for water and low-fat milk, and make sure you eat a healthy breakfast. Having low-sugar, whole-grain cereal and low-fat milk with a piece of fruit is a much better idea than inhaling a donut as you run to the bus stop or eating no breakfast at all. A registered dietitian can give you lots of other snack and menu ideas.

Avoid fad diets. It's never a good idea to trade meals for shakes or to give up a food group in the hope that you'll lose weight—we all need a variety of foods to stay healthy. Stay away from fad diets because you're still growing and need to make sure you get proper nutrients. Avoid diet pills (even the over-the-counter or herbal variety). They can be dangerous to your health; besides, there's no evidence that they help keep weight off over the long term.

Don't banish certain foods. Don't tell yourself you'll never again eat your absolutely favorite peanut butter chocolate ice cream or a bag of chips from the vending machine at school. Making these foods forbidden is sure to make you want them even more. Also, don't go fat free. You need to have some fat in your diet to stay healthy, so giving up all fatty foods all the time isn't a good idea. The key to long-term success is making healthy choices most of the time. If you want a piece of cake at a party, go for it. But munch on the carrots rather than the chips to balance it out.

♣ It's A Fact!!
How many teaspoons of sugar are in a typical can of soda?
Ten—more grams of sugar than in a chocolate candy bar.
Source: The Nemours Foundation.

Get moving. You may find that you don't need to cut calories as much as you need to get off your behind. Don't get stuck in the rut of thinking you have to play a team sport or take an aerobics class to get exercise. Try a variety of activities from hiking to cycling to dancing until you find ones you like.

Not a jock? Find other ways to fit activity into your day. Walk to school, jog up and down the stairs a couple of times before your morning shower, turn off the tube and help your parents in the garden, or take a stroll past your crush's house—anything that gets you moving. Your goal should be to work up to 60 minutes of exercise every day. But everyone has to begin somewhere. It's fine to start out by simply taking a few turns around the block before bed and building up your levels of fitness gradually.

Build muscle. Muscle burns more calories than fat. So adding strength training to your exercise routine can help you reach your weight loss goals as well as give you a toned bod. And weights are not the only way to go. Try resistance bands, Pilates, or push-ups to get strong. A good, well-balanced fitness routine includes aerobic workouts, strength training, and flexibility exercises.

Forgive yourself. So you were going to have one cracker with spray cheese on it and the next thing you know the can's pumping air and the box is empty? Drink some water, brush your teeth, and move on. Everyone who's ever tried to lose weight has found it challenging. When you slip up, the best idea is to get right back on track and don't look back. Avoid telling yourself that you'll get back on track tomorrow or next week or after New Year's. Start now.

Try to remember that losing weight isn't going to make you a better person—and it won't magically change your life. It's a good idea to maintain a healthy weight because it's just that—healthy.

Chapter 51

Choosing A Safe And Successful Weight Loss Program

Choosing a weight loss program may be a difficult task. You may not know what to look for in a weight loss program or what questions to ask. This chapter can help you talk to your health care professional about weight loss and get the best information before choosing a program.

Talk With Your Health Care Professional

You may want to talk with your doctor or other health care professional about controlling your weight before you decide on a weight loss program. Even if you feel uncomfortable talking about your weight with your doctor, remember that he or she is there to help you improve your health. Here are some tips:

- Tell your provider that you would like to talk about your weight. Share your concerns about any medical conditions you have or medicines you are taking.

- Write down your questions in advance.

- Bring pen and paper to take notes.

About This Chapter: Information in this chapter is from "Choosing a Safe and Successful Weight-loss Program," NIH Publication No. 03-3700, Weight-control Information Network, an information service of the National Institute of Diabetes and Digestive and Kidney Diseases, National Institutes of Health, February 2006.

- Bring a friend or family member along for support if this will make you feel more comfortable.

- Make sure you understand what your health care provider is saying. Ask questions if there is something you do not understand.

- Ask for other sources of information like brochures or websites.

- If you want more support, ask for a referral to a registered dietitian, a support group, or a commercial weight loss program.

- Call your provider after your visit if you have more questions or need help.

> ✔ **Quick Tip**
>
> If your health care provider tells you that you should lose weight and you want to find a weight loss program to help you, look for one that is based on regular physical activity and an eating plan that is balanced, healthy, and easy to follow.
>
> Source: Weight-control Information Network.

Ask Questions

Find out as much as you can about your health needs before joining a weight loss program. There are some questions you might want to ask your health care provider.

About Your Weight

- Do I need to lose weight? Or should I just avoid gaining more?

- Is my weight affecting my health?

- Could my excess weight be caused by a medical condition such as hypothyroidism or by a medicine I am taking? (Hypothyroidism is when your thyroid gland does not produce enough thyroid hormone, a condition that can slow your metabolism—how your body creates and uses energy.)

About Weight Loss

- What should my weight loss goal be?

- How will losing weight help me?

About Nutrition And Physical Activity

- How should I change my eating habits?

- What kinds of physical activity can I do?

- How much physical activity do I need?

About Treatment

- Could a weight loss program help me?

A Responsible And Safe Weight Loss Program

If your health care provider tells you that you should lose weight and you want to find a weight loss program to help you, look for one that is based on regular physical activity and an eating plan that is balanced, healthy, and easy to follow. Weight loss programs should encourage healthy behaviors that help you lose weight and that you can stick with every day. Safe and effective weight loss programs should include the following:

- Healthy eating plans that reduce calories but do not forbid specific foods or food groups

- Tips to increase moderate-intensity physical activity

- Tips on healthy behavior changes that also keep your cultural needs in mind

- Slow and steady weight loss. Depending on your starting weight, experts recommend losing weight at a rate of ½ to 2 pounds per week. Weight loss may be faster at the start of a program.

- Medical care if you are planning to lose weight by following a special formula diet, such as a very low-calorie diet

- A plan to keep the weight off after you have lost it

Get Familiar With The Program

Gather as much information as you can before deciding to join a program. Professionals working for weight loss programs should be able to answer the questions listed below.

✤ It's A Fact!!
Is the Alli diet pill right for me?

You may have heard about the new weight-loss pill "Alli" (pronounced: al-eye). Could it be the diet miracle you're waiting for?

Probably not.

Alli (generic name orlistat) is only for overweight adults. The U.S. Food and Drug Administration (FDA) and Alli's manufacturer both say that anyone younger than 18 should not use Alli. That's because the drug has not yet been tested in teens. So experts don't know if it could interfere with the way a teen's body grows and develops, or if it might cause other health problems.

Alli works by preventing a person's body from absorbing some of the fat that's in food. That may sound like a good thing—after all, when fat calories are not absorbed, there's no chance they can be stored in the body as extra pounds. But not getting enough fat could interfere with normal growth and development in both girls and guys. Fat also helps the body absorb and process many of the vitamins we need for good health.

Some potentially unpleasant (and embarrassing) side effects go with taking Alli (the company calls these "treatment effects"). All that undigested fat has to go somewhere, and the only way for it to leave the body is as an oily discharge through the anus. This means the following things could happen to someone taking the drug:

• Gas (farting) with oily discharge that can leak out and stain clothing

• More frequent—or even uncontrollable—bowel movements

• Looser, oilier bowel movements

What does the weight loss program consist of?

• Does the program offer one-on-one counseling or group classes?

• Do you have to follow a specific meal plan or keep food records?

• Do you have to purchase special food, drugs, or supplements?

• Does the program help you be more physically active, follow a specific physical activity plan, or provide exercise instruction?

Alli can also cause problems for people who have certain health conditions, such as diabetes, thyroid disease, gallbladder problems, or kidney stones.

Although Alli is approved as safe and effective for adults, it's no quick fix. For one thing, just like dieting, it takes time to lose weight with Alli. People who take the drug don't see instant results.

Taking Alli requires as much discipline and willpower as sticking to a diet: People using it have to keep careful track of the amount of fat they eat at each meal to be sure they don't get too much. Taking Alli with meals that contain more than 15 grams of fat can worsen the side effects mentioned above (15 grams is about the amount of fat in 2 tablespoons of peanut butter or one chocolate bar). So Alli is not a free pass to eat more fatty foods without gaining weight.

The bottom line is, when you're young, it's best to talk to a doctor about weight loss. Only a doctor can know your personal history—such as whether any recent weight gain is just a temporary part of the growing up process.

Source: "Is the Alli Diet Pill Right for Me?" June 2007, reprinted with permission from www.kidshealth.org. Copyright © 2007 The Nemours Foundation. This information was provided by KidsHealth, one of the largest resources online for medically reviewed health information written for parents, kids, and teens. For more articles like this one, visit www.KidsHealth.org, or www.TeensHealth.org.

- Does the program teach you to make positive and healthy behavior changes?
- Is the program sensitive to your lifestyle and cultural needs?

What are the staff qualifications?

- Who supervises the program?
- What type of weight management training, experience, education, and certifications do the staff have?

Does the product or program carry any risks?

- Could the program hurt you?

- Could the recommended drugs or supplements harm your health?

- Do participants talk with a doctor?

- Does a doctor run the program?

- Will the program's doctors work with your personal doctor if you have a medical condition such as high blood pressure or are taking prescribed drugs?

How much does the program cost?

- What is the total cost of the program?

- Are there other costs, such as weekly attendance fees, food and supplement purchases, etc.?

- Are there fees for a follow-up program after you lose weight?

- Are there other fees for medical tests?

What results do participants typically have?

- How much weight does an average participant lose, and how long does he or she keep the weight off?

- Does the program offer publications or materials that describe what results participants typically have?

If you are interested in finding a weight loss program near you, ask your health care provider for a referral or contact your local hospital.

Chapter 52

Should I Gain Weight?

"I want to play hockey, like I did in middle school, but now that I'm in high school, the other guys have bulked up and I haven't. What can I do?"

"All of my friends have broad shoulders and look like they lift weights. No matter what I do, I just look scrawny. What can I do?"

"It's not like I want to gain a lot of weight, but I'd like to look like I have some curves, like the girls I see on TV. What can I do?"

A lot of teens think that they're too skinny, and wonder if they should do something about it.

Why Do People Want To Gain Weight?

Some of the reasons people give for wanting to gain weight are:

I'm worried that there's something wrong with me. If you want to gain weight because you think you have a medical problem, talk to your doctor. Although certain health conditions can cause a person to be underweight, most of them have symptoms other than skinniness, like stomach pain or

About This Chapter: "Should I Gain Weight?" October 2006, reprinted with permission from www.kidshealth.org. Copyright © 2006 The Nemours Foundation. This information was provided by KidsHealth, one of the largest resources online for medically reviewed health information written for parents, kids, and teens. For more articles like this one, visit www.KidsHealth.org, or www.TeensHealth.org.

diarrhea. So it's likely that if some kind of medical problem were making you skinny, you probably wouldn't feel well.

I'm worried because all of my friends have filled out and I haven't.

Because everyone is on a different sched- ule, some of your friends may have started to fill out when they were as young as 8 (if they're girls) or 10 (if they're guys). But for some normal kids, puberty may not start until 12 or later for girls and 14 or later for guys. And whenever you start pu- berty, it may take 3 or 4 years for you to fully develop and gain all of the weight and muscle mass you will have as an adult.

> ♣ **It's A Fact!!**
> Many guys and girls are skinny until they start to go through puberty. The changes that come with puberty include weight gain and, in guys, broader shoulders and increased muscle mass.
>
> Source: The Nemours Foundation.

Some people experience what's called delayed puberty. If you are one of these "late bloomers," you may find that some relatives of yours developed late, too. Most teens who have delayed puberty don't need to do anything; they'll eventually develop normally— and that includes gaining weight and muscle. If you are concerned about delayed puberty, though, talk to your doctor.

I've always wanted to play a certain sport; now I don't know if I can. Lots of people come to love a sport in grade school or middle school—and then find themselves on the bench when their teammates develop faster. If you've always envisioned yourself playing football, it can be tough when your body doesn't seem to want to measure up. You may need to wait until your body goes through puberty before you can play football on the varsity squad.

Another option to consider is switching your ambitions to another sport. If you were the fastest defensive player on your middle school football team, but now it seems that your body type is long and lean, maybe track and field is for you. Many adults find that the sports they love the most are those that fit their body types the best.

I just hate the way I look. Developing can be tough enough without the pressure to be perfect. Your body changes (or doesn't change), your friends' bodies change (or don't), and you all spend a lot of time noticing. It's easy to judge both yourself and others based on appearances. Sometimes, it can feel like life is some kind of beauty contest.

Your body is your own, and as frustrating as it may seem to begin with, there are certain things you can't speed up or change. But there is one thing you can do to help. Work to keep your body healthy so that you can grow and develop properly. Self-esteem can play a part here, too. People who learn to love their bodies, and accept them for what they are, carry themselves well and project a type of self-confidence that helps them look attractive.

If you're having trouble with your body image, talk about how you feel with someone you like and trust who's been through it—maybe a parent, doctor, counselor, coach, or teacher.

It's The Growth, Not The Gain

No matter what your reason is for wanting to gain weight, here's a simple fact: The majority of teens have no reason—medical or otherwise—to try to gain weight. An effort like this will at best simply not work and at worst increase your body fat, putting you at risk for health problems.

So focus on growing strong, not gaining weight. Keeping your body healthy and fit so that it grows well is an important part of your job as a teen. Here are some things you can do to help this happen.

Make nutrition your mission. Your friends who want to slim down are eating more salads and fruit. Here's a surprise: So should you. You can do more for your body by eating a variety of healthier foods instead of trying to pack on weight by forcing yourself to eat a lot of unhealthy high-fat, high-sugar foods. Chances are, trying to force-feed yourself won't help you gain weight anyway; and if you do, you'll mostly just be gaining excess body fat. Eating a variety of healthy foods, making time for regular meals and snacks, and eating only until you are full will give your body its best chance to stay healthy as it gets the fuel and nutrients it needs.

Good nutrition doesn't have to be complicated. Here are some simple tips:

- Eat lots of vegetables, fruits, and whole grains.

- Eat breakfast every day.

- Eat regular, healthy snacks.

- Eat a variety of foods. That can sometimes include less nutritious ones, like chips and soda. But try to limit them so you don't crowd out healthier food and drinks.

Eating well at this point in your life is important for lots of reasons. Good nutrition is a key part of normal growth and development. It's also wise to learn good eating habits now—they'll become second nature, which will help you stay healthy and fit without even thinking about it.

Keep on moving. Another way to keep your body healthy is to incorporate regular exercise. This can simply be a matter of walking to school, playing Frisbee with your friends, or helping out with some household chores. Or you might choose to work out at a gym or with a sports team. A good rule of thumb for exercise amounts during the teen years: Try to get at least 30 to 60 minutes of activity every day (like walking to school or around the mall) and get more vigorous activity (like playing soccer or skating) for 20 minutes or more at least three times a week.

Strength training, when done safely, is a healthy way to exercise, but it won't necessarily bulk you up. Guys especially get more muscular during puberty, but puberty is no guarantee that you'll turn into a cover model for *Muscle & Fitness* in a couple of years—some people just don't have the kind of body type for this to happen.

If you've hit puberty, the right amount of weight training will help your muscles become stronger and have more endurance. And, once a person's

♣ It's A Fact!!
Our genes play an important role in determining our body type. Adult bodies come in all different shapes and sizes, and some people stay lean their entire lives, no matter what they do.

Source: The Nemours Foundation.

reached puberty, proper weight training can help him or her bulk up, if that's the goal. Be sure to work with a certified trainer, who can show you how to do it without injuring yourself. It can be easy to overdo strength training, especially during the teenage years when there's more risk of injuring bones that haven't finished growing yet.

Get the skinny on supplements. Thinking about drinking something from a can or taking a pill to turn you buff overnight? Guess what: Supplements or pills that make promises like this are at best a waste of money and at worst potentially harmful to your health.

The best way to get the fuel you need to build muscle is by eating well. Before you take any kind of supplement at all, even if it's just a vitamin pill, talk to your doctor.

Sleep your way to stunning. Sleep is an important component of normal growth and development. If you get enough, you'll have the energy to fuel your growth. Your body is at work while it sleeps—oxygen moves to the brain, growth hormones are released, and your bones keep on developing, even while you're resting.

Focus on feeling good. It can help to know that your body is likely to change in the months and years ahead. Few of us look like we did at 15 when we're 25. But it's also important to realize that feeling good about yourself can make you more attractive to others, too.

Part Six

If You Need More Information

Chapter 53

New Research And Clinical Trials On Eating Disorders

How Are We Working To Better Understand And Treat Eating Disorders?

Researchers are unsure of the underlying causes and nature of eating disorders. Unlike a neurological disorder, which generally can be pinpointed to a specific lesion on the brain, an eating disorder likely involves abnormal activity distributed across brain systems. With increased recognition that mental disorders are brain disorders, more researchers are using tools from both modern neuroscience and modern psychology to better understand eating disorders.

One approach involves the study of the human genes. With the publication of the human genome sequence in 2003, mental health researchers are studying the various combinations of genes to determine if any DNA variations are associated with the risk of developing a mental disorder. Neuroimaging, such as the use of magnetic resonance imaging (MRI), may also lead to a better understanding of eating disorders.

Neuroimaging already is used to identify abnormal brain activity in patients with schizophrenia, obsessive-compulsive disorder, and depression. It

About This Chapter: This chapter includes "How Are We Working to Better Understand and Treat Eating Disorders?" and "Clinical Trials, Eating Disorders, Featured Studies," National Institute of Mental Health (NIMH), January 2008.

may also help researchers better understand how people with eating disorders process information, regardless of whether they have recovered or are still in the throes of their illness.

Conducting behavioral or psychological research on eating disorders is even more complex and challenging. As a result, few studies of treatments for eating disorders have been conducted in the past. New studies currently underway, however, are aiming to remedy the lack of information available about treatment.

Researchers also are working to define the basic processes of the disorders, which should help identify better treatments. For example, is anorexia the result of skewed body image, self-esteem problems, obsessive thoughts, compulsive behavior, or a combination of these? Can it be predicted or identified as a risk factor before drastic weight loss occurs, and therefore avoided?

These and other questions may be answered in the future as scientists and doctors think of eating disorders as medical illnesses with certain biological causes. Researchers are studying behavioral questions, along with genetic and brain systems information, to understand risk factors, identify biological markers, and develop medications that can target specific pathways that control eating behavior. Finally, neuroimaging and genetic studies may also provide clues for how each person may respond to specific treatments.

Featured Studies

Some clinical trials include the following. They are listed according to the date they were added to the ClinicalTrials.gov registry, with the most recent studies appearing first.

Pharmacogenomics of Antidepressant Response in Children and Adolescents. *Evaluation study.* This study will identify variations in genes that

---

♣ It's A Fact!!

Eating is controlled by many factors, including appetite, food availability, family, peer, and cultural practices, and attempts at voluntary control. Dieting to a body weight leaner than needed for health is highly promoted by current fashion trends, sales campaigns for special foods, and in some activities and professions.

Source: "Featured Studies," NIMH, January 2008.

may be involved in the development of suicidal events or certain behaviors in youth who are exposed to antidepressant medications.

Evaluating the Brain's Response to Natural Versus Artificial Sweetener in Women Who Have Had an Eating Disorder. *Evaluation study.* This study will compare the brain's ability to distinguish between natural and artificial sweeteners in women with and without a history of eating disorder.

Comparing the Effectiveness of Two Therapies to Treat Signs of Anorexia Nervosa in Adolescents. *Interventional study.* This study will compare the effectiveness of two therapies to treat early signs of anorexia nervosa in adolescents.

Antidepressant Safety in Kids (ASK) Study. *Evaluation study.* This study will evaluate the risks and benefits of treatment with a selective serotonin reuptake inhibitor or serotonin-norepinephrine reuptake inhibitor in children and adolescents with a pre-specified anxiety disorder, depressive disorder, eating disorder, or obsessive-compulsive disorder.

Determining the Response to Sipping Beverages Without Swallowing in People With Eating Disorders. *Evaluation study.* This study will use a sipping and spitting exercise to better understand the brain's response to food intake in people with eating disorders.

Brain Function of Self-Regulation in Women With Bulimia Nervosa. *Evaluation study.* This study will compare brain images of females with bulimia and females without eating disorders to better understand the brain's involvement with self-regulation.

Amino Acids, Serotonin, and Body Weight Regulation. *Interventional study.* This study will assess the behavioral effects of an amino acid mixture thought to influence serotonin function in individuals who have recovered from anorexia nervosa.

Serotonin Transporter Concentrations in Women With a History of Anorexia Nervosa. *Evaluation study.* This study will compare the concentrations of serotonin transporter in the brains of women with a history of anorexia nervosa who are currently maintaining a normal weight to those of healthy women of normal weight.

Cholecystokinin for Reducing Binge Eating in People With Bulimia Nervosa. *Interventional study.* This study will determine the effectiveness of administrating a dose of cholecystokinin during a binge eating episode in reducing this eating behavior in people with bulimia nervosa.

Hormone Release and Stomach Disturbances in People With Binge Eating Disorder. *Evaluation study.* This study will determine whether the disturbances in cholecystokinin release and gastric emptying that occur in people with binge eating disorder are similar to those that occur in people with bulimia nervosa.

Motivating Factors That Play a Role in Bulimia Nervosa. *Evaluation study.* This study will compare the effects of binge eating to the reinforcing effects of frequently abused drugs by determining whether people with bulimia nervosa will exert effort to be able to binge eat.

Effectiveness of Antibiotic Treatment for Reducing Binge Eating and Improving Digestive Function in People With Bulimia Nervosa. *Interventional study.* This study will determine the effectiveness of the antibiotic erythromycin in enhancing gastrointestinal function and decreasing the frequency of binge eating in people with bulimia nervosa.

Effectiveness of a Normalization of Eating Intervention Program for Treating Women With Eating Disorders. *Interventional study.* This study will evaluate the effectiveness of a new approach to a normalization of eating (NOE) program, based on principles of cognitive behavioral therapy, in treating women with anorexia nervosa or bulimia nervosa.

Comparing the Effectiveness of Three Types of Therapy for the Treatment of Anorexia Nervosa in Adolescents. *Interventional study.* This study will compare specific family therapy, standard family systems therapy, and standard individual psychotherapy to determine which is most effective in treating adolescent anorexia nervosa.

Effectiveness of Family-Based Versus Individual Psychotherapy in Treating Adolescents With Anorexia Nervosa. *Interventional study.* This study will compare the effectiveness of family-based therapy versus individual psychotherapy for the treatment of adolescent anorexia nervosa.

Chapter 54

Additional Reading About Eating Disorders

Books

The Beginner's Guide to Eating Disorders Recovery
By Nancy J. Kolodny
Published by Gürze Books, 2004
ISBN: 978-0936077451

Conquering Eating Disorders: How Family Communication Heals
By Sue Cooper and Peggy Norton
Published by Seal Press, 2008
ISBN: 978-1580052603

Eating Disorders for Dummies
By Susan Schulherr
Published by Wiley Publishing, Inc., 2008
ISBN: 978-0470225493

About This Chapter: This chapter includes a compilation of various resources from many sources deemed reliable. It serves as a starting point for further research and is not intended to be comprehensive. Inclusion does not constitute endorsement. Resources in this chapter are categorized by type and, under each type, they are listed alphabetically by title to make topics easier to identify.

The Eating Disorder Solution
By Dr. Barbara Cole
Published by Trafford Publishing, 2006
ISBN: 978-1412075930

The Eating Disorder Sourcebook
By Carolyn Costin
Published by McGraw-Hill, 2007
ISBN: 978-0071476850

Feeding the Fame: Celebrities Tell Their Real-Life Stories of Eating Disorders and Recovery
By Gary Stromberg, Jane Merrill, and Wendy Naugle
Published by Hazelden Publishing & Educational Services, 2006
ISBN: 978-1592853502

Gaining: The Truth About Life After Eating Disorders
By Aimee Liu
Published by Wellness Central, 2008
ISBN: 978-0446694827

The Good Eater: The True Story of One Man's Struggle With Binge Eating Disorder
By Ron Saxen
Published by New Harbinger Publications, Inc., 2007
ISBN: 978-1572244856

Inside Out: Portrait of an Eating Disorder
By Nadia Shivack
Published by Ginee Seo Books, 2007
ISBN: 978-0689852169

It's Not About the Weight: Attacking Eating Disorders
By Susan J. Mendelsohn
Published by iUniverse, 2007
ISBN: 978-0595418831

100 Questions & Answers About Eating Disorders

By Carolyn Costin
Published by Jones and Bartlett Publishers, Inc., 2007
ISBN: 978-0763745004

Overcoming Your Eating Disorder: A Cognitive-Behavioral Therapy Approach for Bulimia Nervosa and Binge-Eating Disorder

By W. Stuart Agras and Robin F. Apple
Published by Oxford University Press, Inc., 2008
ISBN: 978-0195334562

Talking to Eating Disorders: Simple Ways to Support Someone with Anorexia, Bulimia, Binge-Eating, or Body Image Issues

By Jeanne Albronda Heaton and Claudia J. Strauss
Published by New American Library, 2005
ISBN: 978-0451215222

Articles

"Anorexia, Bulimia Prove Gene Related," in *USA Today (Magazine)*, October 2006, Page 11.

"Comfort Food: Is emotional eating ruining your diet? Physical hunger and emotional hunger are not the same," by Matthew Hutson, in *Psychology Today*, July-August 2007, Page 20.

"Does Your Friend Have an Eating Disorder? Here's how to help—you could save her life," by Cheryl Brody, in *CosmoGirl!*, February 2008, Page 56.

"Driven to Be Thin: Millions of teens suffer from eating disorders and many of them are boys," by Lynn Santa Lucia, in *Scholastic Choices*, September 2006, Page 20.

"Dying to Be Thin: Eating disorders are ugly. Here's why," by Andrea Faiad, in *Current Health 2*, a *Weekly Reader* publication, November 2006, Page 20.

"Dying to Be Thin: Even though she was pretty and popular, Jennifer only saw fat and ugly when she looked in the mirror. She shares with us the devastation of struggling with anorexia," by Sandy Fertman Ryan, in *Girls' Life*, February-March 2007, Page 52.

"Eating Troubles," by Emily Sohn, in *Science News for Kids*, February 8, 2006.

"Empty Inside: Eating disorders involve much more than wanting to be thin," by Polly Sparling, in *Current Health 2*, a *Weekly Reader* publication, January 2005, Page 19.

"Food Fight: One girl looks at the consuming problem of eating disorders," by Elyse Bassman, in *New Moon*, March-April 2007, Page 38.

"Health: Battle of the Binge," by Karen Springen, in *Newsweek*, February 19, 2007, Page 76.

"The Heavy Weight of Exercise Addiction: Treating this often-overlooked disorder can save patients' lives," by Edward J. Cumella, in *Behavioral Health Management*, September-October 2005, Page 26.

"The Language of Fat: Are you constantly criticizing your body? Discover how those negative words are masking your true feelings, and learn how to express yourself more honestly," by Leah Paulos, in *Scholastic Choices*, April-May 2006, Page 6.

"Learning to Love My Body: After struggling with an eating disorder for more than a decade, this reader discovered how to heal her body with healthy food and exercise," by Sarah Robbins, in *Shape*, May 2007, Page 190.

"The Lost Boys," by Jenni Schaefer, in *CosmoGirl!*, May 2007, Page 122.

"Mind Over Mirror," by Daniel Williams, in *Time International* (South Pacific Edition), October 30, 2006, Page 50.

"Special Report: Weighing In," by Kristen Kemp, in *Girls' Life*, June-July 2006, Page 64.

"Starved for Assistance: Coercion finds a place in the treatment of two eating disorders," by B. Bower, in *Science News*, January 20, 2007, Page 38.

"Wanna Rexia," by Amelia Mcdonell-Parry, in *Teen Vogue*, February 2008, Page 116.

"Weight Watcher: What happens when you and your mom don't see eye to eye about dieting?" by Kara Jesella, in *Teen Vogue*, October 2007, Page 210.

Internet Resources

About Eating Disorders
Academy for Eating Disorders
http://www.aedweb.org/eating_disorders/index.cfm

Female Athletic Triad
American Academy of Orthopaedic Surgeons
http://orthoinfo.aaos.org/topic.cfm?topic=A00342

Body Image and Eating Disorders
4 Girls Health
http://www.girlshealth.gov/emotions/bodyimage/index.cfm

Body Image: Loving Yourself Inside and Out
Healthfinder®
http://www.womenshealth.gov/BodyImage/

Eating Disorder Treatment and Recovery
Helpguide
http://www.helpguide.org/mental/eating_disorder_self_help.htm

Signs and Symptoms
Love Your Body
http://loveyourbody.missouri.edu/signs.htm

What Can You Do to Help Prevent Eating Disorders?
National Eating Disorders Association
http://www.nationaleatingdisorders.org/p.asp?WebPage_ID=286&Profile_ID=41170

Eating Disorders
TeensHealth.org
http://kidshealth.org/teen/exercise/problems/eat_disorder.html

Binge Eating Disorder
Weight-control Information Network
http://win.niddk.nih.gov/publications/binge.htm

Chapter 55

Directory Of Eating Disorders Organizations

For more information about eating disorders and other related topics, contact the following organizations.

Information About Eating Disorders

Academy for Eating Disorders (AED)
111 Deer Lake Road, Suite 100
Deerfield, IL 60015
Phone: 847-498-4274
Fax: 847-480-9282
Website: http://www.aedweb.org
E-Mail: info@aedweb.org

Anorexia Nervosa and Related Eating Disorders, Inc. (ANRED)
Website: http://www.anred.com

Casa Palmera
14750 El Camino Real
Del Mar, CA 92014
Toll Free: 888-481-4481
Website: http://www.casapalmera.com
E-mail: info@casapalmera.com

About This Chapter: Information in this chapter was compiled from many sources deemed reliable. Inclusion does not constitute endorsement, and there is no implication associated with omission. All contact information was verified in July/August 2008.

Eating Disorders Coalition
720 7th Street, NW, Suite 300
Washington, DC 20001-3902
Phone: 202-543-9570
Website: http://
www.eatingdisorderscoalition.org

Eating Disorders Foundation of Victoria Inc.
1513 High Street
Glen Iris, Victoria 3146 Australia
Helpline (03) 9885 0318 / 1300 550 236
Phone: (03) 9885 6563
Fax: (03) 9885 1153
Website: http://
www.eatingdisorders.org.au
E-Mail: help@eatingdisorders.org.au

The Harris Center
2 Longfellow Place, Suite 200
Boston, MA 02114
Phone: 617-726-8470
Website: http://
www.harriscentermgh.org

National Association of Anorexia Nervosa and Associated Disorders
P.O. Box 7
Highland Park, IL 60035
Phone: 847-831-3438
Fax: 847-433-4632
Website: http://www.anad.org
E-Mail: anad20@aol.com

National Center for Overcoming Overeating (NCOO)
P.O. Box 1257
Old Chelsea Station
New York, NY 10113-0920
Phone: 212-582-0383
Website: http://
www.overcomingovereating.com
E-Mail:
webmaster@overcomingovereating.com

National Eating Disorders Association (NEDA)
603 Stewart St., Suite 803
Seattle, WA 98101
Referral Hotline: 800-931-2237
Phone: 206-382-3587
Website: http://
www.nationaleatingdisorders.org
E-Mail:
info@NationalEatingDisorders.org

National Eating Disorder Information Centre
ES 7-421, 200 Elizabeth Street
Toronto, ON M5G 2C4
Toll Free 866-NEDIC-20
(866-633-4220)
Phone 416-340-4156
Fax: 416-340-4736
Website: http://www.nedic.ca
E-Mail: nedic@uhn.on.ca

National Eating Disorders Screening Program (NEDSP)

Screening for Mental Health, Inc.
One Washington St., Suite 304
Wellesley Hills, MA 02481
Phone: 781-239-0071
Fax: 781-431-7447
Website: http://
www.mentalhealthscreening.org/
events/nedsp
E-Mail:
smhinfo@mentalhealthscreening.org

National Women's Health Information Center

200 Independence Avenue, SW
Room 712E
Washington, DC 20201
Toll Free: 800-994-WOMAN
(800-994-9662)
Website: http://www.4woman.gov

National Women's Health Network

514 10th Street NW, Suite 400
Washington, DC 20004
Phone: 202-347-1140
For Health Information:
202-628-7814
Fax: 202-347-1168
Website: http://
www.womenshealthnetwork.org
E-Mail: nwhn@nwhn.org

Overeaters Anonymous

P.O. Box 44020
Rio Rancho, NM 87174-4020
Phone: 505-891-2664
Fax: 505-891-4320
Website: http://
www.overeatersanonymous.org
E-Mail: info@oa.org

Rader Programs

Toll Free: 800-841-1515
Fax: 818-880-3750
Website: http://
www.raderprograms.com
E-Mail:
Rader@raderprograms.com

Renfrew Center

475 Spring Lane
Philadelphia, PA 19128
Toll-Free: 800-RENFREW
(736-3739)
Phone: 877-367-3383
Fax: 215-482-7390
Website: http://
www.renfrewcenter.com

Walden Behavioral Care, LLC

9 Hope Avenue, Suite 500
Waltham, MA 02453-2711
Phone: 781-647-6700
Website: http://
www.waldenbehavioralcare.com
E-Mail:
Info@waldenbehavioralcare.com

Information About Nutrition

American Heart Association
National Center
7272 Greenville Avenue
Dallas, TX 75231-4596
Toll Free: 800-AHA-USA-1
Phone: 214-373-6300
Website: http://www.amhrt.org

American Dietetic Association
120 S. Riverside Plaza, Suite 2000
Chicago, IL 60606-6995
Toll Free: 800-877-1600
Phone: 312-899-0040 x5000
Website: http://www.eatright.org

American Society of Nutrition
American Society for Clinical Nutrition, Inc.
9650 Rockville Pike
Bethesda, MD 20814-3998
Phone: 301-634-7050
Fax: 301-634-7892
Website: http://www.nutrition.org

Center for Nutrition Policy and Promotion
3101 Park Center Drive, Room 1034
Alexandria, VA 22302-1594
Phone: 703-305-7600
Fax: 703-305-3300
Website: http://www.usda.gov/cnpp

Children's Nutrition Research Center
Baylor College of Medicine
1100 Bates Street
Houston, TX 77030
Phone: 713-798-6767
Fax: 713-798-7098
Website: http://www.bcm.tmc.edu/cnrc
E-Mail: cnrc@bcm.tmc.edu

Food Marketing Institute
2345 Crystal Drive, Suite 800
Arlington, VA 22202
Phone: 202-452-8444
Fax 202-429-4519
Website: http://www.fmi.org
E-Mail: fmi@fmi.org

Food and Nutrition Information Center
National Agricultural Library/ARS/USDA
10301 Baltimore Avenue
Room 304
Beltsville, MD 20705
Phone: 301-504-5414
Fax: 301-504-6409
Website: http://nal.usda.gov/fnic

International Food Information Council

1100 Connecticut Avenue, NW
Suite 430
Washington, DC 20036
Phone: 202-296-6540
Fax: 202-296-6547
Website: http://www.ific.org
E-Mail: foodinfo@ific.org

Iowa State University, University Extension

Food Science and Human
Nutrition Extension
2312 Food Sciences Bldg.
Iowa State University
Ames, Iowa 50011
Phone: 515-294-3011
Fax: 515-294-8181
Ames, IA 50011-1120
Website: http://
www.extension.iastate.edu/
healthnutrition

Kellogg's Nutrition University

P.O. Box CAMB
Battle Creek, MI 49016-1986
Toll Free: 800-962-1413
Website: http://
www.kelloggnutrition.com

Nutrition Information Center

NY Hospital-
Cornell Medical Center
Memorial Sloan-Kettering
Cancer Center
1275 York Avenue
New York, NY 10065
Toll Free: 888-675-7722
Phone: 212-639-2000
Website: http://www.mskcc.org

Nutrition Information and Resource Center

Department of Food Science
The Pennsylvania State University
208 Special Services Building
University Park, PA 16802
Phone: 814-867-1528
Website: http://nirc.cas.psu.edu/
index.cfm
E-Mail: eat4health@psu.edu

U. S. Department of Agriculture (USDA)

1400 Independence Avenue, SW
Washington, DC 20250
Phone: 202-720-2791
Website: http://www.usda.gov

U.S. Food and Drug Administration
Office of Consumer Affairs
Department of Health and Human Services
5600 Fishers Lane (HFE-88), Room 16-85
Rockville, MD 20857
Phone: 888-INFO-FDA (463-6332)
Fax: 301-443-9767
Website: http://www.fda.gov

University of Minnesota
Department of Food Science and Nutrition
Nutritionist's Tool Box
225 FScN
1334 Eckles Avenue
Saint Paul, MN 55108
Phone: 612-624-1290
Fax: 612-625-5272
Website: http://www.fsci.umn.edu/tools.htm

Weight-Control Information Network
National Institute of Health
1 WIN Way
Bethesda, MD 20892-3665
Toll Free: 877-946-4627
Phone: 202-828-1025
Fax: 202-828-1028
Website: http://win.niddk.nih.gov/index.htm
E-Mail: win@info.niddk.nih.gov

Information About Fitness

President's Council on Physical Fitness and Sports
200 Independence Avenue, SW
Room 738-H
Washington, DC 20201-0004
Phone: 202-690-9000
Fax: 202-690-5211
http://www.fitness.gov

Shape Up America!
Website: http://www.shapeup.org

Information About Mental Health

American Academy of Child and Adolescent Psychiatry
3615 Wisconsin Avenue, NW
Washington, DC 20016
Phone: 202-966-7300
Fax: 202-966-2891
Website: http://www.aacap.org
E-Mail:
communications@aacap.org

American Psychiatric Association
1000 Wilson Blvd., Suite 1825
Arlington, VA 22209-3901
Toll-Free: 888-35-PSYCH
(357-7924)
Fax: 703-907-1085
Website: http://www.psych.org
E-Mail: apa@psych.org

American Counseling Association
5999 Stevenson Avenue
Alexandria, VA 22304
Toll Free: 800-347-6647
TDD: 703-823-6862
Fax: 800-473-2329
Website: http://www.counseling.org

American Psychiatric Nurses Association
1555 Wilson Blvd., Suite 602
Arlington, VA 22209
Toll Free: 866-243-2443
Fax: 703-243-3390
Website: http://www.apna.org
E-Mail: info@apna.org

American Institute for Cognitive Therapy
136 East 57th, Suite 1101
New York, NY 10022
Phone: 212-308-2440
Fax: 212-308-3099
Website: http://
www.cognitivetherapynyc.com

American Psychological Association
750 First Street, NE
Washington, DC 20002
Toll Free: 800-374-2721
Phone: 202-336-5500
Website: http://www.apa.org

Anxiety Disorders Association of America (ADAA)
8730 Georgia Avenue, Suite 600
Silver Spring, MD 20910
Phone: 240-485-1001
Fax: 240-485-1035
Website: http://www.adaa.org
E-Mail: AnxDis@adaa.org

Association for Behavioral and Cognitive Therapies
305 Seventh Avenue, 16th Floor
New York, NY 10001
Phone: 212-647-1890
Fax: 212-647-1865
Website: http://www.aabt.org

Body Image Program
Butler Hospital
345 Blackstone Blvd.
Providence, RI 02905
Phone: 401-455-6200
Website: http://www.butler.org/body.cfm?id=123
E-Mail: info@butler.org

Depression and Bipolar Support Alliance
730 N. Franklin St., Suite 501
Chicago, IL 60654
Toll Free: 800-826-3632
Phone: 312-642-0049
Fax: 312-642-7243
Website: http://www.dbsalliance.org

Emotions Anonymous
P.O. Box 4245
St. Paul, MN 55104-0245
Phone: 615-647-9712
Fax: 651-647-1593
Website: http://www.emotionsanonymous.org
E-Mail: infodf3498fjsd@emotionsanonymous.org

iFred
P.O. Box 17598
Baltimore, MD 21297
Phone: 410-268-0044
Website: http://www.ifred.org
E-Mail: info@ifred.org

Mental Health America
2000 N. Beauregard Street
6th Floor
Alexandria, VA 22311
Toll Free: 800-969-6642
Phone: 703-684-7722
Fax: 703-684-5968
Website: http://www.nmha.org

Mental Health Net
Website: http://www.mentalhelp.net

National Institute of Mental Health

6001 Executive Boulevard
Rockville, MD 20892-9663
Toll Free 866-615-6464
Phone: 301-443-4513
Fax: 301-443-4279
Website: http://www.nimh.nih.gov
E-Mail: nimhinfo@nih.gov

National Mental Health Consumers' Self-Help Clearinghouse

1211 Chestnut Street, Suite 1207
Philadelphia, PA 19107
Toll Free: 800-533-4539
Phone: 215-751-1810
Fax: 215-636-6312
Website: http://
www.mhselfhelp.org
E-Mail: info@mhselfhelp.org

Rethink

5th Floor, Royal London House
22–25 Finsbury Square
London, England EC2A 1DX
Phone: 0845 456 0455
Website: http://www.rethink.org
E-Mail: info@rethink.org

SAMHSA's National Mental Health Information Center

P.O. Box 42557
Washington, DC 20015
Toll Free: 800-789-2647
Phone: 301-443-9006
TDD: 866-889-2647
Website: http://
mentalhealth.samhsa.gov

Helplines And Hotlines

Al-Anon/Alateen Hot Line
Toll Free: 800-344-2666

American Anorexia/Bulimia Association
Toll Free: 800-522-2230

Covenant House Nine-Line
Toll Free: 800-999-9999

Eating Disorder Awareness and Prevention
Toll Free: 800-931-2237

Hope Line Network
Toll Free: 800-SUICIDE (784-2433)

Mental Health America
800-273-TALK (8255)

National Adolescent Suicide Hot Line
Toll Free: 800-621-4000

National Alliance For The Mentally Ill (And Their Families)
Toll Free: 800-950-6264

Nationwide Crisis Hot Line
Toll Free: 800-333-4444

SAFE (Self-Abuse Finally Ends)
Toll Free: 800-DONT-CUT
(800-366-8288)

United Way Help Line
Toll Free: 800-233-HELP
(800-233-4357)

Index

Index

Page numbers that appear in *Italics* refer to illustrations. Page numbers that have a small 'n' after the page number refer to information shown as Notes at the beginning of each chapter. Page numbers that appear in **Bold** refer to information contained in boxes on that page (except Notes information at the beginning of each chapter).

Health Reference Series